Playwork

Play and care for children 5–15

Annie Davy

Foreword by Pam Henry

First published 1995 by
MACMILLAN PRESS LTD
Houndmills, Basingstoke, Hampshire RG21 2XS
and London
Companies and representatives
throughout the world

ISBN 0–333–64159–0

A catalogue record for this book is available
from the British Library

Typeset by 7\Tek Art, Croydon, Surrey

Printed in Great Britain by Biddles Ltd,
Guildford and King's Lynn

10   9   8   7   6   5   4   3   2   1
04 03 02 01 00 99 98 97 96 95

Contents

Foreword

Play is an essential part of every child's life, and vital to the processes of human development. Working with children to facilitate and enrich their play opportunities is a responsible and skilled job.

Over the last few years the growing awareness of the play and care issues for school-aged children has been reflected in constant coverage in the media and attention from government. The Children Act 1989 emphasises the need for good-quality care for children under 8 and the need for qualified and experienced staff in playsettings. The Employment Department encouraged the expansion of out-of-school childcare with grants, training opportunities and support through the Training and Enterprise Councils.

The rapid growth and development in this area, together with the launch of the National and Scottish Vocational Qualifications (NVQs/SVQs) in playwork, have highlighted the need for accessible, available and affordable training resources which will enhance and enrich workers' development and their practice.

Playwork is one of the first resources linked to NVQs/SVQs which meets this need. Readers are guided through chapters of practical yet reflective activities, case studies and play theory which will help them gather underpinning knowledge to support NVQ/SVQ assessment.

The book will support and complement other playwork training or study. It is also a wonderful read for those who simply want to explore the many exciting facets of children's play.

Children and parents deserve and expect the very best quality, reliable childcare in out-of-school hours. Throughout this book readers are able to explore the needs of the child and the role of the adult within the playcare setting. The company of other children and adults is the greatest resource a child can have, a resource we must continue to encourage and nurture at all times in our lives as well as in the workplace.

Playwork is a valuable and rewarding workbook for all those working with children in out-of-school settings for play and care.

Pam Henry
Head of Training
Kids' Clubs Network

Acknowledgements

I should like to express thanks to the many people who have helped me in various ways during the preparation of this book:

To those who commented on drafts of the whole text or parts of the text: Wendy Russell, Stuart Sillars, Harry Shier, Emma Lee, Janet and Gordon Osborn, Barbara Slatter, Frances Duffy and Helen Wheeler.

To Pam Henry (Kids' Clubs Network), Keith Clark (Oxfordshire Council for Voluntary Services) and Anne Webster (Macmillan) for their help and advice.

To those who contributed examples or case studies: Tracy Collins (PARASOL co-ordinator), Sharon Crockett (playworker), Mary Januarius (Information Officer, HAPA), Karen King (playworker) and Dolcie Obhiozele (play development officer).

To the children of SS Mary and John School and Isis Middle School after-school clubs, PAWS (Drayton) and Blackbird Leys Adventure Playground for recording their thoughts about themselves and their playsettings.

I would like to give special thanks to Sharon Crockett for her continuous support, comments and encouragement, to my colleagues at Oxfordshire Social Services, my friends Helen, Jane and George, and especially to my family for helping me to find the space and time to complete the book.

Thanks are due to the following for kind permission to use photographs, drawings or other copyright material: Blackbird Leys Adventure Playground – pages 6 (top), 19, 121; Children's drawings: Laura Ashby, Gemma and Loren Green, Polly Lowe, Oswah Osborn, Roberto and Nikita Raskovsky; Sharon Crockett – page 130; HAPA/Terry Beasley – pages 23 (left), 34, 78; HAPA/Tilly Odell – pages 8, 12, 47, 90, 93, 140, 168; Karen King – page 94; Kids' Clubs Network – page 137; Oxford City Council Play Development/ Anthony Cunning – pages 15, 31, 61, 68, 85, 86, 98, 131, 164; Oxford City Council Play Development/Dolcie Obhiozele – pages 53, 59; Oxfordshire Chinese Community and Advice Centre – page 51; Oxfordshire Department of Public Health – pages 116–18; Scottish Council for Voluntary Organisations – page 148; Sue Thorpe – pages 6 (bottom), 13, 17, 23 (right), 49, 73, 166.

I would like to thank the staff and children of the following playsettings for allowing photographs to be taken: Blackbird Leys Adventure Playground, SS Mary and John First School After-School Club, Isis Middle School After-School Club, Oxford City Council After-School Clubs, Project Sparrowhawk and Playday in South Parks, Oxford.

Every effort has been made to trace all copyright holders, but if any have been inadvertently overlooked the publishers will be pleased to make the necessary arrangements at the first opportunity.

About this book

Who it is for

This book is for playworkers: that is, for anyone who works with children between the ages of 5 and 15 years in a setting where play is important. You might work in an adventure playground, afterschool club or holiday playscheme. Perhaps you work on a playbus, in a playcentre, or as childcare worker in your own home. You may work full or part time, you may be a volunteer or you may be undertaking a playwork training course.

Wherever you work, your responsibilities as a playworker are substantial. Playwork requires practical and interpersonal skills. To be a playworker you need at different times to be companion, nurse, builder, artist, story-teller, manager, public relations officer, community worker, book-keeper, counsellor, all-round games player, referee and more.

Many playworkers have to learn their trade on the job. Nothing can take the place of personal experience of working with children. But playwork training can support you and help you to develop your skills, gain understanding and keep in touch with new thinking and legal requirements. It also provides you with the opportunity to share ideas with others.

Playwork is becoming more widely recognised as a profession in its own right – with particular skills, competences and qualifications. Local authorities are required to consider staff qualifications as part of their assessment of daycare and play facilities under the Children Act 1989. In 1992 the National Vocational Qualifications (NVQs) and Scottish Vocational Qualifications (SVQs) in Playwork were launched. There are now numerous accredited courses for playworkers. (See Endword.)

How to use it

The book considers an approach to playwork, its values and the skills and underpinning knowledge required of a playworker. You can use it as a handbook to dip into for ideas and quick reference, or to provide underpinning knowledge for a playwork training course or if you are working towards an NVQ.

The key is flexibility and discovering what works for the children within your particular work setting. While the theory throughout is related to practical examples of work with children, I have deliberately steered clear of being prescriptive about specific activities to be undertaken with children of different ages. The focus is on creating an environment and circumstances in which children can play and using the children themselves as your starting-point in planning for play. Books containing ideas and instructions for activities with different ages – games, art and craft, environmental play, music, drama and cooking – are recommended as further reading.

Structure of the book

The book is arranged in five chapters.

Chapter 1 looks at some of the underlying principles of playwork and creates the framework for the other chapters. It examines the meaning and importance of play, the values of playwork and some of the laws which affect you at work.

Chapter 2 considers why it is important for playworkers to have some understanding of child development and suggests ways of gaining it through observation. The key stages of school-aged child development are summarised, and there are suggestions for how you can encourage social and emotional development within the playsetting.

Chapter 3 is concerned with creating play opportunities within the play-setting – looking at the play environment, resources, and the activities which may be part of it. Good planning and evaluation are key factors. Record keeping has been included in this part of the book because it is important to both these aspects of playwork.

Chapter 4 is about the role of the playworker in ensuring that the play-setting is safe. How can you ensure that your playsetting is physically safe, and that the individual children *feel* safe in terms of their relationships with others? Safety in the playsetting should be considered alongside the fact that play is also challenging, adventurous, fun and offers opportunities for exploration and personal growth.

Chapter 5 looks at working with adults. As a playworker you do not work in isolation. There are the parents and carers of the children who come, and there are your co-workers and managers who form part of your work team. There is also the community in which your playsetting is situated. How can you build strong links with all of these people and use the skills and knowledge of a range of individuals and organisations who can support your work? How can you share your own skills and understanding to enhance and develop the important work you do?

Activities and observations

Throughout this book there are observations and activities to enable you to relate what you have read to actual practice, or to develop greater under-standing of the subject. In most cases it is best if you undertake these activities with the support of your co-workers or a senior worker. Many require discussion with others.

To think about

As well as the activities there are 'To think about' boxes. These ask you to consider wider issues around the points being made and how these relate to the playsetting in which you work. You are not expected to give full or immediate answers. In most cases the questions pick up themes which run throughout the book. As you progress through the book and carry out the activities you will get help in finding solutions to the questions raised.

Further reading

The subject matter of each section could have made a book on its own. I hope you will explore some of the topics further. You will find suggestions for further reading at the ends of sections.

Language used

In writing this book I have tried to steer clear of jargon. Where it has crept in it is because I have been unable to find a suitable alternative word or phrase.

Language changes over time, along with our thinking about what makes good practice in working with children. By thinking about language and being open to challenge and change in the terms we use, we also re-evaluate our working practice.

Children

I have used the words 'child' and 'children' throughout the book to mean people aged 5–15, unless otherwise stated. This is the age range covered within N/SVQs in playwork, although in some cases I have referred particularly to the needs of older children or adolescents. I have tried to keep the different needs of the wide age group in mind throughout.

Playsetting

Playsetting is the term I finally fixed on to encompass the whole range of situations and circumstances in which playworkers work. It is not ideal, as it does not convey the wonderful and diverse range of play projects and environments which exist.

Parent/carer

I have used 'parent' to mean the adult or adults responsible for the child within the family or at home, even though this may not be the biological parent. In some cases I have used 'parent or carer' to emphasise this point.

She and he

I have varied the use of the personal pronouns 'he' and 'she' throughout the book.

Children with special needs

Each child is unique with different abilities and individual needs. The term 'special needs' has been used to raise awareness that some children have needs arising from disabilities, behaviour or learning difficulties which require careful thought and planning so they can be met within the playsetting. These needs may be to do with access or transport, the adaptation of games, activities and play opportunities, or obtaining additional resources or staffing so that you can offer equal opportunities to all children. The term 'special needs' is used in the NVQ/SVQ standards and is currently recognised and used in education and social work.

Variations in legislation, policy and practice

The Playwork standards in the N/SVQs are the same throughout the UK. However, practice will differ to some extent because of the legal and social context in which you work. For example, in Wales, notices have to be in Welsh and English, safety and other legislation differs in Scotland. The law quoted in the book is English law. The principles of good practice are the same, but a playworker moving from one part of the UK to another would be expected to acquire any relevant new knowledge.

Finally – a word about standards

When I first came into playwork there were no playwork qualifications, and playsettings for school-aged children were not required to be registered until the implementation of the Children Act 1989. Playsettings operated often from hand to mouth with voluntary workers and very few materials. We did not have written policies or codes of practice. I recall with retrospective panic several days on an adventure playground with two workers and over 70 children of all ages. We had little training available to us as playworkers but we did meet together and share ideas on everything from new games to constructive ways of dealing with difficult situations. Play facilities were often haphazard and under-resourced, and could not do justice to the children or the workers in the longer term.

The situation may not appear to have changed very much for some of you. Resourcing is still an ever-present problem for many playsettings, and planners and politicians need constant convincing and reminding about the importance of play – to children and to society as a whole.

As you are working through the activities you may find that the standards and expectations are not what you have to work with on a daily basis and that you are not in a position to do much to change them to begin with. Do not lose heart. This book should be used as a source of ideas for you and your colleagues to work with, towards and beyond.

In writing this book I have drawn on the work and ideas of many, and have tried to incorporate the themes which I see as central to current thinking in playwork. As with any author, I am limited by the nature and scope of my own personal life story and circumstances, the current time in history and the place where I live and work. All these factors influence my thinking and similar factors will influence yours. I hope that what you read here will find echoes in the way you want to work. I trust that playworkers everywhere, whatever their circumstances, share the common ground that we have shared from the earliest days of playwork: that play, and children's right to play, is vital to healthy human development.

1 Framework for play

1.1 Play and playcare

ACTIVITY 1.1

Conduct a small survey within your local or neighbouring area. Find out from your local authority (council social services, recreation and education departments) what provision for play is made for school-aged children within this area. There will probably be both supervised settings (holiday playschemes, kids clubs, playbuses) and unsupervised settings (parks, recreation grounds).

If possible, arrange to visit or volunteer to help in one or two different kinds of supervised playsettings. If your area has few such facilities, you may need to look at another area. It is useful if you can visit playsettings in contrasting areas such as an inner city area and a rural one.

Children's play is freely chosen, personally directed behaviour, motivated from within . . .

National Occupational Standards in Playwork 1992, Appendix 2

Playworkers work in many different kinds of playsettings. Each setting will have particular aims and serve different needs, but children's play must be an important part of all of them. If you and your colleagues and managers in the playsetting can agree on what play means to you collectively, it will help you to plan an environment in which that play can happen.

What is a playsetting?

You may work in an after-school club, a playcentre, a holiday play scheme, a playbus, an adventure playground or another kind of playsetting altogether. The following case studies are examples to help build a picture of the range of settings in which playworkers can work. They are fictional examples, but are all based on real settings of their type.

'Play is when one person gets together with other people and they have fun. Sometimes you can play on your own with toys or an imaginary friend.' Loren (aged 8)

CASE STUDY 1.1: THE ADVENTURE PLAYGROUND

The adventure playground has a large portakabin placed on a fenced-in piece of what was once wasteland. It backs on to a large housing estate. Outside there are several large and small structures, built from old telegraph poles, railway sleepers and various other pieces of reclaimed material such as tyres, oil drums and plastic tubing. The structures are always changing under the influence of new ideas thought up and carried out by the children and playworkers. Sometimes there are large rope swings or aerial runways. At other times a tree house or a skateboarding ramp is the main focus of structural activity. The playworker ensures that safety standards are maintained.

There is a large sandpit, big enough for six large 12-year-olds to stand or sit in and create forts or fountains (with water from the outside tap) or bury each other in up to the neck. There is a small vegetable garden, some bushes and trees, and the focal point of the outside area is a large open fireplace with logs in a circle around it for seats. Children and workers gather here to keep warm in winter, to have barbecues in summer, to chat, to brew a cup of tea or make some pumpkin soup at Halloween. The adventure playground borders on a sports field which is used by some of the children and workers for more structured team games.

The building is not used much unless it rains. There are toilets, a small kitchen and office space. There is a big store-cupboard with arts and crafts materials, sports equipment, musical instruments, tools of all kinds and some games. There is a comfortable corner with soft chairs and a settee and an inviting display of books. The walls are covered with pictures, posters and graffiti, created or chosen by the children.

The adventure playground is open every-day after school until 6 p.m. It is open from 10 a.m. until 4 p.m. at weekends and all day in the holidays. Children come and go as they please throughout the opening times. There are always staff there to welcome them and to ensure that the playground remains a safe, as well as an adventurous, place to be.

Many exciting things go on through the different seasons. Festivals are celebrated. Friendships are made and broken. Tears and fears are shared as well as joy and laughter. Most of all it is a place which belongs to the children. Here is a space where they can decide what to do. They create their own challenges and get help and support, if they need it, to put them into action.

> 'It depends what you actually want to do. If you want to play outside you can play outside. If you want to make something particular you can make it.'

ACTIVITY 1.2

If you do not work in an adventure playground, arrange to visit one – either in your local area if there is one, or contact one of the national organisations which promote adventure playgrounds (see useful contacts at the end of the book).

TO THINK ABOUT

- What can children gain from this kind of playsetting, that might not be offered by other types of playsetting?

- What possibilities for 'adventure' are offered by the playsetting in which you work?

'Some people are not allowed home on their own – like me – and there wouldn't be anyone to look after them if they went home on their own and there wasn't an afterschool club.'

CASE STUDY 1.2: THE AFTER-SCHOOL CLUB

The after-school club is based in a community hall in the centre of a medium-sized town. It is open every weekday from 3 p.m. until 7 p.m. The children, aged from 5 to 12 years, are collected from three local schools by the playworkers.

There is one large hall, toilets, and a kitchen. They have use of a small hardcore area which can be used for ball games and such like outside, and a park down the road which is often used by groups of children from the club, accompanied by playworkers.

The playworkers aim to offer a 'home-from-home' atmosphere, with the extra benefits of having a large group of same-age children to play with. The room has to be set up daily as it is used by other groups at other times.

As the décor is drab, the playworkers cover the walls each day with large pieces of coloured fabric stapled to pieces of display-board on the walls. These cloths provide a backdrop for children's artwork. Sometimes they are used to set the scene for a particular theme around which the play opportunities for the week are based: shades of blue and green materials when the theme is water; mirrored fabrics from India when the Festival of Diwali is being celebrated.

They have several movable screens and pieces of furniture – some of which double as pieces of storage equipment for art materials and games. With these they divide the large room into more welcoming small areas – a relaxing area with books and beanbags, a 'messy' area for art and craft and water play, table space for board games.

There are three large trunks (with air-holes in lids) which contain a variety of imaginative play materials – dressing-up clothes, blankets, cloths, hats and props, picnic and tea-sets, dolls, musical instruments and puppets. The children take these trunks, which are mounted on castors, to particular areas of the room in which they wish to build their houses and hideyholes, or create their cafés, islands, doctor's surgeries or theatrical productions.

The after-school club offers a cooked meal to all children and caters for a variety of dietary needs – there is always a vegetarian option, which is particularly important as there is a large local Hindu population whose children attend the club. There is a television in a small side-room, and the children negotiate a limited amount of viewing time with each other and the staff. The children remain at the after-school club until collected by their parents.

ACTIVITY 1.3

Why is it important for this kind of playsetting to have a home-from-home atmosphere?

If you work in a similar setting, make a list of the things you do to develop a homely environment.

Remembering that each child's experience and idea of what makes home will be different, think of one new thing to add to the list.

CASE STUDY 1.3: THE PLAYBUS

The mobile play project is based on the outskirts of a large town. It has an office space, a large storage unit and parking for its two double-decker playbuses. One of these buses goes out to rural areas where the children lack access to other play opportunities. This bus also visits travellers' park-up sites in and around the town. The other bus goes to areas of the town which lack playgroup or other play facilities: a large housing estate, and an area of the town with a lot of temporary accommodation where children and families have little or no play space during the day.

Playworkers on both buses run a variety of play sessions geared to different age groups. During term times they might run an under-fives session in the morning and a youth group for 10- to 14-year-olds in the early evening. They also have holiday sessions for 5- to 9-year-olds. The kinds of sessions they offer will be largely decided by the groups they are working with. Where the bus goes changes over time, depending on where a need for additional play resources is identified.

Both buses are brightly decorated on the outside with pictures designed by children. Inside, the downstairs areas are converted to provide a comfortable seating area with children's books, an information stand with welfare rights advice and health and community information aimed at parents and older children. There is a 'portaloo' with running water in the washbasin. There are pull-out tables for games, puzzles and construction activities.

Upstairs there is a small kitchen area. Most of the upstairs is often used for messy and creative play opportunities of all kinds from potato printing and sandplay to woodcuts and glass painting. Sometimes the whole upper deck is filled with a variety of soft play equipment, for more energetic activity sessions. At other times the area is used to create an imaginative play area – a cave, a Bedouin tent, a spaceship, a Chinese restaurant . . .

The under-five sessions are for children together with their parents or carers. Sessions for older children are usually drop in sessions where children come and go as they please. The bus tries to park close to the homes of the children it serves, preferably with no major roads to cross.

> 'It's fun. It keeps you off the streets. Stops you getting into trouble. I just like it here.'
>
> 'You're never bored here. Never.'

ACTIVITY 1.4

1 Playbus workers have to be adept at working within a very small space. Playworkers in other playsettings may need to break up a large echoing hall into smaller, inviting and comfortable play spaces.

- Look again at Case studies 1.2 and 1.3.
- List the ways in which the space on offer to the children is changed and adapted.

2 How is the space in which you work adapted to create different play opportunities?

The play environment is considered in more detail in section 3.1.

'You get to see your friends when you don't see them at other times. Friends that don't live near me.'

'It's good in the summer because you can get out – but it's good in the winter because it's warm too.'

CASE STUDY 1.4: THE HOLIDAY PLAYSCHEME

Two classrooms and the school hall of a village school are used to accommodate 30 children from surrounding villages and four playworkers. The scheme runs from 10 a.m. to 4 p.m. on weekdays for two weeks in the summer holidays. The playscheme aims to offer a 'holiday' for children and a break for parents. The focus is on group activities, including several day-trips – to the seaside, the zoo, a theme park and so on.

Each day starts with co-operative games in the hall, using soft balls or a parachute. Then there is a choice of art-and-craft activities, board games or team sports outside on the sports field or indoors in the hall. There are limited opportunities for free play: a playdough table, a book corner, face painting, a climbing frame outside.

Children bring a packed lunch. Most children are brought and collected by their parents, but the playscheme organisers have teamed up with a community transport scheme to enable children who are in isolated areas without transport to attend. This transport scheme also enables several children who are wheelchair users to attend. The playscheme staff ensure that all the activities are accessible to all children in the scheme.

ACTIVITY 1.5

The kind of playsetting you work in will affect the way in which you begin each session and plan activities and play opportunities. The workers in Case study 1.4 plan many group activities and begin each day with co-operative games. Co-operative games are games without losers. The object of the game can only be achieved by the players working together.

As a playworker in a similar holiday playscheme, you are asked to plan a 30-minute games session with 7- to 11-year-olds on the first day.

- What games would you play?
- What, if any, materials would you need?

Use a co-operative games book for new ideas (see end of this section for example session plan).

If possible try out your planned session with a group of children in your own playsetting or in another playsetting by arrangement.

Play and playcare

The above case studies are just four examples of different playsettings. Each playsetting is different, and each has its own goals and objectives – even if they are not formally expressed.

Play must be an important part of all playsettings, but some settings also aim to provide a childcare service to parents. In such playcare settings there is a contract between the child's parent or carer and the playsetting that they will look after the child until she or he is collected at the end of the session. In their 1989 Guidelines of Good Practice for out-of-school careschemes, Kids' Clubs Network suggest that the aims of playcare settings may include: 'Providing for the needs of children, including play, safety and security, social, personal, nutritional, behavioural, recreational, leisure and educational'. From this it is clear that play is important, but not necessarily the main or only aim of such a setting.

Play and care

What do you mean by play?
What is play?

> Play is the highest expression of human development in childhood for it alone is the free expression of what is in the child's soul.
>
> Frederich Froebel 1887

As a playworker, you will no doubt recognise play behaviour when you see it – but how is it different from other kinds of behaviour?

How is play different from other kinds of behaviour?

Catherine Garvey (1991) suggests the following points as typical characteristics of play:

- Play is pleasurable, enjoyable . . . positively valued by the player
- Play has no extrinsic goals (i.e. the process of playing is important in itself)
- Play is spontaneous and voluntary . . . freely chosen by the player
- Play involves some active engagement on the part of the player
- Play has certain systematic relations to what is not play (i.e. play is linked with lots of other areas of activity: problem solving, creativity, socialisation . . .)

ACTIVITY 1.6

Look at the following five situations. Discuss with others: in which of them are the children playing and in which of them are they not? Use the characteristics of play suggested by Catherine Garvey (above) to help you decide.

1 Amena, Joe and Suleika are fixing blankets to bamboo canes to make a den. They are concentrating hard, but finding it very difficult to make their structure stand up on its own. Amena makes a suggestion: 'Get some clothes-pegs.' 'Get them yourself,' Joe replies. In spite of some obvious frustration the activity continues for several minutes.

2 Pasquale and Louise are sprawled on big cushions on the floor watching TV. They are both engrossed and ignore everything going on around them.

3 Alison is bouncing a ball on the ground with a bat. After a few minutes she begins to bounce it against the wall.

4 A group of four children are colouring in a picture for a colouring competition. They are concentrating and do not talk, other than to ask for a particular coloured pencil.

5 Sebastian and Natasha are having a game of hopscotch.

Sebastian: 'You stepped on the line'.
Natasha: 'No I didn't'.
Sebastian: 'Yes you did'.
Natasha: 'No I didn't'.

This continues a few times until Natasha says, 'No I didn't and no returns.'

Sebastian says, 'Last one to the bench is a slimy toad'. They run to the bench laughing.

Consider Activity 1.6. If you were watching the children in situation 1, you would probably say 'Yes, of course they are playing'. If you look back too at Garvey's characteristics of play, they all seem to fit. Amena, Joe and Suleika are engaged in an activity which we assume is freely chosen. There is a goal or end product – the den. But the end product seems less important than working out how to make the blanket stay up – the process of building. Although there are signs of frustration, the children continue to try. Is this a sign that they value what they are doing? They are involved in problem solving – how to fix up the blankets. They are interacting with each other and Amena is showing creativity in making a suggestion and wanting to try out a new idea.

In situation 2 Louise and Pasquale may be enjoying themselves, and their activity is presumably freely chosen. There is no specific end product to watching TV, although the purpose of watching might be to gain information, understanding or entertainment. Louise and Pasquale do not seem to be actively involved with each other or their surroundings, and therefore one of the characteristics of play is missing. Perhaps you will conclude that watching television is not play, although it may be a recreational or leisure-time activity.

In situation 3 Alison's behaviour is also presumably freely chosen and enjoyable. Would she stop if she were not enjoying it or finding value in it? She is actively involved with the bat and the ball, the ground and the wall.

She is developing her skills and trying out new ideas by introducing a variation to the activity. The essential ingredients of play are there.

In situation 4 the children who are colouring in are presumably doing so of their own choice and may be enjoying themselves – they are concentrating hard. The aim of the activity is specific – to produce the best-coloured picture in order to win the competition. (Garvey says play has no extrinsic goals.) Whether this goal is more important to the children than the actual process of colouring will depend on the approach that they take to the activity.

In situation 5 Sebastian and Natasha are obviously enjoying themselves – even when they are disagreeing. They are laughing. They change their behaviour voluntarily when they run off to the bench, and they are actively engaged in interacting with each other. They are developing patterns of language use and sharing an understanding of the rules of their game. Sebastian does not 'answer back' when Natasha says 'No returns'. As in situation 1 you would probably agree that these children are obviously playing, and their behaviour meets all Garvey's (1991) characteristics of play.

You can see from these examples that it is not always simple to define what is play and what is not. The same activity – such as modelling with clay – can be play, if it is freely chosen and involves enjoyable exploration of the modelling materials, or it can be a chore – as in making pots to earn a living. Doing high jumps can be play or it can be a competitive sport – where the goal of winning is the most important thing.

Play can be many things. It can be adventurous, challenging, exciting – scary even. It can be calming and therapeutic. It can be noisy or quiet, fast or slow, or a combination of any of these things. Play can be solitary, or undertaken in pairs or groups. Play can involve rules and equipment or neither.

Freedom and choice are important concepts to consider when defining play, as are enjoyment and fun – although play can involve tears as well as laughter. Play can help a child to develop and explore aspects of herself, and extend her relationships with others and with her environment: she can increase her understanding of the wider world.

Play is important in providing children with a means to develop their skills, understanding, self-confidence and self-esteem. The examples and activities throughout this book aim to increase your understanding of how and why this is so.

ACTIVITY 1.7

Spend time watching children wherever you see them: in the street, the park, the supermarket or at home (make notes later). What are they doing? If you think they are playing, what is it about their behaviour that makes you define it as play?

Important note. Such observation should be casual and informal and undertaken in the course of your everyday activities (shopping, etc.). Longer, detailed or recorded observation should only be carried out with prior arrangement and permission from parents or those in charge of a group setting such as a school or playsetting.

Play is important in developing confidence and self-esteem

ACTIVITY 1.8

Look back to Activity 1.7. What are the elements which are common to all your observations of children playing?

Discuss with a friend or your co-workers what they think are the important points in describing what play is and how it is different from other kinds of behaviour or activity.

Write down your own definition of play.

TO THINK ABOUT

Looking at your definition of play, how much of the time do children in your playsetting spend actually involved in play?

What do you do as a playworker actively to encourage play as opposed to other activities?

EXAMPLE Co-operative games session

Game 1. Name game: What's your name?

All move around the room. Each person chooses another and asks, 'What's your name?'. Take that person by the hand and introduce them to someone else: 'This is Ruth'. Then go off and ask the same question to others and introduce them (and be introduced yourself by others).

Game 2. The sun shines

All sit in a circle with one person in the middle. This person calls, 'The sun shines on everyone wearing something blue'. Everyone wearing something blue changes places with each other. Caller says, 'The sun shines on everyone who travelled by bus today' or 'likes ice-cream' or 'feels happy' or 'whose hair smells of shampoo' or any other factor which some members of the groups may have in common. If only one person has to move from the circle, they change places with the caller and become the caller themselves. If the caller has had enough, he or she can choose to join the circle at any stage and the person left without a place becomes the caller.

Game 3. Soft ball tig

Use a sponge ball the size of a football.

The person who is 'it' has the ball (there can be two 'its') and tigs others by throwing the ball. 'It' cannot move while ball is in hands. Everyone else can move in any way he or she likes except by running or walking. Once touched by the ball, players must lie still on the floor until someone frees them by touching their head, shoulders and knees.

Materials needed: one or two sponge balls.

Game 4. Octopus

One person is the octopus who sits in the middle of the room. Everyone else gathers at one end of the room. At a signal they try to get across to the other side without being caught by the octopus. Everyone who is caught becomes part of the octopus (they must stay linked in someway) and tries to catch the others until all players are caught.

Game 5. Dragons and crocodiles

One person is the storyteller. She makes up a story which the others mime along to each other in pairs. From time to time the words 'dragon' and 'crocodile' are used in the story. When dragon is mentioned, both players lie flat on the floor and cover their faces. When the word 'crocodile' is mentioned one player must help the other get their feet off the ground by holding his hands and enabling him to sit on her knees, or climb on her back while she kneels, or any other way possible. You can choose other words to be the given signals, and other actions which must follow the significant words in the story.

General guidelines

All these games can and should be adapted to suit the children you are working with. No one should find themselves excluded because of the form the game takes. If one or more members of the group cannot run but can move by rolling on the floor, you can play tig games with an added rule that everyone must roll. Make rules simpler for younger children, more complex for older children. If there are shy members in the group, play games which involve working in pairs. Develop ways of giving instructions non-verbally, using signs or pictures to explain what happens next. Encourage the children to find their own ways of adapting games to make them more challenging, more enjoyable, more fair or more attractive and accessible to all children in the group.

References

Froebel, Frederick 1887: *The Education of Man* New York: Appleton.
Garvey, Catherine 1991: *Play* Fontana.
National Occupational Standards in Playwork 1992: Sport and Recreation Lead Body, Appendix 2.

Further reading

What is play?

Bonel, Paul 1993: *Playing for Real.* National Children's Play and Recreation Unit.
Moyles, Janet, (ed.) 1994: *The Excellence of Play.* Oxford University Press.
Petrie, Pat 1994: *Play and Care.* London: HMSO.

Books on co-operative games

Dearing, Alan and Armstrong, Howard 1994: *The New Youth Games Book.* Russell House.
Dewar, Palsar Notley 1989: *Games Games Games – a co-operative games handbook.* Woodcraft Folk.
Masheder, Midred Let's Play Together 1991 Peace Education Project.
Orlick, Terry 1978: *The Cooperative Sports and Games Book – Challenge without Competition.* New York: Pantheon Books.
  (This last book is particularly useful if the idea of co-operative games is new to you. As well as useful ideas for games for children of different age-groups, it discusses some of the principles behind co-operative games: why they are important, what they are about, and ways of responding to the child who says 'I don't want to play'.)

1.2 Playwork – underpinning values

> States parties recognize the rights of the child to rest and to leisure, to engage in play and recreational activities appropriate to the age of the child.
>
> *The United Nations Convention on the Rights of the Child,* Article 31

This section considers some of the values which create the underlying philosophy of playwork. Values change and develop over time and are influenced by culture. The themes chosen for this book, and which are drawn from the value statements of the N/SVQs in playwork, are themes which have been associated with play and playwork in the UK for decades, and in some cases centuries. The same themes are threaded through this book.

You may find that many of these themes are obvious and that you take them for granted in your everyday work with children. But we all need to make time to look more closely at how our thinking and practice changes over time and to reflect what the values we believe in mean in the reality of everyday practice.

TO THINK ABOUT

Children have individual and different life stories and expectations. As a playworker you will need to consider how the opportunities you provide in your playsetting will be met by the different children who come to your setting. How can you meet the individual needs of many different children?

Differing life stories – differing values

EXAMPLE Bridget

Bridget was brought up in rural England with no brothers or sisters. Her understanding of childhood will be very different from that of Kumran, youngest child of a family of six, who spent his childhood years partly living with grandparents in a village in Pakistan and partly with his parents in an English city.

EXAMPLE Peter

Since his alcoholic father left when Peter was eight, Peter has had to take the main responsibility for caring for his mother who has severe arthritis. His understanding of what it is to be a child is different from that of Tanya, whose school years were spent in a whirl of gym clubs, music and ballet lessons, pony riding competitions and activity holidays.

Each of us develops values and assumptions about the world we live in and our own possibilities or limitations within it. Using our own experiences and sharing experiences with others, we develop and enrich our understanding of the world and of what it means to be a human being. For each of us the meaning of 'childhood' and 'play' will be different. Values change over time and are closely connected to culture.

The Channel 4 series 'Childhood' explored in depth the differences in the values attached to childhood by cultures in different parts of the world. In the Baka tribe, the children played and learned the skills of survival in the rainforest alongside older siblings and adults. The homeless street children in a city in Mexico created their own 'family' and support network between peers as a means of survival. The family in the USA had children who attended daycare from babyhood. There are often many different cultures represented in one smaller community – a city, a town, a village or your playsetting. Each child and family has their own story.

Where there are many differences there are also similarities. In his book *Childhood* Melvin Konner points out that groups of children join together for play throughout the world, and that similar games, rhymes riddles, songs and chants are found in places which are separated by thousands of miles and thousands of years.

Do not assume that everyone shares your values. For example, you may think it is important for all children to sit down and eat their packed lunches together, sharing conversation and the company of others. Your colleague may not agree – preferring to encourage the children to choose where to sit and when to eat. It is important to look at the underlying values of your work to understand and be able to explain why you think certain things are important. It is equally necessary to be open to change as new experience, new understanding and new children come your way.

You can share with others inside and outside your playsetting your understanding of what it is to be a child. By sharing experiences and ideas with other professionals, with friends and with children you can show others what playwork means to you and gain understanding of what it means to others.

Being child centred

In creating play opportunities your starting-point will be the needs and interests of the children who come or will come to your playsetting. How do you discover what these needs are?

ACTIVITY 1.9

1 Think about the things in your past which have influenced your own attitude to childhood and play.

2 List five things which you see as important values underpinning playwork: e.g. all children should be treated fairly; or children should be able to make choices

3 Share your list with another playworker and ask them to do the same. Are your lists different? Talk about what the differences are and why do you think it is so.

On a personal level you can gain insight into children's needs and interests by:

- talking to the children. Ask them about their needs and interests;
- giving the children the confidence, opportunity and right ('empowering' children) to express their own needs and make their own decisions;
- spending time watching children in general and particularly those you work with;
- studying child development – learning from other people
  (more on this in sections 2.1 and 2.2).

It is not easy to create a playsetting which is truly child centred. There are several questions which need to be addressed:

- what are your responsibilities as a playworker?
- what are the limitations imposed by the physical surroundings, organisation and health and safety considerations and resources?
- what are the expectations of parents or funding bodies?

These questions are important. Some answers could lead to an 'adult-orientated' rather than a 'child-centred' playsetting.

Some people ask 'Do children really know their own needs? At what age have they enough experience and understanding to make judgements and choices?'

Five-year-old Martin wants to eat ice cream and chocolate for every meal. Eleven-year-old Charlotte wants to play computer games all day. Do these activities meet either child's developmental needs? Does either child know of the existence of the other possibilities within the playsetting?

Child centred is not the same as child driven. Children as well as adults are influenced by their surroundings, role models and peer pressure. They are susceptible to the effects of advertising and commercial pressures will influence choices. No child or adult is alone in the playsetting. There is always the need to negotiate between different needs and wishes. An important part of many play opportunities is learning to share and to co-operate.

In his playsetting Martin gets to eat ice-cream, but not every day. This would not be possible within the resources of the playsetting. It would infringe on the choices available to other children and be counter to the playsetting's policy to promote healthy eating. But Martin's interest in ice-cream is acknowledged. He even learns how to make it. He also learns about and tastes other children's favourite recipes. He discovers that Kulfi, ice-cream from India, tastes different from the ice-cream he is used to eating at home.

Charlotte finds it difficult to accept that there is no money or space for computer games within the playsetting. She brings in her own some days and the playworker shows interest and joins in. She introduces Charlotte to Daisy, an equally enthusiastic twelve-year-old computer games expert. At the playsetting they swap games and games magazines. Over time, as Charlotte observes the many other interesting opportunities around her at the playsetting, she becomes increasingly involved in the other activities in progress.

There is often a tension between being child centred, responding to what the child wants, and how you perceive his needs as an adult. You need to consider the needs of all the children, and the requirements or limitations of the playsetting. One key to unlocking this tension is to develop good communication with the children and help them to develop independence, responsibility and the skills to negotiate and reach agreements. This requires an understanding of child development and an ability to form good relationships with children. This is covered in more detail in Chapter 2 of this book.

Your starting-point is the needs and interests of the child

ACTIVITY 1.10

To think about:
How do you involve the children within your playsetting in deciding what should happen there?
Try the following activity in your group:

1 Ask the children to draw or write, or simply talk about, their 'ideal' play setting. What do they like playing? How do they like playing?

2 Discuss with the children what is possible and not possible within the limitations of the playsetting. Your aim should be to try to make as many ideas and suggestions as possible into a reality bearing in mind essential limitations of safety, cost and organisation.

TO THINK ABOUT

How can you encourage the children to be active in determining what happens in your playsetting on an ongoing basis?

Involving children

If your playsetting is child centred, the children will be involved in the planning and decision making. That way they can make choices and discover their own solutions. They can play and develop at their own pace and in their own way. Children throughout the world can and do participate in deciding on and creating their own play opportunities. The way in which they are able to do this within your playsetting will depend on their stage of development, the nature of the playsetting and the opportunities they are given to participate.

You need to be flexible in order to engage actively with each child to discover what he needs. Then you can work with him to meet these needs within the playsetting.

Adults joining in – or interfering?

Play begins from birth. A baby plays with her own fingers in her cot, or with her mother's hair or face while feeding or being carried. The parent or carer

By joining in children's play, adults can show that they think play is valuable and important

can increase the infant's pleasure in playing and her incentive or wish to continue her efforts, by responding positively. The infant will be rewarded by a smile, encouraging words, and being given new play materials at the right time – a mobile hung above the cot to look at, a rattle to hold, bite and shake, or an opportunity to see dappled sunshine through leafy branches, for example. In providing these things the adult is showing the baby that play is valuable and important.

CASE STUDY 1.5: THE ROLE OF THE PLAYWORKER

At the adventure playground, Robert and Hafiz are building a large construction using empty oil drums, planks of wood, plastic milk crates and car tyres. They have amassed their building materials from around the playground site and are attempting to balance the third oil drum on top, but are finding it difficult to get up to the height required to achieve this balancing act.

There are four workers. Each would give a different response to this situation:

- *Worker A* sees what is going on. Does nothing. She believes children should be allowed to 'get on with it'. Adults should not interfere in children's play.
- *Worker B* sees what is going on, calls across the playground, 'Oi. Hold on. That's not safe. Let me give you a hand.' Walks over to the children and balances the oil drum in position.
- *Worker C* sees the situation. Walks over to the boys. 'That looks interesting. How many oil drums do you think you can balance on top of each other?' Both boys look at him and say nothing. 'How do you think we can find out?'
- *Worker D* sees the situation. Approaches close to the boys and watches and listens. She discovers that the boys are trying to build a bulldozer. She asks, 'Do you think the small step-ladder from the store cupboard would help?' As Robert returns with the ladder, she adds; 'There is a pulley in the office which might help in making the bulldozer's lever when you need it. Oh and have you seen the hard hats in the dressing-up box?' She walks on.

Discuss which of the responses is most appropriate? Why?

The case study above shows how adults can respond to childrens play in different ways. Worker A believed in a non-intervening approach. Children will learn for themselves. In many cases this might be true. Alternatively, Hafiz and Robert might have given up in frustration, or the oil drum might have fallen on someone's head.

Worker B was vigilant about safety. However, Hafiz and Robert will have learnt nothing about how to build more safely next time, or how to take responsibility for their own safety. They will become more dependant on adults.

Worker C was interested in what Robert and Hafiz could learn from the situation about building, number and balance. However, the children's motivation for building was lost. They were unresponsive because the focus of their play had been switched from building a bulldozer to building a tower and counting numbers of oil drums. The control of the direction of their play was taken over by the adult.

Worker D spent time 'tuning in' to what the focus of the children's play was. She considered what their needs might be. She made a suggestion and offered resources which would both improve safety and extend the imaginative aspect of their play without taking over control.

The presence of a responsive, sensitive adult who accompanies but does not control children's play can enrich their play experiences. Children learn a lot through imitation and will often take their lead from the adults around them. They need adults to provide some resources which they cannot get for themselves. Adults can also help them acquire new skills – such as how to use tools.

Safety

Children have the right to expect adults to protect them from harm as far as this is possible. Your role within the playsetting will include ensuring not only physical safety, but also emotional security: a space in which children can play free from fear of bullying, racism, sexism or other forms of harassment. Chapter 4 looks specifically at this.

Challenge and risk

Play is not always about playing safe. Perhaps you remember the 'high points' of your own play: the risks (real or imagined) you took when you successfully retrieved your ball from the neighbours yard without getting caught, or when you balanced the length of the high wall down the street, or managed to climb to the top of the tallest tree in your village? Do you remember the achievements of lighting your first match – and maybe burning your fingers? Learning to roller-skate – and the many bruises you had to show for it?

Similar events to these form an important part of growth and development through play for all children. You need to offer opportunities for challenge and risk through which they can explore their surroundings and develop their own skills, independence and confidence.

Play is not always about playing safe

Building confidence and self-esteem

Many challenges which children have to face from an early age set them up for failure. They have to compete against brothers and sisters, classmates, children with more money, children who can run faster, children who are better at maths and so on. From an early age they will learn about stereotypes which limit or distort the way other people treat them or other children around them because of their gender, religion, disability, colour of their skin or other personal family circumstance.

If the challenges and the pace of play are determined by the children themselves, good play opportunities can release children from the fear of failure and the need to compete. Each child can be encouraged to set his or her own milestones or goalposts. For one child this might be beating his own best score in skipping, for another it might be making a friend, learning to juggle with four balls or cooking something which is appreciated by others. At each stage your role is to encourage and extend each child's options and possibilities for being. It is important to start from where the child is at, and to give her the reins in deciding both the pace and direction of the play.

CASE STUDY 1.6: GAINING PHYSICAL CONFIDENCE

Philip wants to join the others in skateboarding on the ramp. He has never tried to skateboard, and is afraid of looking 'uncool'. He confides his fears in Parveen, the playworker. She talks this over with him, reassures him, points out all the things he is good at. Philip is not convinced. Parveen shows him her own inexpert efforts and points out that Sarah over there is also learning for the first time. Philip still hangs back.

Parveen drops the subject for while. Then, one day the following week, she remembers that Philip is a wizard on a BMX. She digs out a couple of bikes from the back of the store shed and suggests that the skateboard ramp should be used for bikes for a couple of days for a change. The children agree.

Philip excels himself to the admiration of all his peers. Parveen encourages him to teach his skills to the expert skateboarders. Three days later Philip's confidence in his image among his peers is sky high. Now he is ready to learn how to skateboard from them.

ACTIVITY 1.11

Read the following two case studies.

1 Meera is 11 years old. Her confident younger sister also comes to the playsetting and teases her mercilessly about the fact that she does not dare swing off the play-platform on the pulley rope. Meera desperately wants to have a go, but on the two occasions she has climbed up on the platform, she has frozen, burst into tears and climbed down.

2 Neville is eight years old. His parents are from Trindad. His mother has mentioned that his school reports say he excels at sport and playing percussion in the school band. You have noticed that he has a quick eye for solving technical problems. One day he asks you to work out how much tarpaulin will be needed to cover the play dome he and his friends have been making. 'About twice as wide as that pole and three and half times as long,' he tells you. You suggest he help you measure it and work out how many metres you will have to order. 'Nah,' he replies, 'I can't do maths.'

What play opportunities could you plan to meet the expressed needs and interests of Meera and Neville? How could you provide them with challenges which would increase their skills, confidence and understanding?

Children can encourage and inspire each other

Children's confidence or lack of it will vary in different activities. One child may be confident in a game of football but shy and withdrawn in a group discussion. Another child is confident in making friends and all sociable activities, but becomes very anxious in activities which are physically challenging, such as running, jumping or climbing.

Lack of confidence can have many causes. You may never discover why a particular child lacks confidence in a particular area, but you can try to help them develop it. Philip (Case study 1.6) was anxious about how he was viewed by peers. This may be just a natural part of growing up or may stem from experiences of being bullied or ridiculed. In either case his self-esteem needed boosting.

In Activity 1.11, Meera appears to have a fear of heights. This is not helped by the teasing of her younger sister. Such fears can be learned or may be inherent phobias. The first step is to take her away from the pressure of her sister's observation and to encourage her to conquer her fear in small stages which she feels happy and ready to undertake.

Neville has already decided he 'can't do maths'. You have observed that this is not the case. Perhaps he is becoming a victim of the old stereotype that black youth are 'good at sport' and 'have natural rhythm' but are not any good at academic subjects?

As playworker you would need to convince Neville that he has shown himself to be good at maths. Look at the skills and language he used in describing how much tarpauline he needed! Perhaps you would offer to help him 'do the maths' the first time, but explain that if he is not able to develop the skills to do this on his own he will not be able to undertake similar tasks independently in future. Maybe you would look for opportunities to enable him to work out the number problems involved with other projects in which he shows an interest: empower him to take increasing responsibility for coping with this kind of challenge, which he will continue to face in his play and in all other aspects of life. Additionally, as playworker in Neville's playsetting it would be important to look at what messages the books, pictures and music of the playsetting are giving him. Do they reinforce the stereotype that the only black people of note are musicians or sports people? Whatever playsetting you work in and whatever the mix of children who come, it is important to be aware of the messages implied in the resources you provide. Such messages may be more significant to children than what you say to them.

Play for all

Play is for all children. Playwork has always embraced ideas of equal opportunities. That is because the concept of equal opportunities is about fairness, and fairness is very important to so much of children's play. That does not mean that playworkers know it all or can afford to be complacent. There are many examples of good and bad practice in respect of equal opportunities within playsettings. I still hear playworkers saying, 'We believe in equal opportunities we treat all the children the same'. Equal opportunities is not about treating all children the same. It is about recognising that we are all different and have different things to offer and different needs to be met.

Earlier in this section I touched on what it could mean for a playsetting to be child centred – recognising and respecting each child as an individual with his or her own life story, needs and expectations. If this is the approach you take to your work, you have an understanding of at least part of what it means to practise equal opportunities in a playsetting. But working towards achieving equal opportunities in a playsetting requires more than a child centred approach alone.

CASE STUDY 1.7: 'IT DOESN'T APPLY TO US'

Mrs Bolton runs an after-school club in a church hall in a suburban town south of London. She says: 'All the children in my club come from the same kind of families. They are all white. So are the children in the school. Equal opportunities isn't important in our case.'

What do you think?

'Equal opportunities' is not only about skin colour. It is about recognising that there are many groups of people who face discrimination in our society and the world over – on the grounds of gender, nationality, race, disability, age, sexual orientation, religious persuasion or other factors. Playwork is concerned with meeting the needs of individual children, and helping them to meet their full potential.

Celebrating differences

People are discriminated against because they are different from the majority or those who hold the power. We are all sometimes afraid of the unfamiliar and the unknown. We can jump to conclusions about why people look, dress, behave as they do.

The world would be a boring place if we were all the same. It is the differences between us that create the interest, the challenge, and that enable us to change and develop ourselves. Differences can be cause for exploration, discovery and celebration.

Many play opportunities can encourage children to accept and value differences in each other. A child who can speak another language or use sign language has a valuable skill to share. Dressing up allows children to try out different roles and images. Talent shows can be opportunities for some children to display their 'hidden talents' but need to be sensitively handled so

---

TO THINK ABOUT

What can be done to ensure such oppression is not present within your playsetting?

Can good play opportunities counter-balance some of the effects of discrimination in the wider world?

ACTIVITY 1.12

Plan two ways in which you can introduce ideas and materials from different cultures into an activity which is currently popular in your playsetting.

EXAMPLE

If building houses and dens is currently popular, you could begin by discussing with the children the different kinds of buildings people live in: flats, bungalows, terraced and so on. Ask if any children lived in any other kinds of accommodation? (In a playsetting I visited recently one child lived on a canal boat, another in a caravan and one had lived in a house on stilts in Indonesia.)

Use books to research other kinds of dwellings – a North American Tipi or a Mongolian Yurt. Some children might be interested in trying to build a copy of one of these dwellings in the playsetting, which may well lead to other kinds of imaginative play, stories and research into appropriate dressing-up clothes, cooking utensils or musical instruments.

that they do not become a platform for only the children who are already bursting with confidence. The best kind of talent shows I have seen have been organised on the spur of the moment. A playworker discovers with delight that the usually quiet and withdrawn 13-year-old Nada with mobility difficulties can juggle with five balls, or that eight-year-old Andrew, who has tried to learn to whistle since he was five has finally cracked it. With the agreement of the new 'star', a small audience is hastily drawn together to watch and show appreciation and applause.

Your playsetting will be a richer, more exciting place for all the cultural materials from all over the world which you bring into it. If you have children from families of different cultural backgrounds you are fortunate to have a first-hand resource. Encourage the children to talk about and, if they are willing, bring examples of different customs, festivals, languages, food, music and clothes.

Whatever topic is currently popular in your playsetting, you can expand and enliven it by introducing ideas and materials from different cultures.

Other play opportunities which are obvious starting-points for including multicultural resources are those involving food, islands, carnivals, festivals, families, clothes, songs and music. You will be able to think of many more. The point is that any theme will be experienced differently by different cultures, and each will be able to contribute another outlook and a variety of ways in which to express it.

Even if you do not have children from a variety of cultural backgrounds in your playsetting you will still be able to research and introduce play materials from other cultures. It is perhaps even more important for these children, with no direct daily experience of other cultures, that they have opportunities to develop understanding of the multicultural world in which they live. These days children may well not stay in the area they are brought up in – knowledge of other cultures equips them to deal with future life experiences.

Educational and play materials supply catalogues now offer a range of multicultural materials from dressing-up clothes to musical instruments, dolls, song

Fashion Show. Some activities encourage children to try out other ways of being

books and cooking equipment. Make contact with specialist 'multicultural resource centres'. (Your local authority education department might be able to help. See also Appendix 2.) Make or develop personal contacts with people from different cultures. Ask them if they are willing and able to share with you their skills, knowledge and understanding. Perhaps you know someone who is prepared to come into the playsetting and talk about their lives within another culture – to tell stories, cook with the children, or help you celebrate a festival. However, do not assume they know everything about their own culture.

A festivals calendar (see Activity 1.13) may be useful in a number of ways. You will know if any of the children of your playsetting has a special or festival day, and can share it with them. For example, you will know the reason why some or all the Muslim children do not come to the setting on a particular day (Eid for example), or why they are wearing special new clothes. If you do not have children from a variety of cultures in your playsetting you will be able to take the opportunity of some of the special days to introduce a taste of the wider world into their lives.

(A calendar of religious festivals is produced by SHAP Working Party on World Religion in Education, available from The National Society's Religious Education Centre – see Appendix 2.)

Anti-discriminatory practice

Anti-discriminatory practice is not just about avoiding discriminatory behaviour within the playsetting. It requires active thinking, planning and evaluation by you and your managers.

A commitment to equal opportunities is essential. But how do you put this into practice? There are suggestions throughout this book and more information and in-depth consideration will be found in the books listed in Further reading at the end of this chapter.

Some of the areas you will need to consider are:

1   *Choosing resources and avoiding stereotypes.*   As well as using play materials from different cultures, you will need to look at how people are portrayed within books, posters or other images. From an early age children become aware of the 'boxes' that different people are put into by society, and the labels that are attached to them. Common stereotypes include:

- 'Girls can't play football';
- 'Disabled people are helpless';
- 'Asian women are docile';
- 'Homosexual people get AIDS'.

These are common and very simple stereotypes. The point about all stereotypes, is that they are generalisations – often based on ignorance and prejudice.

In the playsetting you can counteract some of these common stereotypes by choosing resources and stories which show people with disabilities, women, girls, black people and people from different cultural backgrounds in a variety of roles with positive value attached.

Your own attitude and example is important too. You will need to be sensitive in the language you use and the role models you and your co-workers provide. As a male worker are you always expected to take more responsibility than the female workers for repairs and construction, organising team games or sports and maintaining discipline? Or do you also care for injured or upset children, prepare and serve refreshments or wipe the floor? As a female worker, have you developed skills in woodwork, construction or team sports?

ACTIVITY 1.13

Obtain a calendar or diary which includes the festival days of the major world religions and cultures. Choose one festival – the Chinese New Year, the birth of Haile Selassi, Chanukka or Diwali, for example.

Plan how to introduce this festival to the children of your playsetting – with music, craft, food, props, costumes? Can you enlist the help of some of the children, parents, your colleagues or members of the local community?

Beware of making the playsetting into a classroom. Concentrate on play opportunities and involving children in activities which interest them. Learning new information will be a valuable bonus.

TO THINK ABOUT

Children are human beings who happen to be either male of female. They should clearly have the opportunity of exploring all aspects of human behaviour as children. If you try to make a child stick to the "right sex" then you deprive him or her of half the world.

(From *An Equal Start* published by the Equal Opportunities Commission.)

TO THINK ABOUT

Is your playsetting a place which encourages every child to feel that she or he is welcomed and accepted? Does each child feel that he or she has equal rights to participate in what happens there? How do you know?

2 *Challenging discrimination.* By the time the children are old enough to come to your playsetting, many of them will have learned what it is like to be a victim of prejudice, and will have had their self-esteem damaged by such experiences.

As a playworker you have a responsibility to challenge racist, sexist and other forms of discriminatory language or behaviour within the playsetting. If it is left unchallenged the perpetrator and victim of such behaviour, as well as any children standing by, will assume that you find the behaviour acceptable. The way in which you challenge will depend on the circumstances of the incident, your knowledge of those involved, and the age and development of those involved. Discriminatory language and behaviour may be unintentional and unconscious and learned through imitating adults who are important in the life of the child. In the situation described in Activity 1.14 below, Ronnie may well have been unaware that his language was racist. He may have learned it from people who are very important to him. You will need to be sensitive in the way you challenge and in the way you support.

ACTIVITY 1.14

Consider the following situation:

1 Ronnie, Ahmed and Julia are on the same team. They are friends and have invented their own relay race game. It is Ahmed's turn to run. Ronnie starts shouting, 'Run. Hurry you stupid Paki. Get a move on!' Ronnie and Ahmed have been friends for a long time. They are both aged six. You have never heard Ronnie use the term 'Paki' before.

How would you react? What would you say to both boys?

2 Get two colleagues to play the part of the two boys and practice what you would say to them as playworker. If possible get a fourth person to observe and comment, with positive suggestions for other possible ways of responding.

TO THINK ABOUT

Would your response be different if the incident had involved an older child or a worker? You could try the role play above, raising the age and perhaps changing the name of the people involved. Note whether and how your responses changed.

When you are challenging discriminatory behaviour your body language and tone of voice are important. Aim to be relaxed, informative and unthreatening, and to achieve the following three goals:

- to raise the awareness of the person responsible for the incident. Say clearly what you find unacceptable and why;
- to change the behaviour of the person responsible to ensure that it does not happen again;
- to be supportive of the person who is on the receiving end of the discriminatory behaviour by showing clearly that you find it unacceptable and to help rebuild self-esteem.

You can provide a good role model if you are open to challenge of your own behaviour and language. We all have our own prejudices and areas of ignorance, and people can be very defensive about this. They are worried that they will say the wrong thing. Others dismiss such anxieties by saying, 'I don't believe in all this politically correct language nonsense'.

Language, including social labels, popular jargon and what are considered acceptable terms, changes over time and as our thinking and awareness changes. We need to be sensitive in the language we use. Language carries meaning – and often the meaning it has for the listener is different from and more damaging than the meaning that was intended by the speaker. In Activity 1.14, do you think Ahmed understood the term 'Paki' in the way it was meant or intended by Ronnie?

If you are unsure about whether a word you use might cause offence, ask the person to whom or about whom you are speaking. Raise the subject of language at a staff meeting, preferably before an incident arises. Try to create an atmosphere within the playsetting where it is acceptable for staff and children to question and challenge language which they think might be offensive to others, and where they can explain why they think it is offensive. The responsibility of pointing out a remark which may be offensive should not always lie with the person to whom offence might be caused.

ACTIVITY 1.15

Consider this situation:

Your manager comes to a team meeting. She says, 'I was asked if we could take an eleven-year-old girl with epilepsy. She is also profoundly deaf. Of course I had to say no. We simply haven't got the expertise or staff to cope with a child like that.'

1 How could you challenge the phrase, 'a child like that'? Did your manager meet the child? Did she find out exactly what the needs of this particular child were?

2 What arguments could you use to convince your manager that it is important to give serious consideration to finding a way to offer this child a place, and the potential benefits this would have to the playsetting and everyone within it?

---

3. *Integration.* Including, or integrating, children with special needs in your playsetting can give each child an opportunity to experience play in whatever way is open to them. You can help each child to discover their own possibilities. All children benefit from having children with different needs and abilities around them and being part of their play. They have the opportunity to become more sensitive to the needs of others and to overcome ignorance and prejudice.

There are often barriers to children with disabilities participating, or participating fully in playsettings. These barriers fall into three categories:

- physical – unsuitable access and toilet arrangements, transport, insufficient resources or inappropriate equipment,
- attitude – anxiety, prejudice, lack of interest, understanding or concern of key members of the playsetting
- organisational – the routines, rules, supervision, aims and activities of the playsetting.

If you do not have any children with disabilities or special needs, what are the reasons for this?

You may need to consider whether your playsetting is accessible – wide doors, ramps, transport, and so on. You may need to raise the issues with your supervisor or manager – for example, the need to make adaptations to premises, materials, equipment and activities in order for some children to be able to participate fully in play with their peers. Some children may need extra adult support, medical care or supervision to ensure their safety and give them equal opportunities within the playsetting.

4. *Training and evaluation.* Playworkers need time to consider their own values and attitudes. You will need time to share concerns, ideas and understanding and to learn about new ways of working. It is important that the values of your playsetting are clearly stated in the form of poli-

---

ACTIVITY 1.16

Is your playsetting available to all children?

List the things which you think would help or hinder integration of children with disabilities or other special needs within your playsetting. Use the three headings listed under 'Integration'.

cies which are understood by all. It is equally important to find ways of monitoring that the policies are put into practice. This is covered in more detail in section 5.3.

You need time to reflect on your playwork practice and refresh your ideas. This can be done by choosing a particular topic – safety, say, or creating links with the community – to discuss and work with during a staff development meeting. One or two workers may attend external training in a particular area and bring new ideas back to the rest of the team and the playsetting as a whole.

The wider world

There may be many practical considerations to be addressed to make your playsetting accessible. Do you need to get your information translated into other languages? Will you need additional staff to support children with disabilities or other special needs?

Building links is a two-way activity. Think about what you and your playsetting have to offer the wider community – in particular your understanding of the importance and value of play.

Your playsetting can be a small version of the wider world. Fill it with possibilities for exploration and discovery of nature, science, people, emotions, skills, sharing, caring and lots of fun.

A child's right to play

Children's right to play is recognised by the United Nations Convention on the Rights of the Child (Article 31). World leaders, politicians, educationalists and many others agree that play is valuable, even essential to healthy human development. But many things in our adult society can limit or hinder childrens opportunities for play.

Ideally every street would have a safe play space, each and every child would be able to meet his or her friends and come and go as she or he pleased,

Learning new skills and developing co-operation through play

Play: a child's right

with no roads or other hazards to encounter and overcome. This is not a reality. A study undertaken by Hillman, *et al.* 1990 compared children's independent access to external environments, and compared their finding with an earlier study undertaken in 1971. The study found marked changes in certain aspects of childhood lifestyle. For example, in 1971, 80 per cent of seven- and eight-year-olds were allowed to go to school on their own. By 1990 this figure had dropped to 9 per cent. Parents have become increasingly aware of the dangers of traffic, violence and possible abduction. In many cases traditional play spaces such as the street are now prohibited to children.

Play is seen by many as an unimportant way of letting off steam or passing the time in between real activities such as formal education or work. Play opportunities are shaped by other adult-orientated considerations:

- *Politics, money and town planning.* Towns, cities and roads are built with adult needs in mind and opportunities for play are often overlooked or catered for in a token or inappropriate way: for example, small parks with limited play equipment next to busy roads.
- *Early responsibilities.* Some children need to work from a very young age. They have to care for younger brothers and sisters, or a parent with disabilities, or they need to work outside the home to contribute to the upkeep of the family.
- *Parents at work, school, leisure time classes.* Children's time is often structured by the needs of parents' work schedules, school timetables and organised leisure activities such as gym classes, swimming, dancing or music lessons.
- *Consumerism and entertainment.* In our society, where there is a wealth of bought games, toys and equipment, children may have fewer opportunities to develop resourcefulness, to invent or to try out their own ideas. Toy manufacturers rush to produce more attractive and entertaining, or so-called educational, toys. They encourage the children to receive this entertainment or education rather than be active in discovering and exploring the environment in which they live.
- *Television.* The content and timetable of television programmes is also adult determined. Watching TV does not need active participation from the child, and often takes up a large proportion of children's free time.

As a playworker you need to be aware of the conflicting nature of some of these issues. On the one hand you need to provide a safe playsetting with play opportunities which interest and attract the children. But you are not there to provide entertainment to be passively absorbed by them, or which is attractive primarily to parents. You are an advocate and facilitator of the child's right to play.

ACTIVITY 1.18

1 Conduct a small survey among a group of children aged 5–8, 8–11, or 11–14 in your local area and ask them:

- where do they spend most time playing?;
- where would they like to spend most time playing, if there was no restrictions or limitations?

Note: It is probably best if you arrange to carry out this survey by making contact with a school in the area and getting permission to carry out your survey within the school.

2 Compare this survey within your finding about facilities available in your local area (Activity 1.1). What do these two surveys tell you about play opportunities in your chosen area? Does the provision meet the needs and interests expressed by the children?

Adults need to take the lead in actively campaigning for and creating play-settings. In circumstances which are indifferent or even hostile to the child's right to play, children must continue to have access to play opportunities which expand their horizons and their potential for all-round development.

Legislation

Play opportunities should always be provided within the current legislative framework relevant to children's rights, health, safety and well-being.
National Occupational Standards in Playwork 1992, Appendix 2

The legal aspects of your work are raised in relevant chapters throughout this book. Some particular pieces of legislation relate to your playsetting as a whole and to the underpinning values discussed in this chapter.

The Children Act 1989

This is a very wide ranging piece of legislation which brings together many other previous laws and regulations relating to the needs of children and the responsibilities of local authorities and other agencies. The main themes of the Children Act are:

- the best place for the child to be brought up is usually his or her own family;
- children in need are best helped by local authorities and other support agencies working together with parents to provide appropriate support, advice and protection;
- local authorities have a responsibility to support families, review provision, identify needs and plan to meet these needs;
- children and their parents need to be kept informed of all matters relating to them to have the opportunity to make their wishes known, and to participate in decision making.

Daycare and play services

The part of the Children Act which particularly relates to play and playcare services is laid down in *The Children Act 1989 – Guidance and Regulations*, Vol. 2 (1991). All daycare services which cater for children under eight years of age, which are open for more than two hours a day and for six days or more in one year, are required to be registered by, and have an annual inspection from, their local authority. The term 'daycare services' here includes childminders, day nurseries, playgroups, out-of-school clubs, holiday schemes, and mobile projects such as playbuses. Some facilities such as open access schemes, adventure playgrounds and some supervised activity sessions (sport, music, art and craft) for example are also required to register. These facilities do not necessarily set out to provide daycare or meet the childcare needs of working parents.

Promoting good practice

The aim of the legislation is to encourage and promote good practice in play and daycare services for children under 8 years of age. How local authorities interpret and assess what is meant by good practice will vary somewhat from one authority to another, and will change over time, as new ideas and research are accepted into our way of thinking about childcare and play.

General issues which are seen as affecting good practice are set out as follows:

- children's welfare and development are paramount;
- children should be treated and respected as individuals whose needs (including special needs) should be catered for;
- parents' responsibility for their children should be recognised and respected;
- the values deriving from different backgrounds – racial, cultural, religious, and linguistic – should be recognised and respected;
- parents are generally the first educators of their children; this should be reflected in relationships with other carers and providers;
- parents should have easy access to information about services in their area and be able to make informed choices.

The Children Act 1989 Guidance and Regulations, Vol. 2, Chapter 6 Section A

Meeting needs

The Children Act gives local authorities a duty to safeguard and promote the welfare of children in need by providing a range of appropriate services. A child in need is defined as one who is:

(a) . . . unlikely to achieve or maintain, or to have the opportunity of achieving or maintaining, a reasonable standard of health or development without the provision for him or services by a local authority . . .;

(b) his health or development is likely to be significantly impaired, or further impaired without the provision for him of such services; or

(c) he is disabled.

The kinds of services to be provided for children in need will include play and childcare services. The local authority do not have to own services, but can 'buy in' services through subsidised or sponsored places.

Registration and inspection by local authority

Your local authority will have its own guidance notes about its requirements for registration. Your playsetting should have a copy. The guidance notes will include information on:

- the procedures for registering your service;
- the requirements in terms of number of places, size of groups, premises and space standards, staff/child ratios, number of toilets and washbasins;
- other staffing issues – police and health checks, references, qualifications, experience and training, requirements and approach to health and safety, food preparation, record keeping, activities, toys and equipment, and involvement of parents.

Equal opportunities and discrimination

The legislation relating to these issues has implications for staff employment and the rights of employees, and for working with children and their families within the playsetting.

The Children Act is the first legislation regarding childcare which specifically refers to a child's religious persuasion, racial origin and cultural and linguistic background, and actively encourages good anti-racist and anti-discriminatory practice. It promotes the idea that good childcare includes meeting the needs of individual children, providing resources which are of value to them and promoting positive images of children from different family types and backgrounds.

The Race Relations Act legislates against direct and indirect forms of discrimination on the grounds of race, colour, nationality, ethnic or national origin. It also outlaws segregation and victimisation. The Sex Discrimination

TO THINK ABOUT

How do you decide what is good practice within your playsetting?

Many of the activities in later chapters of this book will help you look at this in more detail.

ACTIVITY 1.19

Is your playsetting required to be registered under the Children Act 1989?

If the answer is no, what are the reasons for this?

If the answer is yes:

- find out which department in your local authority is responsible for registering and inspecting your playsetting

- ask for a copy of your authority's guidance notes and requirements for registration relevant to your playsetting.

TO THINK ABOUT

What things would you see as direct or indirect discrimination in the playsetting?

Act 1975, legislates against discrimination on the grounds of gender. You can get further information, publications and advice from: Commission for Racial Equality and The Equal Opportunities Commission (see Appendix 2: Useful contacts at back of this book).

> Indirect discrimination is important because it may not be intentional, but be a result of long-held practices which have the effect of discriminating.
>
> Jane Lane 1990

Jane Lane, from the Commission for Racial Equality, points out that refusing to admit a child to a play- or daycare setting simply because she is black (or white) would be direct unlawful discrimination. An example of indirect discrimination she gives is one where a setting sets conditions which can be seen as 'fair in form' but which put certain groups at a disadvantage – for example, if places are allocated to children whose parents are part of a circle of friends and acquaintances who have spread the word among themselves. This would be unlawful if it excluded a particular racial group and could not be justified.

Discrimination does not have to be intentional to be unlawful. There is at the present time no legislation which gives comparable rights to staff or children with disabilities or other special needs. New legislation is currently going through Parliament, and the principles of equal opportunities for children with special needs are embedded both in the Children Act and legislation relating to education. This is an area where the policies of the playsetting may need to go beyond the law (this is considered further in section 5.3).

Other relevant legislation

There are many other laws affecting individuals and organisations which can have a bearing on playwork. Mostly these relate to management responsibilities in a playsetting and establishing its legal status as an organisation:

- The Town and Country Planning Act 1990 will affect which premises are suitable or allowed to be used for play facilities, and will also need to be considered if a new building or alterations to an existing building are planned.
- If you are part of a small business you can consult your local Small Business Advice Service or Training and Enterprise Council (TEC) for information. Local authority economic development officers or departments may also have useful information and advice.
- If your playsetting is a voluntary organisation with charitable status you will need to comply with the Charities Act 1992 and adopt a constitution which is recognised by the Charity Commission. Kids' Clubs Network have a model constitution in their 'Here's How' publication (see Appendix 2, Useful contacts).

Health and Safety legislation is covered in Chapter 4 of the book.

Summary

The values of playwork introduced in this section are referred to throughout the book:

- that the child should be the centre of the process;
- that children have rights and should be consulted and able to participate in decision making about their play;
- that children's play opportunities can be enriched by sensitive adult involvement;

- that through appropriate play experiences children can develop confidence and self-esteem;
- that while play which offers challenge and risk is important for development, it is equally important for children to feel physically and personally safe;
- that each child and each family has their own life story and the right to consideration and respect from others;
- that there is no place for prejudice and discrimination in any playsetting – play should promote equality of opportunity;
- that play promotes understanding of the wider world. It involves co-operation within, and with those outside the playsetting – a sharing of skills and sensitivity to the needs of others;
- that adults should support children's rights to accessible play environments.

Finally, playwork must be carried out within the framework of current legislation.

References

1984 (1994): *An Equal Start*. Equal Opportunities Commission.

Department of Health 1991: *Guidance and Regulations to the Children Act 1989*, Vol. 2. London: HMSO.

Guidelines for the Selection of Toys and Other Resources (WGARCR).

Lane, Jane *'Sticks and Carrots' Local Government Policy Making* Vol. 17 No. 3.

Hillman, Adams and Whitelegg 1990: *One False Move . . . A study of Children's Independent Mobility*. The Policy Studies Institute.

National Occupational Standards in Playwork 1992: Sport and Recreation Industry Lead Body.

Further reading

About playwork values

The Charter for Children's Play 1992: National Voluntary Council for Children's Play. (A booklet outlining a charter for children's play which has been adopted by many national organisations and local authorities.)

Guidelines of good practice for out-of-school care schemes. Kids Clubs Network 1993.

Lubelska, Anna (ed.) 1993: *Better Play*. The National Children's Bureau. (A series of articles on different aspects of thinking about play.)

About involving children

Hart, Roger 1992: *Children's Participation: from Tokenism to Citizenship*. UNICEF International Development Centre.

Westland and Knight 1982: *Playing, Living, Learning*. Venture Publishing.

About equal opportunities

Melville, Sandra 1994: *Gender Matters*. Playboard.

1993: *Equal Opportunities: Some Guidelines* Journal 10 HAPA.

1995: *Playing Fair*. The National Early Years Network and Save the Children. (A readable booklet with practical suggestions for helping children to resist bias.) Early Years Trainers Anti-Racist Network (EYTARN) and

HAPA produce several other relevant publications. The Working Group Against Racism in Children's Resources (WGARCR) have produced guidance, and resource lists for selecting books, toys and resources and finding suppliers of multicultural and anti-racist resources. See Appendix 2 for the addresses for these organisations and others who support and promote playwork.

Legislation

Forbes, Duncan, Hayes, Ruth and Reason, Jaki 1990: *Voluntary but not Amateur.* London Voluntary Service Council. (This book outlines the legal responsibilities of voluntary organisations, including premises, liability, insurance and accounts.)

2 Play and child development

2.1 Understanding child development

> Through play the child explores the world and her or his relationships with it, elaborating all the while a flexible range of responses to the challenges she or he encounters; by playing the child learns and develops as an individual.
>
> *National Occupational Standards in Playwork* 1992, Appendix 2

This section considers some of the ways in which you can look at child development. It encourages you to reflect on why it is important for you, as a playworker, to have some understanding of child development. Learning to observe children is seen as an important way for you to gain understanding of children's behaviour and development. Good observation can be a key to discovering their needs within the play setting.

Child development is a vast subject, and suggestions for further reading are given at the end of this section. For centuries people have been fascinated by child development. What makes each child unique? What makes many children of a similar age go through the same phases? Why is it that we think a five-year-old should be ready for school, for reading and writing, a twelve-year-old to travel across town, and a sixteen-year-old to leave home?

Nature/nurture

Children have two biological parents: the two people who provide the sperm and the egg from which the child is conceived. Every child inherits traits from two sets of genes. Their combination will determine the child's physical appearance and may influence many other things about the child. There are different theories about how much the child's character, growth and development are formed by inherited genes (that is, 'nature'), and how much is influenced by things which happen to the child after he has been conceived and born (that is, 'nurture'). A child's development can be affected by:

- nutrition;
- the care she receives;
- the response he receives from other people after birth and during childhood;
- family make-up and circumstances (for example, poverty, wealth employment);
- the environment in which she lives (for example, housing, town, country);
- family culture and religious beliefs;
- illness;

- other circumstances and experiences of stress (for example, accidents, bereavement, abuse);
- opportunities to mix with other children and adults;
- opportunities for education, leisure, play.

By the time a child is five years old, and maybe comes to your playsetting for the first time, she will bring with her a range of individual experiences and expectations and will have individual needs for you to discover and help her meet. She will generally have reached over half her adult height and achieved the greatest milestones of development: walking, talking and independent feeding, dressing and hygiene.

Ages and stages

As well as noting the differences in individual children, people studying child development have also identified that all over the world children go through similar stages in a similar order. Before children can read or write they need to be able to recognise shapes, understand symbols and hold and control a writing tool. Before a child can dress himself he must be able to co-ordinate his hands and fingers well enough to do up buttons or handle zips. Before a child can cross a busy road safely she must be aware of the danger, be able to judge the speed of oncoming cars, and know how to be consistent in looking to the right and to the left to see if the road is clear.

Each child develops at his or her own rate. No two six-year-olds will be at the same stage in terms of their skills and knowledge and understanding. But it is useful to look at broad stages of what you can expect at different ages, so that you can plan activities which are appropriate. It is no good planning a game with complicated rules for five- to six-year-olds, or one which involves a lot of reading or writing. Equally a ten-year-old may object to 'babyish' ring games, and lose interest in activities that are not challenging enough. Section 2.2 looks more closely at stages of development.

Knowledge of child development can also help you recognise that a child is nowhere near the stage you might expect for her age. You can then look

No two children will have the same skills, understanding and experience

for the causes of this and, if possible, identify what she needs to enable her to keep up with other children of her age. Remember, children are individuals. Knowledge about stages of development is useful, but it should not stop you from recognising that each child is different and will develop in his own way.

Family and culture

Cultural and family background will have a major influence on many aspects of development. Every culture has different expectations of its children. Every family has different physical, social and economic circumstances. For example:

- what is expected of boys and girls in terms of behaviour, dress, later work?
- what social contacts do they have?
- what resources are available?
- what opportunities are there for education, leisure, work?
- what are the religious beliefs and practices?

Each culture has different adult role models, and will provide different opportunities for development. The way the child is perceived by those within and outside of her family culture will also have profound effects on her development. Where she is accepted, respected and loved, her sense of identity, confidence and self-worth can blossom. Where she is rejected, humiliated or discriminated against, her possibilities for development will be impaired.

Children who face particular challenges in their development

Every child develops at an individual pace. He or she will develop some skills and understanding easily and face challenges in other areas. Tying shoelaces may be easy for one five-year-old but difficult for another seven-year-old. Some children face additional challenges to the majority of children in their peer group. They may be particularly gifted in a particular area or have impaired sight or hearing, or have learning difficulties or muscle control problems. Each child so affected, will cope with such challenges in a different way and his or her overall development will be affected accordingly.

Find out as much as possible about the challenges facing children with special needs in your group, by talking to the child and/or the child's parents or carers. In some cases the child may have difficulty speaking or communicating, but do not make assumptions about this. Always try communicating directly with the child. Get specialist help, information or advice.

Through observation, sensitivity and ongoing communication with those involved you can plan play opportunities which help the child to become fully integrated into the playsetting, and enable the child to reach her full developmental potential within it.

SPICE

SPICE is a way of remembering five different aspects of development: Social, Physical, Intellectual, Creative and Emotional.

Children need to develop in different aspects:

- socially (how they relate to other people);
- physically (using their bodies);
- intellectually (in their knowledge, ideas and understanding);

- creatively (applying their personality, ideas and skills to artistic work or imaginative activities);
- emotionally (how they feel about themselves and the world about them, and how they cope with these feelings).

There are also spiritual and moral aspects to development: how children make sense of their world, their 'inner life', religious beliefs, and sense of right and wrong or good and bad.

Opportunities for development in play

As a playworker it is useful for you to be able to recognise different aspects of development and ensure that your playsetting gives opportunities to the child for:

- social interaction;
- physical activity;
- intellectual stimulation;
- creative expression;
- emotional stability.

Some activities or play opportunities will encourage one or two aspects of development more than others. Some will offer opportunities for all-round development.

EXAMPLE Opportunities for development: chain tig

Rules of the game

One person is 'it' and tries to catch the others. When the it 'tigs' another child, the two link hands and try to tig more children together. As more and more children are caught, the 'it' becomes an ever longer chain of children. The chain must not be broken. The game ends when all children have been tigged and all belong to one chain.

Chain tig (Gemma aged 6)

Opportunities for development

Social development. As in any game the children need to agree on the rules. This may include negotiating and changing them. The children need to work together as parts of the chain. Older children need to gauge the pace so that younger children don't fall over (that is, consider the needs of others). There are no losers and co-operation is more important than competition to achieve the end of the game.

Physical. Children develop their large muscle movements, agility and build stamina through running, ducking, stretching and twisting.

Intellectual. Children need to understand the rules of the game. They may also need to work out strategies for how best to catch others when they are part of the chain.

Creative. Working out ways to avoid being caught. As part of the chain, working out strategies for co-operating to tig others.

Emotional. Sense of being an individual but part of the larger group, and therefore a sense of belonging to a group. Experiencing and coping with emotions such as fear of being caught and elation at catching, or avoiding being caught.

EXAMPLE Opportunities for development: junk modelling

Instructions

Using a variety of 'junk' materials (paper, card, egg boxes, fabric scraps, corks, cartons), glue and scissors, make a model of your choice or on a particular theme – transport, house, aquarium, dragon or castle.

Opportunities for development

Social. If done as a group, this activity can encourage children to work together, share ideas, talk about what they are doing and share materials.

ACTIVITY 2.2

1 Choose one of the play activities you provide in your playsetting. Write down what opportunities it offers for social, physical, intellectual, creative and emotional development (as in the examples above).

2 Look at the activities you provide over one session or one week. Does your setting offer opportunities for all aspects of development?

3 Think about:

- what play opportunities are particularly good for encouraging each particular area of development? For example physical development – 'obstacle course'; emotional development – topic about 'ourselves' or 'my family' or roleplay
- Which play opportunities offer greatest possibilities for 'all round' development?

Opportunities for all-round development

Physical. Through cutting, gluing and sticking, children develop their manipulative skills and their hand–eye co-ordination (getting their hands to do what their thoughts and eyes want them to do).

Intellectual. Planning, designing, measuring, estimating (the piece of fabric I want for a sail will need to be about – long), anticipating (what will happen if I stick this cheese carton on top of this drinking straw?), evaluating (the wheels on my truck won't go round because . . .). Possibly also counting, matching, making comparisons and much more.

Creative. Inventing, designing, achieving the desired result, problem solving (how can I make the wheels on my truck turn better? Or how many ways are there to make a cotton reel into a wheel? Which different ways can I stick this piece to that piece?)

Emotional. Sense of achievement and self worth, independence, pride in a finished result, expressing feelings, dealing with frustration.

Observing children

One of the best ways of learning about child development and in particular about the development of children in your playsetting is to watch what they do. Most of what child development theorists know and have written about children comes from their direct experience of working with and observing children. This may seem obvious. You know the children in your groups and observe them every working day. But you are also doing a huge range of other things while at work – preparing materials, supervising, sorting out problems, communicating with children and adults, preparing food, joining in play, mediating in disagreements, keeping records. How often do you have the time to stand back and watch what is actually going on over a period of time? The value of this has been recognised in teacher training and early-years work for many years.

Regular observation in your place of work can help you to:

- gain a better understanding of the children in your group: their stages of development, interests, behaviour and needs;
- identify what leads up to an individual child behaving in a particular way. This is useful if a child is giving cause for concern (for example, not settling into the group, causing disruption, appearing to be bored) as it can give clues as to why the child is behaving in this way;
- discover which activities and play opportunities are particularly successful or unsuccessful, with which children, and why this might be so;
- plan and evaluate future activities and play opportunities;
- identify what adult behaviour is helpful or unhelpful in encouraging play;
- discover whether particular times of day in your playsetting are likely to cause disruption or stress and think about ways of making changes to alleviate this;
- share what you have observed about an individual child or activity or structure of session with colleagues so that you can plan as a team;
- agree where staff can most usefully be deployed.

There are many useful ways in which to observe. This book gives observation exercises in many chapters to help you become more aware about particular aspects of your practice. Observing children is a skill which needs practice. It gets easier (and more useful) with practice. There are many types of observation and ways to record observations (see Further reading at the end of this section for ideas on this).

Some general points about observing children

1   *Make time to observe.* You will need to get agreement from colleagues about when you can observe. It is important that while you are observing you become as unobtrusive as possible. Get your colleagues to agree about when you can leave your usual work and concentrate on observing. Don't feel guilty – observing is important, even if done only for a few minutes at a time.

2   *Decide what you are going to observe and why.* What are the aims of your observation? Are you observing to find out: more about an individual child?; about how a group of children relate to each other?; about a particular activity within a session?; or about how the space is used in order to evaluate and make changes? You may observe more than one of these things at once – but keep your aims simple to begin with.

3   *Decide how to deal with interruptions.* Until children get used to your observing they will be interested in what you are doing and may interrupt with requests for assistance or advice. It may be best to tell the children that you are going to observe before you begin. You can then answer their questions and explain that while you are observing you cannot do anything else and that they should go to another staff member if they need anything until you have finished. Although they may at first change their behaviour if they think or know you are observing them, the more accustomed they become to your observing as a regular activity the less interest they will take.

4   *Decide on a method of observation and recording your observation.* Where will you observe from? How long and how often will you observe for? How will you record your observation?

   For observation to be most valuable you will need to record what you have observed. This can be done in written form, and sometimes with the assistance of a small tape-recorder (resources and acoustics permitting!). It takes practice to record written observations as quickly as you need to and it helps if you can develop your own shorthand way of note taking. To save time, have some prepared sheets or pages in a notebook with details to fill in such as aim of observation, date, time and duration (see illustration, p. 37). Write up your notes more fully when you have time. Some observations are done with the help of check-lists, sketches or tick boxes (there is an example of such an observation in section 3.1, Activity 3.6).

5   *Record what you see not what you think.* Observations need to be as objective as possible. The language you use to record the observation should not be judgemental: 'Tipu drew a single line with a red felt-tip on his piece of paper. He dropped his pen. He walked over and said "What are you doing?" to R (who was building a den). He did not wait for R's answer but went to the book corner. Picked up a book and put it down. Ran outside to join S, B and P in a game of Unihoc.' This is what you might see. 'Tipu went from one activity to another and did not concentrate on anything' is what you might think (see p. 37 for how you might record this sequence).

6   *Be aware of confidentiality.* Use initials or first names only when recording observations. Do not write anything you would not want somebody else to read. Keep your observations in a safe place. Be ready to explain why you are observing if asked by parents or visitors.

7   *Evaluating what you have observed.* When you have completed your observation, or series of observations, go back to your reasons for observing and ask yourself some questions. See if what you have observed can suggest answers.

If you were observing a group activity, for example, you might want to ask: did the activity go as planned? (you will need to know how it was planned); how many children joined in?; which children did not?; why might this be?

You might want to find out how different children enjoyed the activity: Did all children join in in the same way? Did they seem to be enjoying the activity? How long did each child spend at the activity? Did any child leave the activity before it finished? Why might this be?

There may be practical lessons you can learn from your observation. Were there enough materials and equipment? Was there enough, too little, or too much adult support or intervention? Were there any health and safety considerations?

There may be other things you can put into practice for the future. Could the activity be developed to appeal to more or different children or to extend their concentration and enjoyment in it? Is this activity particularly good at encouraging social interaction, physical activity or creative expression or emotional stability?

Use what you observed to answer the questions if possible. If you cannot get the answers, longer or more frequent observations may be necessary.

As you get more experienced in observing you may find it useful to carry a notepad and pen in your pocket to record quick observations, ideas for changes to be made or issues which need to be raised with your co-workers at a staff meeting. A child's incidental comments or behaviour can be very significant in giving clues to greater understanding. But if you do not record them on the spot, they are often lost in the 'busy-ness' of a session or inaccurately remembered at a later stage.

OBSERVATION NOTES

AIM OF OBSERVATION: *To observe single child: Tipu*

Date: *8.8.95*   Time: *10.35 a.m.*   Place: *Playsetting*

Duration: *2 Minutes*

	ACTIONS	LANGUAGE
1035	At drawing table	
	T drew red line/dropped pen	
	Walking - den area	T→R "What are you doing?"
	Did not wait for answer	
	Walking - book area	
	Picked up book & put it down	
	Running outside	T→S + B "What are you doing?"
	Joins unihoc game	
1037		

If you find it difficult to observe and make notes at the same time, practice observing without recording to begin with. If you make time to stand back at regular intervals and practice concentrated observation with a clear aim in mind you can train yourself to notice and remember things more accurately.

ACTIVITY 2.3

1 Observe three or four children, one at a time, who are of the same age group (within the age group of the children you work with). It is helpful to begin observing children outside your worksetting, so that you can concentrate on developing your observation skills without being influenced by what you already know about the children or feeling guilty about time taken out of work. You might observe in a park, at a friends house, in the street, on the beach or in a playsetting other than the one in which you work (get permission from the parent, carer or supervisor first.)

Spend up to ten minutes at a time recording what the child says and does. Develop your own shorthand way of recording/coding what you have seen. (Some of the books listed at the end of this chapter suggest ways of doing this.)

2 Write up your notes.

3 Ask yourself: what was the child doing?; what was his main focus or interest during the observation?; did the child relate to any other children or adults during the observation?; did the observation reveal anything about aspects of the child's development: social, physical, intellectual, creative, emotional, his skills, understanding or experience?

4 Did the observations of different children have anything in common? Can you tell anything about the common interests, needs or development of children of this age group from your observations?

Further reading

Child development

Bartholomew, Lynne and Bruce, Tina 1993: *Getting to know you – a guide to record keeping in early childhood education and care.* Hodder & Stoughton.

Lindon, Jennie and Lance 1993: *Caring for the Under-8s.* Macmillan.

Morris, Beverley 1993: *Understanding children.* New Zealand Play Federation.

Moyles, Janet 1989: *Just Playing?* OUP.

Steinberg, L., Meyer, R. 1995: *Childhood.* McGraw-Hill.

2.2 Children's development 5–15

> Childhood is not from birth to a certain age and at a certain age
>   The child is grown, and puts away childish things.
>   Edna St Vincent Millay, from a poem in: *Wine from the Grapes* 1934

In section 2.1 it was stressed that each child develops in his or her own way and at his or her own pace, but that there are common patterns of development which relate broadly to certain age groups. This section looks at these patterns as they relate to children aged 5–15. What might children of these age-groups be like? What do they say about themselves and their playsettings?

Children aged 5 to 7
Physical development

A five-year-old may be able to tie his own shoelaces, or learn this shortly after starting school. As well as gaining in independence in tasks relating to personal care, children in this age-group are often learning or developing expertise in a range of other physical skills such as swimming or riding a two-wheeled bicycle.

There is often a noticeable growth spurt, sometimes called the 'five-to-seven shift', in children's height or weight, although not as noticeable as the growth spurt in puberty. They also begin to lose their milk teeth and develop a new set of back molars. The rapid growth in head size will have slowed down, and brain growth will be almost complete.

Fine motor skills are developed for holding and using tools – scissors, pens, sewing needles – for more precise and delicate craft and construction (building, drawing, threading, collage, knotting, modelling).

Intellectual development

Children gain increasing hand-eye co-ordination at this stage and begin to recognise shapes and symbols in the formal ways required for reading and writing.

There are major developments in terms of the child's ability to understand concepts related to logic and rational thought. This is the stage of intellectual development which the child psychologist Piaget (1896–1980) called the stage of conservation. The child who has reached this stage will be able to use reasoning and no longer relies solely on what her eyes and other senses tell her. For example, she will understand that the mass of a ball of dough does not change when it is rolled into a different shape.

'Me and my friends playing' (Polly)

A child who has reached the stage of conservation will know that the tall thin glass still holds the same amount of liquid, even though it looks more (the level of liquid is higher up the glass). Most four-year-olds will not be able to understand this. They can be misled by the evidence of their eyes: unable yet to apply powers of adult-type reasoning to what they have seen.

Creative expression and self-esteem

Developing physical and intellectual skills will also enable the child to plan and carry out more complex creative projects from building dens to baking cakes. She will develop the capacity to follow a plan with an end product in mind and be clear about whether and what assistance she requires from an adult. Adult encouragement and a positive attitude towards creative efforts is particularly important. Sadly, without this encouragement, a seven-year-old can already believe it when he says 'I can't draw', and will begin to judge his own efforts by the reaction of others.

Fantasy and imaginative play may still be strong, but will increasingly be influenced by what is popular in the culture of peer groups with whom the children mix.

Social and emotional development

Generally, children become less dependent on their parents or long-term carers than in their pre-school years. Friends and peer groups take on increasing importance. The development of language and social skills will have been influenced by pre-school experiences. Some children will already have had a great deal of experience of being in a group, for example in a playgroup or nursery setting, or by mixing with older siblings and their friends. Others will have had no pre-school group experience, and may take longer to settle in to your playsetting. Sections 2.3 and 5.2 look in more detail at how this relates to your role as a playworker.

An increasing ability to understand rules will enable children to participate in a greater variety of games. But many five-year-olds will still have only vague notions about fairness and taking turns and may rely a great deal on imitation in this respect. They will learn rules by participating and imitating rather than by having them explained. Many will still enjoy the traditional, pre-school circle and singing games or follow my leader, which may be considered babyish by the time the child reaches eight.

While children in this age-group are increasingly less dependent on their family, they are becoming more aware of how others see them. They are entering a phase when they begin to feel great shame and embarrassment on being shown up in front of friends.

How they cope with this will depend partly on the confidence and self-esteem (or lack of it) built up in their pre-school years experience. It will also depend on whether the environment encourages them to try out and practise new skills, and challenge themselves physically and mentally, without fear of ridicule if they do not succeed immediately (see John Holt: *How Children Fail*, Penguin 1964).

Play can be very therapeutic in allowing a child to express her feelings about the world as she experiences it, and perhaps 'act out' some of her hopes and fears through imaginative play (see Axline Virginia: *Dibs in search of self* Penguin 1971). But be cautious about reading too much into a child's free play, without knowledge and understanding of psychology or play therapy.

Boys and girls tend to stick to friendships of their own gender, and play becomes increasingly differentiated for boys and girls during these years, although this separation can begin even earlier.

'They have art and sewing that you wouldn't be able to do at home.'

'I like cooking mostly ... painting too and reading books sometimes. I like making cakes out of junk modelling.'

'We make up our own plays ... like a different version – once we did "Home Alone 3".'

'You make loads and loads of friends.'

TO THINK ABOUT

How do you encourage children to take pride in their creative achievements in the playsetting? (This is covered in more detail in section 2.3.)

TO THINK ABOUT

How can you encourage children to be sensitive to the needs, abilities and achievements of others?

Some play opportunities may be particularly good at encouraging children to develop awareness of each other. Consider the example of 'chain tig' given on pages 33 and 34. There are other examples in later chapters.

ACTIVITY 2.5

Observation

1 Observe a boy and a girl between the ages of five and eight involved in 'free' play (that is, not organised group activities).

2 Observe each child on three separate occasions for a period of of several minutes.

3 Write up your notes on your observations.

To think about

Were there considerable differences in the kinds of play the boy and the girl engaged in?

Did either or both children tend to play more with children of their own sex?

Do you think there was a difference in opportunities for play open to them?

If there were differences, what might be the reasons for this and is there anything you could do as a play-worker to extend the opportunities open to each?

Read *Gender Matters* by Sandra Melville (1994) published by Playboard for ideas on countering gender stereotypes in the playsetting.

Children aged 8 to 11
Intellectual development

These years are often seen as the period of most stability within childhood. The eight-year-old will generally have settled in or become accustomed to school, and will be building on the foundations described in the previous section on five- to eight-year-olds. During these years children become increasingly able to fend for themselves and to make reasoned judgements. However, they still need to work things out using trial and error and hands-on practical experience with physical play materials rather than using abstract theories or working things out on paper.

EXAMPLE Finding the answer through practical experience

Salima and Naseem are nine years old. They are playing in the sand. They want to fill a large old-fashioned milk-churn with water. They estimate it will take about six trips to the outdoor tap with the yellow bucket to

What children say

achieve this. In fact, it takes six-and-a-half buckets to fill the churn, so they are very close. They are quite clear that the churn will always take the same amount of water, and will not have to estimate next time, although they do not understand about working out the mathematical volume of things on paper. At five years old they would not have been able to make this estimation, nor would they have been so sure that the churn would take the same number of buckets to fill it from one day to the next.

'I like juggling' (Oswah)

Physical development

Physically, children will grow steadily in strength and co-ordination. By the end of this period many children will be able to cook and use sharp tools independently of an adult. They continue to lose their first teeth and develop the permanent ones. Children enter puberty at different ages, and girls usually earlier than boys. Some may be entering puberty at the end of this period.

Social development

Socially, peer groups continue to be very important and most children, given the opportunity, prefer to play with friends outside, or out of adult range, riding bikes or roller-skating in the street, or making their own way to the local park or adventure playground.

Children aged nine or ten understand complex rules and realise that they can be subject to change. They can make up their own new rules. This ability to understand rules has been associated with the development of moral reasoning in children. Research cited by Konner suggests that peer groups may have a much greater influence on this aspect of development than parents, teachers or religious leaders. Through play, children sort out sophisticated concepts of fairness, equality, right and wrong. They understand the consequences of breaking rules and begin to identify how their actions affect others or make them feel.

A child of this age can begin to be able to put himself into the the shoes of another, and to realise that other children can also be expected to understand his point of view. At this age children continue to associate predominantly with members of their own sex.

Emotional development and creative achievement

Emotionally, middle childhood has been called 'the latency period' by psychoanalyst Sigmund Freud (1856–1939), in that strong sexual feelings experienced in pre-school years are repressed until puberty.

Through imaginative play they continue to try out new roles, and explore the world around them. Imaginative play is still important, although this may be more personal and private, without the need for any adult involvement. Many hours may be spent by creating imaginative play spaces – whether they are camps or dens, or miniature worlds of model space stations, insect gardens, desert islands or dolls' houses.

A child of this age may take up her first hobby. It could be taking an interest in a particular animal (and she will now be able to take prime responsibility for the care of a pet) or making collections of things, from stamps, stickers or badges to shells, conkers or sweet-wrappers. Small toys (the particular type varies with popular fashion) become prized items to collect and swap with great satisfaction. But these can also be a source of resentment and conflict, particularly as some children have parents or carers who are more willing or able to afford them than others.

ACTIVITY 2.6

Talk to the children in your play-setting about their hobbies and interests.

Plan one activity in the play-setting which builds on a currently popular interest or hobby.

If collecting shells and fossils is popular you could suggest to the children that they might like to create:

- a shell museum (with items made by the children out of shells),
- a prehistoric cave in a corner of the room or outside, or
- a fossil landscape out of doors. (Small fossils can be made of clay, large ones of papier mâché.)

Add model dinosaurs or dressing up clothes.

If some of the children in your playsetting are more interested in physical skills – skipping, acrobatics, juggling – perhaps you could create a circus ring.

The children's hobbies and interests are a good starting point for art, craft and drama activities. You can also help them to extend their knowledge and interest by providing relevant books. But don't turn the playsetting into a classroom. Your aim should be to create play opportunities which are initiated by the children and which they can take in the direction they choose.

The ability to apply creative thinking to problem solving becomes more sophisticated. Confidence and skills development can be encouraged through opportunities for creative achievements. Some children's skill at drawing, construction or use of technology may surpass your own.

Puberty and adolescence

Physical development

The term 'puberty' refers to the physical changes which need to occur for a child to become a biologically mature adult. Adolescence refers to the social, emotional and psychological changes which take place over this same time and which will be completed only when the person is recognised as an adult. As with other aspects of development children will reach puberty at different ages, girls usually maturing before boys of their age-group. During puberty the body produces hormones. In girls this leads to the development of the ovaries, breasts, pubic and underarm hair, and the onset of menstruation (periods). In boys, other hormones lead to growth in the testes and penis, body hair, sperm production and deepening of the voice. These changes are accompanied by an overall 'growth spurt'.

Emotional development

Emotionally, adolescence can be a difficult time as the rapid changes in hormone levels and bodily changes need time for the emerging adult to adjust to and accept. As children develop at different rates they may worry if they mature much earlier or later than their friends. They have to deal with new aspects of personal hygiene such as body odour and periods and may become acutely conscious of body hair or spots.

Social development

Socially, peer groups still play a very important role. Increased physical and financial independence allow more opportunities for potentially negative peer pressure to be exerted to drink alcohol, smoke, take illegal drugs or have sexual intercourse earlier than individual free choice would allow.

It is a time when children are often trying to break free from or feel alienated from parents, teachers or other carers, and the less formalised or structured atmosphere of the playsetting may enable the playworker to have an important role in giving guidance and support.

'If we've got a problem we can always talk to them [the playworkers]. They're good company.'

'Playing on the pulley . . . doing parachute games. Gymnastics . . . listening to music . . . football, face painting . . . helping the little kids draw and colour.'

'We can look after ourselves more. I know the streets around here.'

'Play in balance' (Laura)

Intellectual development and creative achievement

Intellectually and creatively children may be reaching their peak during this period. They will be full of questions about the world around them and developing skills and discovering talents which may lead them to future vocations and work or leisure pursuits. They are able to think about problems in an abstract way and work out solutions in their heads without relying solely on direct experience. They may be more aware of environmental and social concerns

Children with different abilities

Within the broad stages of development children may develop quickly or more slowly. Some have uneven development. They may be intellectually mature for their age, but socially less so; advanced in creativity but emotionally much younger.

Children with disabilities or learning difficulties may need support in one area but surpass their peers independently in another. A child with autism may be gifted at numerical arithmetic, a child in a wheelchair may well enjoy physical activity. A child with learning difficulties may have astounding drawing skills and a profoundly deaf child can enjoy and be very skilled in music, using the senses of sight, touch and rhythm. Whatever her age, and however she compares to what may be considered 'usual', each child needs to be given opportunities to discover and develop her individual skills and talents.

Other factors affecting development

Children's development is affected by many things (see section 2.1). If you see that a child is obviously a long way behind others of his or her age, you need to ask why. Illness, stress, changes at home such as divorce, bereavement, moving house, bullying, child abuse, pressures from school or home, can all cause delayed or uneven development.

A sudden change of behaviour or marked uneven or delayed development should not be ignored. It may be a sign that the child is ill or needs specialist help.

If you are concerned you can:

- discuss your worries with a senior member of staff;
- spend time observing the child to see if there is something within the playsetting which is affecting her, or whether her play gives any other 'clues';
- talk to the child's parents or carers and see if they can throw any light onto things;
- contact the child's teachers, and see if they share your concerns.

Health visitors, social workers and GPs can give advice on making referrals to other specialist sources of advice. The first step, though, is to discuss the situation with your supervisor or manager.

Meeting the development needs of a wide age range in the playsetting

EXAMPLE Puppets

5- to 7-year-olds
Making a variety of simple puppets: paper bag, paper plate, sock puppets, using junk materials, glue, sewing. Using puppets in imaginative play, storytelling, talking to each other.

ACTIVITY 2.7

1 Plan and carry out two activities for adolescents in a playsetting. If you do not have this age group in your place of work, arrange if possible to carry them out in another playsetting or youth group.

For example, more complex creative projects can be undertaken (resources permitting), such as photography, paper or jewelry making, air brushing, drama productions, mural painting or work with video.

2 Evaluate the activity with the children involved.

Ask them whether they enjoyed the activity, whether they would like to do it differently if given another opportunity. Have they any ideas on how they would like to extend the activity? What other activities would they enjoy?

ACTIVITY 2.8

Plan one activity which will cater for the whole range of ages within your playsetting. Include details of what aspects of the activity you think will appeal to different age-groups.

8- to 10-year-olds

Making more complicated puppets: papier mâché or clay heads, puppets on sticks and puppets on strings. Making cardboard box puppet theatre. Inventing own shows, including writing short scripts. Performing shows to each other (and parents?) including 'selling tickets' and serving biscuits/squash refreshments.

11 and over

Making a variety of still more complicated puppets: marionettes, life-size puppets, plaster moulds, shadow puppets, etc. Building a puppet theatre (including scenery and lighting). Creating a show to be put on to the local community as a fund-raising event (including designing tickets and posters, budgeting, selling tickets, preparing and serving refreshments).

All ages

Free play with all kinds of puppets. Exploring a variety of materials which could be used in puppet making. Using books and stories from a variety of cultures for ideas, inspiration and information. Making music to accompany puppet play.

Note: Don't make children stick to the opportunities planned for a particular age-group. Older children will enjoy and participate in those planned for younger ones, and vice versa.

See sections 3.2 and 3.3 for books with ideas for other activities.

Some playsettings do not cater for the whole age-range of 5- to 15-year-olds at the same time. However, where there is a very wide age-group, older children will often play an active role in caring for, supervising and encouraging younger children. Many older children will occasionally enter into the play of younger ones (perhaps under the pretext of helping) – dressing up, face-painting, constructing bridges or dams in the sandpit.

In a playsetting catering for adolescents as well as younger children, their physical and social needs must be considered. Adolescents will require more privacy for matters relating to personal hygiene in washrooms and changing areas, and availability of sanitary towels and tampons. There will also need to be comfortable areas in which they can sit and relax and talk or listen to music, perhaps with tea and coffee or other facilities for preparing refreshments (although these should not be accessible to younger children for safety reasons).

In a playsetting catering for a very wide age-range it is possible to have play activities and projects which can involve all individuals, with each child contributing something at an appropriate level to his or her development.

As a playworker you will work with children of different ages. Within each age-band, individual children will be at different stages of development. Observing what children do and talking to them about how they think and feel are two ways of finding out about their development. Knowledge and understanding about theories of stages of development and how they relate to different ages can give you a framework in which to place your understanding of the individual children who come to your playsetting.

References

Axline, Virginia 1971: *Dibs in Search of Self*. Penguin.
Holt, John 1964: *How Children Fail*. Penguin.
Piaget, Jean (1896–1980) – see Further reading.
Freud, Sigmund (1856–1939) – see Further reading.

ACTIVITY 2.9

1 Look at the illustrations in this chapter drawn by children of different ages.

What can you tell about the child from each drawing?

- what age do you think the child is and how did you come to this decision?
- what, if anything, can you tell about the artist's interests and the way he or she perceives the world around him or her?

2 Look at what children said about themselves and their play-settings in the quotations in this chapter. What do they tell you about how these children perceive their own development?

3 Write down three ways of finding out about a child's stage of development.

Further reading

Bee, Helen 1995: *The Developing Child* (7th ed.) HarperCollins. (Chapter 16 looks at development relating to different age-groups.)

Einon, Dorothy 1985: *Creative Play*. Penguin. (Child development 0–10 with a focus on practical play activities.)

Konner, Melvin 1991: *Childhood*. Educational Broadcasting Corporation Little Brown and Co. (Looks at child development through observations and research in different countries and across several cultures. Chapter 7. 'Marbles and morals' is particularly interesting on moral and social development and play in middle childhood.)

Leach, Penelope 1983/1991: *The Parent's A to Z – A Guide to Children's Health, Growth and Happiness*. Penguin. (The section on Adolescents is particularly useful.)

Petrie, Pat 1990: *The Adolescent Years*. Michael Joseph.

For an introduction to the theories of Piaget, Freud and others who have contributed to child development theory and research, try Davenport G. C. 1991: *An Introduction to Child Development*. Collins Educational.

2.3 Forming good relationships with children

Grown ups never understand anything for themselves, and it is tiresome for children to be always and forever explaining things to them.

Antoine Saint-Exupery, *Le Petit Prince* (The Little Prince), 1943

Developing and maintaining good relationships with children is a theme which runs throughout this book. It assumes a basic understanding of child development (see sections 2.1 and 2.2) and relates to many of the underpinning values and assumptions of playwork (as outlined in section 1.2).

'When you're down, and you've had a hard day at school and you come to (the playsetting) and, like, K and P always cheer you up. They encourage you to join in games and they'll like never leave you out. They'll like fuss kind of.'

'Sometimes when you've got nothing to do and you want to play a game but no one wants to play a game with you, they'll play a game with you.'

'They [the playworkers] look after us and make sure we're safe.'

'They're [the playworkers] good for a laugh and everything. They're good fun. They're not like teachers at all. They don't act like teachers. You can call them by their proper name.'

'I nearly always need an adult . . . It's not when I'm upset it's just sometimes other people bully on me and I have to tell M about it 'cos then she'll sort it out.'

ACTIVITY 2.10

Think about new situations which you have faced in the past, for example:

- the first day of a new job or course;
- going to a social gathering where you did not know most of the people present;
- a holiday in another place.

How did you feel? How did you behave?

Write down:

- things which made you feel uncomfortable;
- what put you at your ease?

Find out from friends or colleagues what helped them in new situations.

This chapter focuses on how you can form relationships and support and promote children's social and emotional development within the playsetting by:

- the way you introduce the child to the playsetting;
- planning play opportunities to develop self-esteem and self-reliance;
- the way you participate in children's play;
- through effective communication;
- through observation and monitoring;
- by helping children to recognise and deal with their feelings.

New children settling in

Activity 2.10 asks you to think about how you felt when facing new situations in the past.

It may be that you felt shy, staying on the sidelines to observe the codes of conduct and the nature of interaction between other people. Perhaps you asked yourself, 'What is expected of me in this situation? How do I fit in?'

Things which made you uncomfortable might have included:

- being overloaded with information which you didn't have time to take in;
- being excluded or ignored;
- other people making false assumptions about why you were there;
- being expected to join in activities or take on tasks which you had not been prepared for or were unwilling to do;
- getting conflicting information from different people.

Things which helped you feel more comfortable may have included:

- having clear and accurate information in advance about what the situation would involve;
- knowing why you are there;
- a friendly and welcoming reception from others;
- individual attention from someone who supported you through the situation, making introductions and explaining anything you didn't understand;
- other people understanding your reason for being there;
- having time to adjust at your own pace without being pressurised to conform or perform before you were ready.

Most people, children and adults need support in adjusting to a new situation. When a new child visits or comes to the playsetting for the first time, ask yourself: 'Who is this child? What brings her to the playsetting? What does she bring with her in the way of interests, skills, past experiences, values, beliefs and expectations?' Try to draw close to the child and think about how she might be thinking.

A named worker

In some settings new children are given a particular named worker (sometimes called a key worker) – someone who will take special responsibility for the welfare of that child and help her to settle in. This worker is someone who can also exchange information with the parent about the child's adjustment to the playsetting or her behaviour and progress within it. Often the child will choose the adult with whom she wishes to form a particular bond – to share information or concerns with, to ask for help or advice or simply to join in companionship in play and other activities. Even if there is a named worker policy in your setting there should be flexibility between the staff to offer the child the freedom to make such choices.

TO THINK ABOUT

Think about the last two or three children who were new to your playsetting. How do you think they felt? What did you, your colleagues and the other children do to make them feel comfortable?

What does this child bring to the playsetting in the way of interests, skills, past experience?

ACTIVITY 2.11

Consider the following situations:

1   François is six. He has very recently come to England with his parents who are attending a three-year course of study. He visits your playcare setting with his mother, who wants him to start next week. He speaks very few words of English. His mother speaks fluent English. He looks anxious, holds his mother's hand and hides behind her back.

2   Yulan is 13. She comes to your open-access play-setting one Saturday with her friend Amanda, who has been coming for several months. Yulan settles in quickly in a game of 'Twister' with a group of other girls. When you go to talk to her, she appears to withdraw.

You offer her an information leaflet and emergency contact form, but she refuses, saying, 'I don't know if I'll be able to come again.'

3   Christopher is nine. You have been asked by the duty social worker to collect Christopher from school along with your usual children for the after-school club. Christopher's mother has been admitted to hospital as an emergency. Christopher has been informed by the social worker and his teacher. The social worker will visit during the session and his grandmother will pick him up.

What might you do to help each child settle into your playsetting? Which of the suggestions listed below would be appropriate and why? What else could you do?

Setting the scene

Consider Activity 2.11. There are many things you can do to help enable a new child to feel comfortable in the playsetting. Each child may need a different approach, depending on the type of playsetting and the child's individual needs and circumstances.

1   Offer a smile and greeting.
2   Introduce yourself and others in the playsetting.
3   Find out the name of the child (the full legal name will go on the records, but you also need to know the name by which the child wants to be known – shortened name or a nickname).
4   Make sure you can pronounce the child's name correctly. If it is an unfamiliar name to you, practise it and ask the child if you have got it right. If you do not do this it can make a child feel unimportant, or singled out as odd.
5   Explain any routines – where to hang coats, where the toilets are, what refreshments are available and when.
6   Introduce the child to others. Encourage other children to involve the new child in their play and to show her the ropes. This will be particularly important if the new child does not know any other children in the playsetting.
7   Give plenty of time for the child (and parents if they accompany the child) to ask questions. You may need to arrange a time for them to visit when this will be possible.
8   Give information (verbal and written if appropriate), including factual information (about opening times, typical pattern of a session, fees) and information about policies relating to attendance, behaviour and equal opportunities. Try to give the information as answers to questions, rather than overloading them with information which will not be taken in.
9   Young children may find it easier to settle if they can make their first visits with their parents. Try to make this possible for as long as is needed by the child and is possible for parents.
10   Provide a play environment which offers interesting and stimulating opportunities for play.
11   Respect each child as individual and unique. Show that she is valued in the playsetting for the qualities, skills and attributes she brings with her – of herself and of her family, culture and past experience.

ACTIVITY 2.12

Involve the children in designing 'Welcome' posters for your door, entrance hall or noticeboard.

Encourage them to explore different ways of conveying a welcome message, for example:

- a smiling face or friendly group of faces;
- the word 'welcome' in different languages (this will require some research) or in different types of script or symbols (e.g. braille, semaphore).

Getting to know you

The way in which a child settles into the playsetting will depend partly on her age, temperament, stage of development and previous experience. Some children have had more experience than others of adjusting to new settings and circumstances. However, a child who has undergone considerable changes in play and care settings, might find it just as difficult or more difficult to settle than a child who attends a playsetting for the first time. He may be insecure and vulnerable because of the many changes he has faced.

An older child may come alone to visit the setting. You will need equal sensitivity to recognise and meet what the older child or adolescent needs to help her settle. She may want just to observe for a while and to find her own way into making social contacts and getting involved in activities. She may appreciate your involvement and help in making introductions. Offer her the same information and time to ask questions or share concerns as you would a younger child and his parents.

In an open-access setting a child may come with friends, loiter around the edges of the playsetting for a while, and come back for longer the next day. He may initially shy away from any prolonged contact with adults. In this case, give him a welcome greeting. Let him know you are available if he wants to know anything. Give him basic verbal information together with any written information and registration form to take away. Leave him to determine for himself the pace at which he wants to make contact and join in.

Get to know as much as you can about the child as soon as possible, ideally before she comes to the playsetting. This does not mean prying: ask only questions which have direct relevance to your being able to meet her needs Such information includes:

- language(s) spoken;
- dietary requirements;
- medical conditions which might require medication or emergency treatment;
- family and emergency contacts;

Let the children determine the pace at which they want to join in – but observe for ways in which you can help them feel included

- particular hobbies or interests; and, in playcare settings;
- who will collect the child from the play setting.

Confidentiality

Some children and parents will be very forthcoming about other aspects of their lives: income, divorce, medical or other problems in the family. Such information must be kept confidential. Share with colleagues only information which is essential for them to care adequately for the child within the playsetting, or information which leads to concerns about the safety or well-being of the child (see section 4.3). Never share personal information about one child with another child or his parents.

Meeting individual needs

If you provide food, make sure you can provide for any dietary requirements of individual children.

A child may have special needs in terms of mobility, communication, support with personal hygiene or feeding. She may require special adaptations or equipment to enable her to play or carry out tasks relating to personal independence.

If a child does not speak fluent English and you do not have a worker who speaks her 'mother tongue', you will need to consider ways to help her communicate with you and you to communicate with her. You might use signs, gestures and picture symbols, and/or learn some basic words in her language. Take time to help her learn English words. Encourage other children to join in. Use your contacts with other agencies (see section 5.3) as sources of help and advice.

Maintaining relationships with children

It takes time to develop trusting and confident relationships. You need to get to know the children. They need to get to know you. The way in which you communicate is very important. There are many ways to work towards building and maintaining good relationships in the playsetting.

Being consistent

In order for a child to learn to trust you and feel confident in the playsetting, you need to be consistent.

Try not to treat children in different ways according to your mood: smiling one day, distracted the next, with humour the third day and with sternness on the fourth. Of course different circumstances and events will affect the way you react on particular days, but be clear about the reasons for this and explain them to the children. If you don't do this, they may wrongly blame themselves for your behaviour or lose confidence in you.

There should also be consistency between staff, particularly in behaviour management (more on this in section 2.4). While you may need to give particular attention to one child at certain times because of their special needs, this should not be done to the detriment of other children who also require your attention.

Developing self-reliance and self-esteem

Sections 2.1 and 2.2 looked at how opportunities for play contribute to healthy development. Part of this development relates to how the child learns to

---

TO THINK ABOUT

Discuss with the person responsible how he or she makes sure that you can meet a child's special needs before offering her a place in your playsetting. Are there links with other agencies (see section 5.3) to get advice and support to help meet such needs?

ACTIVITY 2.13

Make a list of all the things you do to help welcome new children into the playsetting. See if you can add at least two new things to try.

ACTIVITY 2.14

1 Go through the list of children in your playsetting. Try and identify those whom you know less about. Perhaps they are quieter, less demanding, or shy away from adult contact.

2 Spend time observing each of these children in the playsetting. What are their interests? Who do they play with? Is there one particular adult who they talk to more than others?

3 Discuss your observations with your colleagues.

4 Decide, with your colleagues, what you do to make sure you spend time talking to, or getting involved in play or activities with, these children as well as those with whom you have had more contact.

TO THINK ABOUT

How can play activities and the way they are set up help to dispel negative stereotypes?

opportunities to take on nurturing and caring roles and tasks?

Example 1

If football is a game dominated by boys with more confidence and experience in your playsetting, you could initiate a girls only team to enable them to develop their skills in an unthreatening way. Are the boys given

Example 2

In painting, drawing and craft activities you can make sure that there is a sufficient range of colours (paper, paints, crayons, fabric) to enable children to reproduce a whole range of skin tones, including their own.

ACTIVITY 2.15

1 Look at two or three of the play activities you are planning for the coming week. Consider the resources you will be using and ask yourself whether each promotes self-esteem and values diversity or whether it promotes stereotypes and a limited world view. (See also section 1.2.)

2 Notice how often you praise children's positive qualities, talents, skills, behaviour and achievements. Try to count how many times you do this naturally in one session. You could take turns with another colleague to observe this in each other. Compare this with the number of times you rebuke, control or limit a child or groups of children (see also section 2.4 on behaviour management).

The way you respond when she shows you her creative achievements can increase or diminish her self-esteem

perceive himself in relation to others. There are many opportunities in the playsetting for a child to develop his own self-image and self-esteem. This will be affected by the recognition and respect received from other children and adults towards his language, culture, skin colour, family, appearance, particular skills, abilities, achievements, beliefs and needs. With older children dress codes and sexuality or sexual orientation may also be important factors.

Selecting and using resources, activities and images which reflect diversity in all these areas are important parts of enabling all children to develop both self-esteem and increased understanding and respect for others. Pictures, posters, books, toys and activities can reinforce stereotypes and therefore limit potential role models with which children can identify. On the other hand you can provide books and posters of people with disabilities, from different parts of the world, of both genders, with all kinds of skin tones and dress codes in a variety of positive circumstances and roles. Other factors can affect children's image of themselves because of the way others see them. Think back to your own childhood and your own experiences of children (perhaps you yourself) being called names or bullied in other ways because of size, glasses, ears or hair.

Draw attention to and praise children's particular individual talents and achievements and encourage children to recognise them in themselves and others. Give praise for social skills as well: 'I think it was great the way you made Kumran feel welcome today Tariq' or 'It's good to have someone like you Alice to cheer us up with your jokes.'

As children develop confidence and self-esteem they also develop self-reliance. They learn to trust their own skills and judgements – about their ability to care for themselves, to assess the risks and safety of a situation, to take responsibility and care for their environment.

Children's play can provide discussion and activities based on all kinds of issues which will extend their shared understanding of the world: behaviour, race, poverty, environmental issues, religion, festivals. But beware of turning the playsetting into a classroom.

Plan activities which present a challenge but which are achievable with the minimum assistance. Make sure resources are available and accessible to children within safety constraints.

Talk to parents about their expectations of their children's independence: when, for example, do they think their child is or will be able to use matches safely or walk home alone? There may be occasions when a child gets a very different view of the world from you than the one he gets from home. You need to be sensitive in how you deal with mixed messages – in particular where there is a conflict between the values of your playsetting and the values the child has learned from other people who are important to him.

Give children opportunities to be involved in decisions within the play-setting: about rules, range of activities, food on offer, trips out, the design and décor of the outside area, the garden or the new 'quiet area'. Give them the freedom to choose their own relationships and develop their own strategies for dealing with disagreements providing they are within the agreed framework for behaviour within the setting.

Joining in is an important and enjoyable part of your role in taking part in children's play. This can enhance children's play because it:

- provides them with role models;
- helps them to feel safe;
- shows them that their play is valued;
- gives new ideas, experience and (sometimes) play materials.

> **TO THINK ABOUT**
>
> How can you use your knowledge about child development and particularly that of individual children to help them develop self-reliance?

ACTIVITY 2.16

Discuss with another playworker how you would get involved if you were faced with the following situations at work? It is helpful if you can actually practice what you would say and how you would intervene. Where possible, ask others (your co-workers or playwork trainees) to roleplay the parts of the children so that you can try out direct responses to one or two of these situations.

1 Osse and Tamari are eight and nine respectively. They have discovered several piles of leaves swept up by the caretaker the night before. They are throwing them at each other and laughing. Osse takes a dive into the middle of one of the piles. Tamari covers him with leaves. Three other children join in and are about to scatter the leaves in the other piles.

2 Lara, aged 11, has spent a long time painting a picture of herself and friends playing in your playsetting. The playworker would like to put it on the wall or in the scrapbook which is kept in the playsetting to record special events. Suddenly Lara starts flicking bright-red paint over the whole page.

3 Lucy, Gemma and Alexandra are seven. They have built a cardboard box train. They go to the playworker, who is helping two other children make some papier mâché, and ask if he will come and be the engine driver and take them to the sea-side.

Be sensitive when you involve yourself in play. You need to remain detached in some respects to fulfil your role and responsibilities in playwork.

Make sure that the main goal of your involvement is to enhance the value of the play for the children. You may have witnessed how this often does not happen in a family situation: a parent gets so involved in building a sand-castle and moat, or an elaborate train-set layout, that she or he ignores or becomes irritated with the interests and 'interference' of the child.

Your participation must be appropriate to the age and development of the children involved. The initiative and responsibility for the direction and success of the play must remain with the child or children. Don't be tempted to 'save' or direct creative achievements such as a painting, a puppet show or construction, if the child wants to change or even destroy them. In play it is the process which is important and the child who is the director.

Keeping the boundaries

As well as being a companion and a resource you may have several other roles when participating in children's play. In particular you may need to be the keeper of all kinds of boundaries. Your role will be easier if you enlist the children's support in this and involve them in establishing the boundaries in the first place. You may be the timekeeper who can introduce and explain a new activity but will also be responsible for bringing it to an end by ensuring that time is available for any essential clearing up. You may be called on to be a referee in a dispute or disagreement. Encourage the children to discuss and sort out their own ideas on what is fair and unfair, or right and wrong, in such situations.

You are the boundary keeper in terms of safety. The more you involve the children in this the more effective you can be but the ultimate responsibility is yours. You are also the boundary keeper in terms of behaviour. (See section 2.4.)

Make sure that the children feel safe within their relationship with you. Don't push them to do things which they are unwilling or unable to do, or which make them feel humiliated or uncomfortable. Be clear about the boundaries of appropriate physical contact, in rough-and-tumble play or imaginative roleplay for example, and do not give grounds for your behaviour to be misinterpreted. (See section 4.3.)

Developing relationships with others

Encourage children to share their skills and use them to support each other in the playsetting. Provide opportunities for them to discover their own talents and discover and value those in others. A child who who cannot run fast or has little confidence to climb or skip might be exceptionally good at using woodwork tools or organising a team game. A child with verbal communication difficulties may excel at art or construction.

Encourage children to relate and to become aware of each other's needs by enabling them to care for each other. They can prepare, serve or even grow food, if you have a spare piece of ground or even a windowbox or growbag. (Lettuce or cress grows quickly and easily for salad sandwiches.) One child can cheer another when he is down, or sit and read or talk to him if he is feeling unwell. Co-operative games enable children of all ages and abilities to work in pairs or in groups, to communicate, be inventive and develop trust.

Communicating with children

Many of the skills of effective communication are the same whether you are dealing with children or with other adults. Some are referred to in sections 5.1 and 5.2. The main difference in communicating with children is that you need to apply your knowledge and understanding of child development. Most children will not have the range of vocabulary that you have, so you may have to choose your words carefully and check that they are understood. Children will also have various levels of understanding of rules, expected behaviour and particular concepts, such as safety and fairness. They may have shorter concentration spans and memories. You may have to communicate the same information many times before it is taken in.

Listening

Listen actively by looking at the child and by trying to find out what the child is trying to communicate.

Talking about the cake we made

Don't interrupt, interpret or judge what is being said.

Do give the child your full attention, or let the child know when this will be possible.

EXAMPLE

Child, 'My sister's gone to Italy.'

Don't fob him off or jump to conclusions with 'How lovely' or 'Lucky thing' . The child is telling you this piece of news because it is important to him. It may not seem lovely or lucky to him. Try some thing like, 'Just let me finish pouring this paint and I'd like to hear all about it.'

Your body language is as important as any words you speak in letting the child know you are listening.

Look interested – make eye contact, nod, smile. Don't fidget, look at your watch, out of the window or walk away. Beware of putting false interpretation onto cultural differences in the way people use and interpret body language. For example direct eye contact in some African and Asian cultures is a sign of insolence not respect or listening.

Giving feedback

Check that you have understood what is being said. Use phrases such as 'I think your feeling angry because . . .'; 'I understand that you want to . . .'. If you are not sure that you have understood correctly, ask open questions which encourage the child to expand more fully rather than closed questions which can be answered with one word.

EXAMPLE

A child is complaining that another has spoilt her game.

Say, 'Tell me what happened from the beginning' rather than 'Who started it?'

Developing assertiveness

Explain clearly your feelings and expectations, while acknowledging and respecting the feelings and expectations of others. Be prepared to negotiate, and if possible find a win–win rather than a win–lose solution. For example, you might say: 'I understand that you expected us to go to the park today, and that you are feeling very disappointed. It was not possible for me to take you because I had to have an emergency meeting with the social worker. If the weather is OK I will take you to the park tomorrow,' Make sure you can keep your promises!

Try to communicate in ways which will not provoke a defensive response. Avoid judging a child by her behaviour or being certain that you can provide the superior solutions. Don't use phrases such as 'You always' or 'Why can't you ever', 'You are', 'The best way to'. These phrases label and judge the child and undermine self-esteem. They do not constructively criticise behaviour, help the child to change or invite her to contribute her own views. Try phrases which begin: 'It hurts when you' or 'It was unfair when you' or 'Have you thought about'.

Encourage children to participate in finding solutions to problems. Provide options and try to be flexible without being passive and over compliant yourself.

ACTIVITY 2.18

Get a friend or colleague to play the part of a child asking questions which you might find it difficult to answer. Here are two ideas to get you started:

1 Shamira, six years old, and just learning to read, brings a newspaper over from the craft table, 'What is HIV?' she asks. Fourteen- year-old Brendan is standing close by and says, 'My sister says you can get AIDS from kissing. Is that true?'

2 Eight-year-old Maria says: 'My grandma died. My mum says she's gone to heaven. Betty says there's no such thing as heaven. Where do you think my Grandma is now?'

Discuss what was easy/hard about answering these questions. Share ideas about other ways you could have answered.

Think about questions you have found difficult to answer in the past. Ask others about questions they find difficult.

Answering children's questions

As a trusted adult you will be asked questions about important issues. Questions about sex, death, religion, illness and politics may be difficult to answer for many reasons.

- You recognise that there are many social taboos around the subject.
- You are uncertain how to explain a complex issue to a very young child.
- There are many different answers depending on what you believe.
- You don't have enough information to answer the question.
- You think the parent should answer such questions.
- You don't want to be accused of indoctrinating the child.

Whatever your reasons for finding the question difficult, the child has a right to an honest answer. If you cannot answer in an appropriate way immediately, explain why. You can ask for time, 'That is a very interesting question and deserves a proper answer which I do not have the time to give today. I will talk to you about this tomorrow/on . . .' Then make sure that you do – having got the appropriate information or having shared ideas with colleagues about the most appropriate ways to answer the question. There are always several ways to answer a question honestly. Give answers in language which will be understood by the child. You can say, 'People believe different things or think differently about this. I think. . . but others think . . .' It is useful to practice giving answers to questions about subjects which we find awkward to deal with – and to consider how the answer should be phrased differently to children of different ages and stages of development.

Recognising and dealing with feelings

Part of emotional development is about recognising and dealing with feelings. A baby expresses feelings of hunger, tiredness, cold, anger, frustration or boredom by crying. A two year old can throw a tantrum – lying on the floor, drumming feet, screaming and even holding his breath – for the same reasons. As a child develops increasingly complex and sophisticated means of communicating her feelings (particularly through the development of language) she has less need to resort to such extreme measures to let her feelings be known. In a playsetting young children may still have a limited vocabulary to express their feelings and limited understanding of their causes.

CASE STUDY 2.1: DEALING WITH STRONG EMOTIONS

One day, Rita, a six-year-old girl, was late for school, had no time for breakfast, was told off by her teacher and had an argument with her best friend at lunchtime. The final straw was being told she couldn't have a second biscuit on arrival at the afterschool club, because the playworker had just eaten the last one. She flies at the playworker, hitting and punching and screaming 'I hate you, I hate you.'

The emotions Rita experiences may be anger, frustration or simply hunger – but probably not the hate she is expressing. She cannot not relate the various causes of her emotions to each other, or to how she is feeling at present. She may also be frightened at the strength of her emotional outburst and be unable to find a way out of it.

In such cases it will be important for the child to have your understanding, support and reassurance. You may need to hold her for your own or her safety – or just give her a reassuring hug. Wait for her to calm down before helping her to sort out what happened and why.

Playsettings can provide opportunities for children to express and explore some of their feelings in a safe and accepting environment. Through play they can learn to recognise and name different emotions and practise ways of dealing with them. Many children learn to suppress their feelings, and 'put on a brave face' or to 'pull themselves together', which may make it difficult for them to identify or express their feelings.

Be wary of interpreting a child's expressed thoughts, feelings and play. Remember each child has learned different ways of dealing with feelings, which may not be the same as your own. Cultural and social background shapes our attitude to emotion and acceptable ways of expressing it.

From the time we learn to talk we may learn that outward displays of emotion (crying, shouting, laughter) are not generally accepted in everyday or public situations. On the other hand, we may be brought up in a situation where open displays of emotion are encouraged.

ACTIVITY 2.19

Initiate a series of play opportunities and activities around the theme of expressing feelings (you may want to call it something else).

With younger children (under ten) you could begin with a discussion about 'Things which make me happy and things which make me sad' or 'Things which make me angry and things which calm me down'.

Develop what comes out of the discussion into art-work, co-operative games, imaginative or dramatic play situations. Use music and musical instruments and dis-cover what feelings are provoked by different sounds and tunes. Look out for books and stories relating to feelings. Develop the theme using your own ideas as suggestions, but remain flexible and sensitive, enabling the children to take the initiative and decide how they want to develop any play opportunities you suggest.

With older children you might want a more specific but less personal starting-point. Perhaps they could bring in records which they like or don't like, and describe what emotions they conjure up.

Children with communication difficulties

An increasing amount of expertise concentrates on developing skills and resources for working with children who find it difficult to communicate. What is required will depend on the reason for the communication difficulty. Speech therapy and non-verbal languages (such as as British Sign Language, Makaton and Signalong) can provide a hearing-impaired child with vital opportunities for expressing himself. Other aids to communication use signs and symbols (such as Braille). There is steady growth in computer and other technological developments to assist people with communication difficulties. If there are indications that a child has communication difficulties, you should discuss the appropriate course of action with the supervisor of the playsetting. He or she will involve the parents before possibly contacting other agencies, such as the child's school, to plan how to meet the child's needs most effectively.

Be positive: a child who can use sign language or speak more than one language, has a very valuable communication skill to share with others in the playsetting. The difficulty here may be your and the other children's inability to understand them.

Monitoring children's progress

Schools and educational establishments monitor childrens progress in terms of measured educational achievements. Healthcare workers measure development in terms of physical and mental milestones. Both use standard tests and measurements. But these are less appropriate for monitoring childrens progress within the playsetting. In play it is the process rather than the goals, the means rather than the ends, which are important. So how can children's progress be monitored within the playsetting? You can develop your observational skills and apply your understanding of child development and play in evaluating what you have observed. You can do this with individual children, with particular activities and with the play environment as a whole. Many of the activities give suggestions on how to do this.

Children and parents can be involved in monitoring progress.

- The children can be encouraged to contribute to a group diary or portrait or photo gallery. Diaries can be compared to those of previous years to see what changes have occurred.
- You can also use questionnaires and discussions to find the views of children and their parents.
- Photographs can record major achievements, significant events and progress during a child's time within the playsetting.

If you have particular concerns about a child's development or behaviour it may be appropriate to keep written records of your observations over a period of time. You can share these with parents and colleagues and make a joint decision about what actions to take. You may just decide to continue to observe and monitor for a while, or you may need to seek additional support. Remember to record only what you have observed, not your opinions or interpretations. Keep all records in a safe place.

ACTIVITY 2.20

1 Make a note of three things which you do, or plan to do to help you form and maintain good relationships with children in your playsetting.

2 Find two examples of how one particular child's progress is monitored in the playsetting. These could be formal written records and observations, informal ways, such as discussion at staff meetings and conversations with parents, or involving the child in assessing his own progress.

Children moving on

All children need to move on from the playsetting. Some playsettings cater for a particular age band, and have contact with the playsetting which takes the next age band up. Some older children evolve from users of the playsetting to volunteer helpers. Other children leave because they may move house, out of choice or for other circumstances (their own or their parents). You can help a child prepare for moving on by seeing his next step positively. Encourage him to talk about his feelings: what are his hopes, fears and expectations? It may be possible for you to visit a new playsetting with him if it is close by.

Develop links with play and youth facilities in your area which enable you to exchange information. Children and staff of neighbouring playsettings can get to know others through exchange visits, shared social events, trips and outings.

Further reading

Crompton, Margaret 1990: *Attending to Children*. Edward Arnold.
Petrie, Pat 1989: *Communication with Children and Adults*. Edward Arnold.
Kerr, Susan 1993: *Your Child with Special Needs*. Hodder & Stoughton.
Quillan, Susan 1994: *Childwatching – a Parent's Guide to Body Language*. Ward Lock. (Many excellent photographs illustrating points about body language.)
Stenhouse, Glen 1994: *Confident Children – developing your child's self-esteem*. Oxford University Press.

2.4 Setting a framework for behaviour

Conflict is part of life and growth. Without conflict there would be no change and no challenge.

Playing with Fire: Training for the creative use of conflict,
Fine and Macbeth 1992

This section looks at behaviour management in the light of the underpinning values of playwork (see section 1.1). Children are individuals with individual needs. They have the right to respect from others and to participate in decisions affecting their lives. In order to play and develop within the playsetting they need to feel safe from all kinds of abuse – from adults or from other children. This includes: intimidation, harassment, discrimination, verbal (including name calling and abusive shouting) and physical harm. We live in a society which is rife with examples of these kinds of behaviour – within families, on television and in the street. Some children, and sometimes adults, will bring these kinds of behaviour into the playsetting. It is therefore necessary to establish a framework for acceptable and unacceptable behaviour, and for what should happen when unacceptable behaviour is evident.

What is acceptable and unacceptable behaviour? What are appropriate rewards and sanctions? Should children be involved in determining limits on behaviour within the playsetting? The answers to these questions will depend on the attitudes, beliefs, experience, understanding and the social and cultural background of those answering them.

There are different approaches to dealing with behaviour in different play and playcare settings. There are also different theories as to how you can best help a child overcome consistent behavioural difficulties or problems.

> **WORD CHECK**
>
> **Sanction** is used here to mean a penalty or consequence of ignoring or stepping outside the agreed framework of behaviour.

Personal feelings about behaviour

ACTIVITY 2.21

Try this activity first on your own, then with colleagues (at a team meeting perhaps?).

What do you see as positive behaviour?

1 Write a list of the kinds of behaviour which you would encourage within the playsetting.

Are these types of behaviour consistent with:

- the values of playwork;
- the aims and objectives of your setting;
- age and stage of development of the children?

2 What is unacceptable behaviour?

Write down as many examples of unacceptable behaviour within the playsetting as you can think of within three minutes.

Take each example in turn and ask why it is unacceptable.

Try to distinguish between rules which relate to health and safety (e.g. no smoking, no unsupervised access to the kitchen, not more than two at time on the aerial swing) and types of behaviour which are unacceptable because they violate another person (physically, socially or emotionally) or limit the shared use and enjoyment of the play environment.

3 Look at your first list. Do you approve of the same positive behaviour in adults? Look at your second list. Is the behaviour you find unacceptable in children the same as the behaviour you find unacceptable in adults? What are the reasons for your answers?

The kinds of behaviour you might want to encourage in your playsetting include co-operating with each other, playing imaginatively, looking after others, being creative, being helpful, attempting new activities, challenging your own 'best score'. Examples of unacceptable behaviour include hitting, stealing, swearing, racism, sexism, destroying equipment and name calling.

Behaviour and development

Behaviour is closely linked with development. Behaviour is largely determined by a child's experiences and role models. It can be affected by other factors such as inherited or acquired physical and mental abilities (including physical disability and learning difficulties), illness, trauma, cultural background and family circumstances. You can expect different behaviour from children at different ages and stages of development. Some we consider acceptable, desirable even, others we may not approve of.

For example:

- A five-year-old in an afterschool club may well be getting used to starting a long day at school. He may be physically exhausted and less able or willing to join in some of the more active play opportunities. Another five-year-old may use offensive language without any understanding of its meaning (and therefore the offence it causes).
- A nine-year-old may consider the approval of her friends more important than the approval of the playworker. This may lead to increased co-operative behaviour and understanding of the rules of a game, but it may also lead to playing 'chicken' or getting involved in other physically dangerous dares.
- A 14-year-old may have developed a great sense of responsibility. He may be able and willing to care for younger ones or lead a cooking activity.

Playworker explaining

He may also see smoking or experimenting with drugs as part of the transition from childhood to adulthood.

By the age of five most children will understand that different kinds of behaviour are acceptable and expected in different settings. What may be accepted at home is not necessarily tolerated at school. The behaviour expected in the supermarket is different from that allowed in the park. Young children will have varying levels of experience of different settings. They may well not understand the reasons why they are encouraged to run around in the park but are told off (or receive greater punishment) for doing so in the supermarket, or why they can draw whenever and whatever they like at home but are expected to sit still and finish colouring in a pre-designed sheet at school. It takes time for children to learn the codes of behaviour which many older children and adults take for granted. They may need to have the rules explained to them many times and to be frequently reminded about what is acceptable and unacceptable behaviour in a particular setting.

Laying the ground-rules – behaviour policy

What is considered acceptable and unacceptable behaviour in your play setting may be influenced by:

- your personal beliefs, experience and background;
- the views and policies of management and staff;
- the participation of children;
- the involvement of parents;
- the nature of the setting and its aims;
- other people with an interest in the premises, service or community;
- the law.

It is important that everyone involved in the playsetting understands and follows the behaviour policy. The policy should be drawn up in consultation with management and staff, children and parents. The more the children are able to participate in this process, the better understanding they will have, although the way in which you involve them will depend on their age and understanding.

It is useful to provide information about the behaviour policy in written information for parents, carers and older children. This can take the form of a written statement about general principles.

EXAMPLE Statement of principles

All children coming to the playsetting have a right to play and enjoy what is on offer without fear of intimidation, harassment or physical or verbal abuse. We strive to promote behaviour which encourages respect for each individual, co-operation with each other and opportunities for play and adventure within a safe and caring environment. Racism, sexism and other kinds of discriminatory behaviour will be challenged and will not be allowed to continue within the playsetting. (For further information: ask for a copy of our behaviour policy.)

Some playsettings involve the children in discussion about what they consider acceptable and unacceptable behaviour, and the resulting lists (No bullying, No swearing, No racist or sexist language or behaviour) drawn or painted by the children are put up as reminders on the wall. But rules are not written in stone. Discuss and review them regularly and do not forget examples of positive behaviour.

ACTIVITY 2.22

1 Go back to Activity 2.21. Try it with the children in your playsetting (perhaps in groups of different age bands).

Make sure you have planned this in advance with the rest of the staff. Encourage in-depth discussion about why particular kinds of behaviour are unacceptable. You could follow up these discussions with relevant stories, drama or artwork (for example, about a child who has to deal with discrimination or bullying).

2 Compare what you hear from the children with your own attitudes and those expressed by your colleagues in Activity 2.21. Do you need to revise the behaviour policy?

Behaviour and safety

Playworkers have legal responsibilities to ensure the safety of themselves and others within the playsetting and to abide by the health and safety policy of their employers (see section 4.2). There need to be health and safety procedures (for the use of equipment or access to kitchen, for example) which must be followed. Depending on the age of the children, these procedures may include limiting children's access to some activities and ensuring adult supervision for others.

The age, developmental stage and skills of the children should be taken into account in drawing up these procedures. But children need to learn to take responsibility for their own safety; it is part of a playworker's role to empower children to do this within the playsetting (this is covered in more detail in sections 4.2 and 4.3).

There are times when rules will be different for a child and for a playworker, for obvious reasons such as health and safety. In most cases playworkers will not ask or expect children to abide by rules or behave in ways which they do not do themselves. This would be contrary to the underpinning values of playwork which see children as individual beings with human rights and deserving respect.

Smoking is a health issue which applies to all ages. The damaging effects of smoking are well known. It is unreasonable to expect a child or adolescent to refrain from smoking if the adults do not also abide by this rule within the playsetting.

Behaviour in a shared premises

The premises and nature of your playsetting will have a bearing on your behaviour policy. Some out of school clubs and playschemes are housed in schools or community centres. This can cause problems if codes of conduct are imposed on the playsetting by other groups. The playsetting needs to be

Empowering children to take responsibility for their own safety

able to develop its own identity. Children in the playsetting will choose their activities, have access to resources and relate to adults in a different way from how they would in a school, place of worship or other setting. Playworkers will need to be clear about the objectives of their setting which are the reasons for adopting a particular behaviour policy. There needs to be continuous communication with other users of the building, so that these objectives can be explained. Negotiation and some compromise will often be required.

Different approaches to behaviour management

Once you have agreed on what behaviour is positive and what is unacceptable you need to think about how you can encourage the first and discourage the second. You also need to agree on how you will deal with unacceptable behaviour when it occurs. This usually involves developing a system of rewards for positive behaviour and sanctions for negative behaviour. Applying these rewards and sanctions is called behaviour modification.

Pat Petrie (1994) observed three different approaches to behaviour management which were based on the underlying values of the playsettings she visited and of their staff. The first was a democratic approach where the children were treated as individuals and fellow cititzens. The children in playsettings with this approach were actively involved in discussions and negotiations about what is fair and unfair, and in finding just solutions to problems. They were encouraged to take responsibility for their own behaviour and its consequences.

The second approach appeared to be a broadly democratic approach in that the playworkers also appealed to the children's sense of fairness about keeping other people waiting or spoiling other people's fun. The difference here was that the emphasis was on group control and keeping children amused.

> Children were seen to some extent as *passive*, as customers or perhaps more accurately as *the children of customers*.
>
> Pat Petrie 1994

The third approach was a more punitative one, where the emphasis was on work rather than choice. Children were seen in a different light.

> These children were not citizens with rights, nor customers to be wooed, they were subordinates, rather who were to be obedient to the staff; they had no autonomy and no right to adult respect for their point of view.
>
> Pat Petrie 1994

This book looks at issues of behaviour with reference to the underlying values and assumptions of playwork as outlined in section 1.2. With this in mind, it suggests behaviour management in playwork should hold the rights of the individual children as central, and should seek participatory and democratic solutions to problems arising within the playsetting.

Good communication is important

Good communication is essential in establishing and maintaining a framework for behaviour: it allows you to negotiate and explain rules and codes of behaviour.

When dealing with unacceptable behaviour you will need to:

- gain the attention of the child(ren) concerned;
- listen to what the child is saying about what happened, what led up to the incident and the reasons behind the actions;

TO THINK ABOUT

Which of the three approaches outlined comes closest to the policy and practice of your playsetting?

You should be aware that there are different approaches to behaviour management in playsettings, and that these are influenced by:

- the aims of the playsetting (what it sets out to achieve and for whom);
- the approach of the staff (how they view children and the meaning they attach to what it is to be a child).

ACTIVITY 2.23

1 Make a list of all the kinds of rewards and sanctions which are used to modify behaviour in your playsetting.

2 Refer the *Playwork* values outlined in section 1.2. How do the values relate to the rewards and sanctions you use? If you think that they do not match up, or you are unclear about the issue, discuss with a senior member of staff or ask for this to be discussed at a team meeting or staff training day.

- explain what the child has done wrong and why;
- criticise the behaviour not the person, for example 'That is a racist thing to say' not 'You are a racist'; 'That was an unfair thing to do' not 'You inconsiderate child!';
- explain what will happen as a consequence of the action;
- have good communication, consistency and support from other team members;
- ensure that the child has the opportunity to make amends and continue to be part of the group once the incident has been dealt with. There should be no further recrimination from staff or other children.

Body language is also important. Try to make sure you are on the same eye-level as the child when discussing important issues such as behaviour. Threatening body language such as towering over a child or pointing or shaking your finger at him may make him feel unsafe and unable to contribute. After dealing with a situation involving unacceptable behaviour, your friendly pat on the shoulder or hug can help reaffirm that you still like the child concerned, even though you did not approve of his behaviour.

Rewards and sanctions

Rewards

Rewards should build up the self-esteem of the child displaying positive behaviour and give an incentive for that child to continue. Rewards for positive behaviour can include giving praise, thanks or encouragement and should offer opportunities for the child to build on the positive actions he or she has taken.

> *EXAMPLE* Rewarding positive behaviour
>
> A child who has attempted a piece of artwork or modelling for the first time or with particular effort, can feel rewarded by having the finished product displayed. You may like to comment about it not only to the child, but also to other staff, children or parents. You could build a 'sharing time' into a wind-down activity at the end of the session or day, when individual children can show or tell something they are pleased about or proud of, to the other children.
>
> A child who has joined in a co-operative game for the first time without attempting to mess it up, can be asked if she would like to choose or lead the next game.
>
> You can acknowledge and reward a child who has shown particularly responsible behaviour in one area (looking after the woodwork tools, for example) by giving more responsibility in other areas (tending an open fire, running a library area, lighting the cooker) albeit still with appropriate adult supervision.

Giving a child responsibility, can be a way of encouraging co-operative behaviour, not just rewarding it.

The role models you and others provide within the playsetting are also important. A child is quick to pick up on double standards and cannot be expected to appreciate rewards for behaviour which you do not value in yourself. Give praise honestly or it will be quickly recognised as patronising: you can nearly always find something to appreciate in another person.

The rewards you offer need not encourage competition They should be based on the individual needs and merits of each child. Learning to catch a ball is a great achievement for one child; for another it is easy. It takes some children more time to learn to co-operate in their play. Your rewards should be consistent with the aims of your setting and the values of playwork.

Sanctions

Dealing with bad behaviour, and 'discipline' are frequently seen by play-workers as major concerns. The role models you provide and the rewards you offer can encourage positive behaviour within the playsetting and can reinforce the values of respect and providing for individual choices and needs. This approach can only succeed with the co-operation of all involved. Every playsetting will have its share of negative or unacceptable behaviour. What sanctions are appropriate for particular kinds of behaviour need to be agreed. Children, parents and workers need to know what they are and in what circumstances they will be applied. Sanctions can include ignoring the behaviour, challenging the behaviour, exclusion from particular activities or trips and temporary or permanent exclusion from the setting.

1 *Ignoring*. Some kinds of non co-operative or disruptive behaviour (a five-year-old making insistent rude noises, for example) are best ignored, at least in the short term. The behaviour may be a bid to get extra attention. Extra attention is usually best directed at positive behaviour. Be aware that the child still wants attention, however. Working as a team helps: another playworker could distract a disruptive child into a different activity. A longer-term strategy would be to help the child to develop more positive ways to gain the attention he needs.

2 *Challenging*. Bullying, intimidation, racism, sexism or other discriminatory or abusive behaviour needs to be challenged at the time. Explain why the behaviour is unacceptable and, if necessary, what will happen if it is repeated (as laid out in the agreed framework for behaviour of your setting). Be sensitive. Don't judge or interpret too quickly what you have seen or been told.

   Give priority to supporting the recipient of the abusive behaviour, who can all too easily be forgotten while the trouble-maker gets all the attention (even if it is in the form of a challenge to and discussion about why his remarks or behaviour are not acceptable)

3 *Exclusions*. Exclusions from activities, trips or the playsetting are more extreme measures, and should only be applied in consultation with the senior member of staff. Parents will also usually need to be informed, particularly in a caresetting. A child may need to be excluded if she consistently presents a danger to herself or others or prevents others from benefiting from what is on offer.

The sanctions used in your playsetting and the way in which they are applied will depend on the nature of the setting and the age of the children. In an open access setting for older children you will be less likely to need to involve parents. Adolescents will be more able to negotiate the framework for behaviour. They are more able to understand another point of view and to understand the consequences of their actions. In an open access setting there is also no contract of care with parents – the children come and go as they please (see section 1.1).

Violent or physical punishments or those which involve shaming or humiliating the child are not acceptable in the playsetting, or in keeping with the values of playwork. There may be occasions where physical force is required to restrain a child from causing harm to himself or others. Stay calm and always use the minimum amount of force to hold the child until the danger

> ### ACTIVITY 2.24
> Discuss with your colleagues how violent or potentially dangerous behaviour should be dealt with and how you can best work together to support each other.
>
> At what point would you need to call on support from outside the playsetting?
>
> Who would provide such external support? How would you contact them?

is passed or help and support arrive. Remember your aim is to safeguard the child and anyone else present. Safe techniques for holding children whose behaviour may cause them to endanger themselves or others are best learned through training and practice through roleplay.

Similar issues need to be considered in the event of unwelcome intruders from outside the playsetting.

ACTIVITY 2.25

1 Ask one colleague to take the part of the child, and another colleague to act as observer.

2 Think of a situation you have found difficult in the past in which you have had to challenge a child's unacceptable behaviour. Explain the situation to the person taking the part of the child – how he or she behaved and a little background to the the incident.

3 Roleplay the situation for a few minutes. The observer should keep time and tell you when to stop.

The observer tells you:

- three things you are doing well (e.g. keeping calm, making eye contact, listening, explaining);
- three things you could improve (e.g. speak louder or more quietly, make eye contact, adopt a different body position, say more or less).

4 Continue the role play for a further few minutes or until the situation is resolved to your satisfaction. The observer announces the end of the role play.

Make sure you detach yourselves from the roles you have been playing Then discuss the roleplay, asking:

- how each player felt during the role play;
- has the observer any new comments to add?

5 Agree on three things you can do to help you to deal more confidently with a similar situation in the future. Write them down.

This activity may work best if each person has an opportunity to take the part of the observer, playworker and child, with a new situation being roleplayed each time.

Developing your skills in dealing with difficult situations

Dealing with unacceptable behaviour is never easy. You may find it difficult to challenge racist or sexist remarks or intervene in a potentially violent situation. It is useful to practice ways of dealing with such situations before they actually occur. When you are dealing with a conflict situation, it is easy to let anger, fear or embarrassment interfere with your ability to deal with it effectively. Practicing your strategies for dealing with difficult situations can build your confidence and ability to deal with the real thing. If you can practice with colleagues it can also increase your understanding of each other and the ways in which you each react in conflict. This will enable you to be more supportive and consistent with each other in your work in the playsetting.

ACTIVITY 2.26

Look at the following examples of unacceptable behaviour. Discuss different strategies for dealing with each situation with another playworker.

What (if any) immediate action would you take in the following situations:

1 You find two children aged 11 and 12 sniffing glue behind the shed.
2 You overhear a seven-year-old say to another child, 'Go away, I don't like brown people. You can't play.'
3 You ask a nine-year-old to help to clear away an activity he has been involved in. He tells you to 'get lost'.
4 You come outside to find two children locked in a fight, rolling on the floor. A group of other children has surrounded them and is cheering them on.

What follow-up action would you take?

Consider the situations described in Activity 2.26. There are no right answers in deciding how you would deal with such incidents. Each situation will be different in practice, and you will need to judge and assess the situation on the spot, drawing on your knowledge of the children and the environment, the support available and your past experience. You can however consider your approach, and practice what you would say and do in a similar situation. Ask yourself what might cause particular types of behaviour. Can you do anything to increase the child's understanding of why the behaviour is unacceptable, and therefore perhaps prevent it from happening again?

In some cases you will need to attend to safety considerations. In the first situation in Activity 2.26, it is important that you assess the physical and mental state of the children sniffing glue before dealing with the behaviour issue in itself. You might need to call for medical assistance. In the fourth situation you will need to diffuse the situation by distracting the supporting crowd of onlookers before separating and dealing with the children who are fighting. Again you might need to seek the support of a colleague.

In the third situation you may not be able to insist the nine-year-old clears away the activity. You will need to consider the reasons behind why he or she was rude to you. You could discuss the ground-rules for behaviour with the children of this age (see Activity 2.21), and agree with them and your co-workers the sanction which will be imposed. A child who refuses to help clear away an activity even when reminded to do so might not be allowed to have access to that activity again for the following week.

In the second situation, you will need to challenge what has been said immediately. You might say, 'That is a very unpleasant thing to say', then explain why it is unpleasant. You will also need to show support to the child who has been rejected, perhaps by putting an arm around him or her. Over the following days, look for opportunities to build up this child's self-esteem by praising his or her positive skills and attributes.

Follow up the reasons behind why the incident occurred. Look at your resources, think about the activities you offer. Encourage discussion and develop those activities which give positive value to differences in children and the world as a whole (see section 1.2).

In all cases remember also that the children may have learned the behaviour from other adults or older siblings who are important to them. Be sensitive in how you challenge behaviour. Your aim should be to increase the child's understanding of other views, not to censure the child or his family.

Dealing with persistent unacceptable behaviour

Negative behaviour can be a symptom of underlying problems for the child. It can be caused by the child's lack of self-esteem, developmental difficulties or anger or confusion about being unable to live up to expectations made of him. Alternatively, perhaps other people or events have not lived up to his expectations of them.

Try to identify the causes for persistent negative behaviour.

- Listen to the child. Listen to the parents. Listen to other members of the team.
- Is the child unhappy? What reasons might there be? Do they stem from home, school, playsetting or other environment? Does the child choose to come to the playsetting?
- Is the child bored? Are the play opportunities varied and stimulating? Are they relevant to the child's age and stage of development? Could new play opportunities be developed based on the child's particular interests?

ACTIVITY 2.27

Choose a child within your playsetting whose behaviour gives you cause for concern. If this child's behaviour is extreme, or frequently unacceptable, you may like to go straight to section B. If it is less critical but gives you ongoing concern, complete section A first, and then try section B.

Section A

Observe this child every 20 minutes for a period of five minutes.

Record what he is doing with whom. Write up your notes.

Ask yourself:

- What were the main activities he engaged in?
- Who are the people (children and adults) he relates to most?
- Is the child unhappy?

Repeat this on several days over a period of two or three weeks to build up a fuller picture.

Share your observations with a colleague or senior member of staff.

Section B

Observe the child only at times when he is behaving unacceptably. Get colleagues to deal with the child when you are observing. After several observations, consider:

- What events led up to the incidents?
- Is there a pattern to them?
- Are there any warning signals, e.g. the child be-comes withdrawn or particularly noisy. (One child I know gets bright red ear tips shortly before he 'blows'.)
- Do the incidents occur at a particular time of day (e.g. before or after food, before going home, on arrival, during large group activities)?
- Do they involve other people? Are they the same people (children, member of staff) every time?

If you identify a pattern, discuss with colleagues the reasons for it. Can the pattern be predicted, and therefore prevented?

What strategies can you think of to help this child deal with his or her behaviour?

Consider Activity 2.27, one strategy might be to distract the child at danger times. You might need to avoid particular activities for a while or talk with his or her parents.

Sometimes a child will show deeply disturbing or consistently unacceptable behaviour within the playsetting and may need specialist advice (see section 5.3). Such a child may require a psychodynamic or therapeutic support to enable her to find the causes of her problems and to develop manageable behaviour patterns. Where such support is not available you may need to exclude the child from the playsetting for a time. The reasons for this must be clearly explained. Always tell the child why you are doing this. Contact your nearest Social Services Department for advice.

Behaviour management and groups

ACTIVITY 2.28

Consider this situation:

It is the first day of a holiday playscheme. You and the two other playworkers employed have basic information about the children who will be attending from their registration forms, and you have met some of the children and parents at the registration evening. The children come from different schools and do not all know each other. You have set up several different play areas and activities within the community hall in which you are based, and an obstacle course outside.

1 What would you expect them to do first?

2 How would you stop them from feeling over-whelmed, or from rushing about and misusing equipment?

3 How would this be different for a group of 5- to 7-year-olds and a group of 11- to 12-year-olds?

You will need to have activities which introduce the children to each other and to get to know the possibilities available to them in the playsetting. Playing a 'name game' can be a good way to start.

EXAMPLE Name games

With 5- to 7-year-olds this could be a circle game: small groups, with a playworker throwing a ball back and forth and saying their names as they throw. After a while, ask the children to say the name of the child they are throwing the ball to.

Older children could be given cards with pictures or words on as they come in. Ask them to find another child with the same picture (there are several pairs of cards). When they have found their match, they introduce themselves with their name, and find two things which they have in common: brown eyes or a pet dog, for example. Then they fetch another card and start again.

Think of interesting ways to divide large groups into smaller ones or teams.

EXAMPLE Creating smaller groups or teams

Cut up two or three large pictures into several pieces and stick them around the playsetting with Blu-tac. The children find one piece and then look for children with the other pieces to make the 'puzzle' whole.

The children can be introduced to what is available by asking small groups to find and collect certain items (a blue sequin, a sponge ball) from around the playsetting. For older children you could set up a more complicated treasure hunt, with cryptic clues and maps.

Some kinds of playsetting have more group activities than others. In these cases it may be necessary for you to adopt a more controlling role. One playworker, regularly takes groups of children (aged 8–14) she doesn't know very well for environmental activities in the woods. These activities include

Group activity to focus on listening and co-operation

charcoal making and the use of sharp tools such as whittling knives, chisels and saws, and are based around an open camp fire. In order to do this safely she feels it is essential to be able to gain every or any individual's attention at any time. She has a particular call which she teaches the children means 'stop what you are doing and pay attention'. She explains and practices this with the children before embarking on her activities session. The children are also taught and practise signals to use in emergency if they get lost in the woods or feel themselves to be in danger. Some workers use whistles or hand gestures to call a group together.

When you take children on a trip, particular codes of group behaviour may be required: crossing roads together, not running off, meeting at a particular place, not giving the playsetting 'a bad name' by dropping litter or causing disruption. These codes of behaviour need to be explained and agreed with the children in advance – including any signals which may be used.

Within the playsetting itself, methods of group control are not usually necessary as you get to know the children and work with them to establish a framework for behaviour. The strongest fabric for this framework is space for individual freedom and choice, respect for and co-operation with each other and valuing diversity within the group.

References

Fine, Nic and Macbeth, Fiona 1992: *Playing with Fire – Training for the creative use of conflict.* Youth Work Press.

Petrie, Pat 1994: *Play and Care.* HMSO (pp. 122–34 in particular).

Further reading

Leach, Penelope 1994: *Children First.* Michael Joseph and Penguin, Chapter 6.

Steinberg and Levine 1992: *You and Your Adolescent.* Ebury Press, Chapter 2.

Yapp, Nick 1991: *My Problem Child.* Penguin.

Train, Alan 1993: *Helping the Aggressive Child.* Souvenir Press.

3 Planning in action

3.1 Planning the play environment

> The pleasures of childhood should in the main be such as the child extracts from his environment by means of some effort and inventiveness.
>
> *The Conquest of Happiness,* Bertrand Russell

This section looks at various starting-points you can use when thinking about and planning the environment within your playsetting.

The environment is the setting into which the children come, in which playworkers work. It includes both the physical space – the rooms, building, size of play areas, heating, lighting and ventilation; and less tangible factors such as the mood, appeal, and the possibilities for action and experience that it offers.

Factors such as legislation and safety, covered in other chapters, have a bearing on planning a play environment. Here, however, we are looking at the environment from the child's point of view: to see how to plan for a play-setting which is child centred (see also section 1.2).

Asking children to take you on a journey around their play spaces (Activity 3.1) will probably give you a different insight into how children experience their environment and their preferred play spaces than simply asking them to tell you. You will be able to use this insight when planning the environment.

Your surroundings are important. Different environments will have a different impact on how you feel and want to behave. It follows then that the the environment of your playsetting will affect the way the children feel and want to behave and is an important factor in planning opportunities for play.

What space do you have? What kind of service do you provide?

Your playsetting may share the premises of a school, church hall or community centre, or you may work in a purpose-built playcentre, adventure playground or other designated playsetting. You may have to meet a range of care needs as well as providing play opportunities – for example, providing nutritionally balanced meals for children whose parents are at work or otherwise engaged.

Your premises and the kind of service you offer will affect the kind of environment which can or needs to be provided. If you intend to provide meals you will need a kitchen and somewhere comfortable to eat. If the

ACTIVITY 3.1

Look back at the survey you were asked to carry out in Activity 1, section 1.1. What did the children in the age range say about where they liked to play?

If possible ask a couple of children of different ages to take you around some of their favourite play spaces and tell you what they like about them.

Explain what you are doing and get permission from parents or carers first.

TO THINK ABOUT

How do different kinds of spaces affect you?

For example, how does it make you feel to be:

- in a room with a fire on a wet winter's day;
- in a large institution such as a hospital or Department of Social Security building;
- in a dark forest;
- on the top of a high tower;
- at the seashore on a summer's day?

ACTIVITY 3.2

Look at your own playsetting.

Consider the following list of issues which can cause difficulties for playworkers in creating an environment. Are they a challenge in your case?

Can you think of other issues relating to space which cause difficulties for you and your co-workers in planning and preparing the play environment?

	Difficult	Adequate	Fine
1 Sharing a space with other organisations			
2 Can you leave most of your play materials in place or do you need to recreate your play environment every session?			
3 Do you have enough suitable furniture and equipment?			
4 Can you provide for outdoor play?			
5 Are you able to display the children's choice of artwork?			
6 Do you have enough storage space?			

Discuss your findings with your co-workers. Are there any areas in which you can think of ways of making improvements?

---

children are to spend several hours in the facility they will need comfortable spaces to sit, relax, talk, rest and maybe even doze off. If your facility is required to register under the Children Act 1989 you will need to meet the requirements of your local authority (see section 1.2).

Whatever the challenges, as long as the basic facilities are there (enough space, toilets, washing facilities, kitchen if needed and office space) there are nearly always options and very often solutions if you are prepared to think creatively, and give enough time to planning.

Sharing a premises will require good communication with the other organisations involved. You will need to be clear about the needs of your group and accommodate the needs of others. For example, you may need to take down displays every day. It will be helpful if a representative of your playsetting is 'link person' with a representative of any other organisation which uses the same premises. He or she can make time to discuss shared interests and concerns. In particular, your play facility will need to negotiate adequate storage space and how various spaces can be used. Can any equipment be shared?

Transforming a hall or bare school canteen is challenging. Ingenious playworkers can use screens, plants, coloured cloths, rugs, cushions, pictures, tables and movable shelving or other furniture, such as child-sized tables and chairs, to create several different spaces within the larger whole.

Children should be able to play out of doors as well as in. Sadly the time spent in your playsetting may be the only opportunity some children get to do this. If you do not have interesting, safe and easily accessible outdoor play space as part of your playsetting, you will have to be creative. How can you make the best use of the space you have got? Can the children grow things in pots? Can you use paint to cheer up stretches of concrete or tarmac? Build up a stock of materials (milk crates, planks, tyres, hoops, skipping-ropes) with which the children can transform and use the space they do have. Look around your local community. Where are the nearest parks, or other open spaces? Are there any wilderness or conservation areas for you to explore?

Making flexible and creative use of space is just as important if your play facility has sole use or is the main user of your building. There should be spaces in which children can be noisy as well as spaces in which to be quiet;

spaces in which to be active – run, jump, climb, play ball – and spaces in which to be still. There should be opportunities for creativity, even if it is sometimes messy, and places which lend themselves to sociable play and inter-action as well as places which afford privacy when desired (hidey-holes and dens). Use equipment which is versatile and easily moved. Overall the play environment should foster the child's inborn motivation to learn and devel-op, to be curious and to explore.

Using the senses

Your memories of childhood play and the descriptions of other people's mem-ories (see Activity 3.3) will conjure up impressions relating to your senses – sights, sounds, smells, textures – as well as social and emotional experience. It is through the senses that a baby first awakens to the world: through sight, sound, touch, taste, smell and movement that she gains information which leads to an understanding of the environment in which she finds herself. This awakening through the senses continues throughout childhood and later life. Children of all ages will enjoy activities and play opportunities which appeal to their senses.

EXAMPLE

Food

1   Try tasting different foods with a blindfold on: food from different countries and cultures, sweet, sour, salty.
2   What effect does sight have on taste? Try adding unusual colour to foods to make: green orange juice, blue baked beans, purple rice and peas, for example. Think about different ways we make food look appetising. Try out different garnishes. (*Note:* some food colourings can cause allergic reactions in some children. You could use natural edible colours such as beetroot juice.)
3   Does sound affect taste? Try eating in silence, eating with music playing, eating while chatting.
4   Touch and taste. Try eating the same food with fingers and with cutlery or chopsticks. Does food taste different if served from china/ wooden/metal/plastic bowls, cups or serving dishes?

EXAMPLE

Sensory walks

1   Everybody walks around the playsetting discovering things which they like or don't like in terms of touch, smell, sound. (With younger children it is probably better to choose just one or two senses at a time.)
2   Everybody finds a partner. One person wears a blindfold and the other person leads the blindfolded partner on a 'sense walk': asking them to listen to, touch, smell the things they have discovered for themselves. Can they guess what each thing is? Do they share the same likes and dislikes?

You will be able to think of other activities and play opportunities which focus on and enrich the children's sense experiences. There are endless possibilities for the use of different fabrics, for example, from sack-cloth to rich velvets or pieces decorated with mirrors and embroidery. Use them for

---

ACTIVITY 3.3

Think back to your own child-hood, to times and places you remember as times of happy play.

● Where did the play take place?
● Were you alone or with others?
● Was there an adult present?

Think about one particular fav-ourite play space. What did it feel like? What were the sounds, sights, smells and textures?

Ask others to recall their experiences to you or read auto-biographical accounts of child-hood play.

ACTIVITY 3.4

1 Walk into any play setting and squat or sit so that you are the same height of the children using the facility. Ask yourself what the setting has to offer to each of your senses.

Take hearing, for example: what noise is being made by the children and adults present? Laughing, shouting, excited screaming or contented babble? Is taped music played continu-ously in the background? What kind of music? At what volume? Does the room echo disconcert-ingly? Can children get away from unwanted sound?

Ask similar relevant questions relating to touch, sight, smell, taste.

2 Talk to older children in your playsetting about how they experience the play setting with each of their senses.

Spaces to relax

discovery and comparison, particularly if you can get hold of pieces of fabric from around the world. What is it made from? How does it feel? What does it smell like? Is it brightly coloured or pastel? You can use fabric for sewing, for dressing up, for wrapping round furniture, draping round walls, numerous art and craft activities, or for creating hidey-holes and many other things.

The senses then, can be a starting-point when looking at how children experience the play environment. Use your senses, and your discussions with children to help you plan the design of your playsetting.

Structure time and rhythm

Play and playcare facilities usually have opening and closing times. Within those two markers a variety of things happen. Some places will have meal-times, story-times, and maybe a programme of activities which will be more or less structured. But play is not about structured activities, and the definition of play quoted earlier in this book that 'play is freely chosen, personally directed behaviour, motivated from within' precludes any form of structured timetabling (but see section 3.2 on how a programme of activities can be a useful planning tool).

Rhythm, on the other hand, is a natural part of the development of all living organisms. Babies need to develop rhythms of sleeping, eating and activity to survive in the world, and repeated interruption or distortion leads to disorientation and breakdown of normal functioning. You can help children gain a sense of security and confidence in the way you plan for play to incorporate familiar rhythms. There should be times to be active, times to be quiet, times for sitting together and talking, planning and sharing food. You can develop a sense of rhythm by paying attention to the pacing of the session or an individual activity: that it has a beginning, a middle and an end, and that time is allowed for clearing away. The week can also have its own rhythm, with opportunities for different types of activity on different days of the week, and the rhythm of the year may be incorporated through seasonal activities, the celebrations of birthdays or festivals of different faiths and cultures.

ACTIVITY 3.7

Observation

Observe your playsetting as a whole for a few minutes at regular intervals – every half hour or 45 minutes, say – throughout one day. Make notes on the level and types of activity in progress.

At the end of the day, ask yourself:

- Did the level of activity vary at different times of day?
- Were there times which seemed more active and energetic, and times where the energy was winding down?

- Were there times when the children came together in larger groups or a whole group to share food, discussion or a co-operative game?
- Were there times which were noiser and times which were quieter?

Think of two activities which you think would be particularly good at the beginning of the day and two which might be better suited to the end of the day. Why?

Rhythm can have endless variations and the children in the setting should be able to initiate and develop it. Some will want a faster more complicated rhythm, others will prefer a simpler pattern. You as playworker can keep the beat: ensuring that individual needs are met, but that one child's or small group's rhythm is not allowed to dominate or obliterate another's.

Underpinning values

The underpinning values of the playsetting contribute greatly to the environment in terms of mood, appeal and the possibilities for play and development for all children through the ways in which:

- children are involved in planning and decision making – do they feel the playsetting is truly theirs?;
- relationships between people are developed and maintained;
- individual children are recognised for their unique abilities and valued for what they bring to the playsetting;
- the play environment relates to the wider world.

Each of these aspects of playwork is considered in more detail in other chapters of this book. Here we look at some examples of how the underpinning values relate specifically to planning the play environment.

Involve the children

Children need to feel that they belong to and have rights within their play environment. They should be involved in the decisions about what happens there, and be able to get what they need without adult help whenever possible. Older children, with greater experience and maturity, will be able to consider the wider needs and limitations of the playsetting. They can be consulted more formally about what resources should be provided and what activities are on offer. A younger child's choices and decisions will relate to his or her own needs and the way he wants to play within the possibilities open to him.

A child-centred environment for play will enable the children to initiate and take their play in many directions at a pace they feel comfortable with. Sometimes the play opportunity may take the children on adventures unknown while still leaving them with the power to stop or change direction. Consider Case study 3.1. Mary Januarius, information officer for HAPA (see Appendix 2: Useful contacts) describes part of a day at an adventure playground as seen through the eyes of Steven.

CASE STUDY 3.1: A PLACE FOR ADVENTURE

Steven is six, fair-haired, with a freckled, round face. He wears blue jeans with green monster patches emblazoned all over. He has a moderate learning difficulty and he is an extremely demanding child, with a very short attention span, who needs to be constantly amused. Steven has an engaging manner and attaches himself to the playworker who will help him do what he wants to do.

Steven usually wants to make masks. Today is no exception. We go over to the arts and crafts corner, find silver paper and white card, green pens, scissors and sticky tape. Steven draws a face, with eyes, nose, ears and big green horns. We cut out the mask, attach string to the ears so it fits over his head. Arms and legs also require adornment, so we make bracelets out of silver card to go round his wrists and over his ankles. All togged out, Steven surveys himself in the mirror and sets off, roaring fiercely at those he encounters. The green monster is eager for an adventure today.

He finds it in the jungle. Slashing the undergrowth he goes deeper and deeper into the jungle, on the lookout for tigers and dragons. Stray branches slow his progress, the way ahead is unclear. But wait . . . help is at hand. Another explorer of uncharted territory, Jonathan, is on the scene. He offers us his own hand-drawn map, to help us find our way. Urging us to keep the map and warning us 'be careful!' he waves us off into the bush.

Before long, we encounter Jonathan, our trusty map bearer, once again. Together, we press on, successfully avoiding being eaten by tigers and dragons. At last we reach our destination – the castle.

At the castle (a slide and climbing structure to the less imaginative), we are joined by other children who are playing a game with a tennis ball. Children take turns to roll the ball down from the top of the slide to the child sitting at the bottom, who then runs up the slide with the ball. Several turns and the game exhausts itself. Time for something new . . ..

There's a little old man who lives in a house. The house is made of three big foam rings, stacked one on top of the other, red, green and blue. It has a removable black roof. Inside is the little old man, with moustache and beard – he's eight, going on eighty-eight. At first, Steven is definitely not welcome. But the little old man relents and lets him in. Once in, there appears to be no way out except by burrowing a tunnel through the wall of the house. And then more unwelcome guests arrive. They clamber onto the roof and are unceremoniously kicked off by the residents. A new game! How long can the guests stay on the roof, before they are kicked off and the house collapses?

HAPA *'Adventure play – a child's experience'* Annual Review 1992/3

ACTIVITY 3.8

1 If Steven (in Case study 3.1) had come to your play-setting, with his green monster patches and wish to make a mask, what possibilities would there have been for him to achieve his wish and take the lead in the way he wanted to develop his play?

2 Think of an example you have observed within your own playsetting where a child was able to develop their choice of play at her or his own pace and in her or his own way. Look out for further examples of this in your observations.

Do the children in your playsetting know what play materials are available to them at any time? If the answer is No there may be good reasons. Some materials may be too expensive or in short supply to allow unlimited access. Other materials are potentially too dangerous to allow unsupervised use by the children, particularly by younger children if you have a wide age-range. In either case however there is no reason why the children should not know of the existence of all play materials and equipment. Only then can they know to ask when they need something. Limited or inaccessible storage space or the fact that children may 'spoil' equipment should not be reasons to limit access. These are issues of behaviour management (see section 2.4), choosing appropriate equipment and materials and enabling the children to feel that the playsetting belongs to them. Your aim should be to encourage children's independence and sense of responsibility towards the playsetting.

Some playsettings hold children's meetings to help plan activities or make changes to the environment. You should at least have a regular time for informal discussion about these issues – perhaps when you are sharing a drink or snack. You will also learn a lot about what the children want and need from the playsetting through careful observation of individuals and groups, and informal chats with individual children. Involving children does not necessarily mean always giving them what they want. A child may want to destroy all the other children's carefully constructed models, or to do nothing but watch TV. These are not play opportunities. The children will need to understand the choices on offer – the possibilities and limitations of the playsetting. Limited 'screen time' may form part of what a playcare setting has to offer. Children attending an afterschool club each day may be very unhappy if they are not able to watch a favourite TV programme which forms part of the conversation and culture of the children who go home after school.

TO THINK ABOUT

Some playsettings, catering for older children, have a children's representative (elected by the children) on their management.

- What are the potential advantages of this?
- What are the possible difficulties?

The children can create a sense of identity for the setting

If you share a building you can foster your group's own sense of identity by giving it an interesting name, displaying children's artwork and having a noticeboard with posters, newsletter, photos or publicity material. The children of one afterschool club I visited had each made their own distinctive name badge out of beads and metallic paint. These were worn when the club met and left on the noticeboard in between times, making a very attractive display. The children of the same club also had their own self-made cushions, each decorated with the individual's name and made from a wide variety of fabric scraps. They were large enough to sit on at story times or just to relax. Each child had also decoratively painted his or her own cheap enamel mug for use while in the club.

In this way children's creative achievements can also be used to develop the identity of the playsetting as a whole. Even if you have to take down displays each night it is well worth encouraging the children to take pride in their creative achievements and in their playsetting by making them part of the same thing. Try fabric painting on large sheets, for example, which can be folded and put away. Use chalkboards or other wipe or washdown surfaces for creating screens. Page 77 shows an idea for a quick wall display or room divide which can be easily folded up and put away at the end of the day. Use large sheets of thick paper or card. The children can choose how they will use them: a collage on a particular theme for example. The pieces are held together with ticker tags through holes punched in the corners. You can use individual pieces of artwork, or create a group mural with different children completing sections of one picture.

A foldaway screen display drawn by Polly, Roberto and Nikita (aged 6, 7 and 8)

Individuals and differences

Planning a child-centred environment requires you to take note of the individual needs that each child has.

Children need to know about their own and other cultures in order for them to understand the world in which they live. Children from all cultures need to have their own family culture acknowledged, and you can introduce positive images of different cultures into the play environment and the activities available.

One idea for such an activity is to adopt a particular culture as a theme for a week's activities. If you chose China, for example, you could:

● collect books, posters, magazine articles with positive images of China, its people and their lives;

ACTIVITY 3.9

1 Plan an activity or series of activities which involves the children in finding out about families or cultures which are different from their own.

2 If you have children from different cultures within your playsetting, encourage them to share their knowledge and experience and take pride in the differences. If you do not have children from a variety of cultures in your playsetting you will need to enlist help from books or people outside of the setting, (see also sections 1.2 and 5.3).

- find out about their major national festivals – how are they celebrated?;
- prepare and eat Chinese food, using Chinese cooking and eating implements;
- borrow or make Chinese clothes for dressing up or drama;
- read Chinese stories. Try out Chinese games and art and craft activities. Listen to Chinese music. Look at Chinese pictograms, listen to Chinese language.

This may seem quite ambitious, but will definitely be easier and come alive more if you can enlist the help and support of people with first-hand, daily experience of Chinese culture.

Another way of tackling this activity would be to use a theme of 'Ourselves'. Take photos of the children. Encourage them to draw themselves and their families (be sure you have paints and paper which can reproduce a variety of skin, hair and eye tones). Older children could interview each other about their lives and their families. Perhaps they could present 'This is your life' or 'This is my life' type stories and take their own photographs. Such activities need to be undertaken with sensitivity and the emphasis should be on celebrating diversity: everyone has something to offer.

Meeting special needs

Some children have special needs which are more difficult to meet if all children are to benefit from play facilities. In planning the play environment, physical access (ramps, toilets, handles, location of resources) needs to be considered for wheelchair users or others with mobility difficulties.

In the case of sensory impairment, the environment may be particularly important in enabling the child to make sense of the world. Textured surfaces will be much more interesting than complicated patterns or colours to a child who cannot see.

Boys and girls are also quick to pick up any bias as to what kinds of play are 'suitable' or 'acceptable' for their gender. In planning the play environment you need to ensure that children of both sexes have opportunities to develop

Appealing to different senses

ACTIVITY 3.10

1 Draw or sketch a plan of your play setting.

2 Label each area A B C D E, etc.

3 Every 15 minutes for one session, scan the indoor and outdoor area and mark how many children are using each area.

4 Add any additional information, such as children walking between areas.

5 After the session ask yourself:

- Are any areas hardly used or not used at all?
- How can I change little-used areas so that they are better used or more attractive to children who currently don't use them?

Talk to the children about your findings. Have they any ideas?

a range of skills, and that one play area (dolls corner or ballplay area) is not always dominated by children of only one gender (see section 1.2). Activity 3.10 may also help with this.

Evaluating the play environment

It is important for you to be able to reflect on, analyse and evaluate your workplace environment: how is it being used, and when and where it should be changed in order to continue to meet the needs of the children who use it. Activity 3.10 provides you with one tool for undertaking this on a regular basis.

It is a very useful form of observation, so keep your plan of the play-setting and a copy of the blank observation sheet. You can use the format of this observation to find out many things about how the play environment is used and by whom. For example if you wanted to monitor whether boys and girls are getting equal access to different play opportunities you would mark the information on your observation accordingly ($\female$ = females, $\male$ = males):

Area A 7($\female$) 2($\male$)
Area B 1($\female$) 1($\male$) every 15 minutes

Then ask yourself where there are obvious differences in the way either gender uses particular areas and why this might be.

You can do the same thing to determine whether some areas of the environment appeal more to younger or older children in your playsetting by marking numbers of children over 7 (7+) and under 7 (–7), for example, in any area at a given time.

You can also use this observation exercise to discover something about adult involvement in your playsetting. For this you will need to mark the

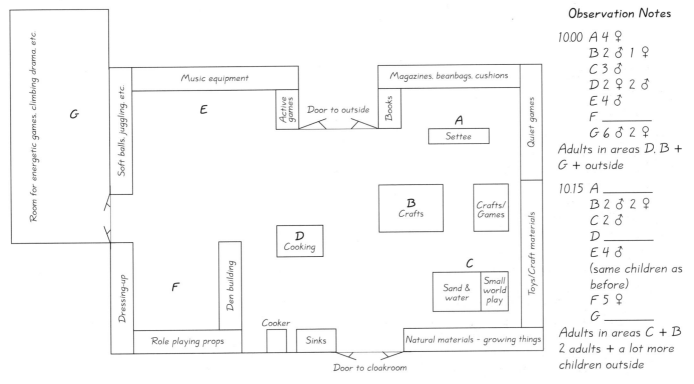

Plan of playsetting

Observation Notes

10.00 A 4 ♀
    B 2 ♂ 1 ♀
    C 3 ♂
    D 2 ♀ 2 ♂
    E 4 ♂
    F _____
    G 6 ♂ 2 ♀
Adults in areas D, B + G + outside

10.15 A _____
    B 2 ♂ 2 ♀
    C 2 ♂
    D _____
    E 4 ♂
(same children as before)
    F 5 ♀
    G _____
Adults in areas C + B 2 adults + a lot more children outside

number of adults present in particular areas as well as numbers of children. Are some areas used by children only if adults are present? Why might this be?

References

Russell, Bertrand 1930 Ed. (1960) *The Conquest of Happiness.*
HAPA 1992/93: 'Adventure play – a child's experience', *Annual Review.*

Further reading

HAPA publications on adventure playgrounds and integrated play. (See Appendix 2.)
Kids Clubs Network 1994: *Out of School – In School!* (On working in the school environment.)
PLAYTRAC booklets on play and play for children with special needs. (See Appendix 2: Useful contacts at the end of this book.)
Titman, Wendy 1994: *Special Places, Special People.* Learning Through Landscapes. (School-based research on how children feel about the outdoor environment and the effects of different environments on how children feel and behave.)
Ward, Colin 1978, 1990: *The Child in the City.* Bedford Square Press (see especially Ch. 8 'Adapting the imposed Environment').

3.2 Opportunities for play – activities and play materials

> Children love their seashell toys,
> and with them they learn about the ocean,
> because a little piece of ocean
> inside the child, and inside the toy
> knows the whole ocean.
>
> Rumi, *trans.* Barks 1991

Where section 3.1 looks at how the play environment affects opportunities for play, this section focuses on the activities and play materials which may be on offer within it.

Some playsettings use a programme of activities as part of their planning for play. This section looks at how this can be used as a tool for creating and evaluating play opportunities, rather than imposing a rigid structure to what happens in the playsetting.

Why use a programme of activities?

A programme of activities which is displayed on a notice-board or given to children to take home can make some children feel more secure. Many children (and their parents) like to know in advance what activities will be on offer in their playsetting.

You can use a programme of activities to plan a whole term's work in an afterschool club, a week-long playscheme or a one-off special playday. It can help you to:

- work more effectively together with your colleagues
- share ideas about what you wish to offer and how it is to be organised and supervised
- be sure you have the right resources and equipment for the activities that are planned
- plan trips and outings
- link play activities to development opportunities

(Ensure that there are opportunities for SPICE – see section 2.1.)

The children who come to your playsetting are the first consideration of all the play opportunities. However in a holiday playscheme, at the start of the year, or in a new playsetting, you may not have all the information and participation you would like before the scheme starts.

Activities versus play opportunities?

You may think that play is incompatible with any kind of structured programme (see definitions of play, section 1.1). But a programme of activities within a playsetting can be very useful in helping you and your co-workers to plan together. A programme does not in itself ensure the provision of good-quality play opportunities. If planned and carried out too rigidly it could hinder children's play – particularly when many children already spend much of their time in structured activities. Key elements in good programme planning include

---

ACTIVITY 3.11

Programme planning checklist

You can use this checklist to plan an individual activity or play opportunity, or for a whole week's programme.

Try it first when planning a single activity with a group of children.

You can refer to it if an activity did not go well, to help you decide why.

Children
How many children are you planning for?

What are their ages?

Do you know their interests, language, cultural backgrounds?

Have you considered the needs of all children including those with disabilities?

Will your activity (or programme) cater for the whole age-range or have you provided alternatives to suit different stages of development and abilities?

Materials and equipment
What materials and equipment will you need? Make a detailed list.

Do you have enough materials?

How much will they cost?

Do the materials and equipment comply to Health and Safety regulations? Will the children need to wear protective clothing?

Have you got materials and equipment for related activities if children want to extend or change direction?

Activity
Have you planned for variety, choice, stimulation and fun?

Does your planned activity promote positive images of children from different family types, cultures or circumstances and avoid negative stereotypes?

Will all the children have the opportunity to participate regardless of gender, race, ability, religion? How will you encourage this?

What will your own involvement be?

What will you do if an activity flops because children are not interested or find it too difficult?

Adults
Are all staff in agreement as to how your activity fits into the session (or how the programme fits together) and the roles or responsibilities they are each expected to take?

Will extra supervision be needed to carry out particular activities?

Do you need special parental consent or approval?

How will you make use of special skills within your team, or do you wish to bring in other adults from outside?

providing children with choices and involving children in the planning. The programme and the way in which you use it should be flexible, responding to the children's ideas and enthusiasm. Used in this way a programme of activities can help create varied and stimulating play opportunities.

First considerations

The activities on offer will depend on the purpose or objectives of your setting and the children who use it. They will also be affected by the premises, storage space, opening hours and resources available as well as skills and preferences of staff and children, the age range of children and the time available.

Remember, spontaneity is an important element of play. Be flexible. You may have to adapt even the best laid plans. A week's programme may have to be altered because Monday's activity is so successful the children want to continue and extend it for the rest of the week.

It is a good idea to have some contingency activities up your sleeve. These could be games which can played with no equipment and might be suitable for confined spaces (when the coach breaks down on a trip for example). Activities for the end of the session or the end of the day, when children are feeling very tired or excited, are also important.

The role of the playworker

Your role in planning and implementing a programme of activities within the playsetting may include:

- providing choices in materials, equipment, ideas, space;
- enabling children – as far as possible – to carry out their own ideas, make decisions and carry out plans;
- acting as referee when required to ensure that the playsetting's boundaries of behaviour are observed, including challenging anyone stepping outside them;
- being aware that each activity is set within the limits of opening times or other limitations and balancing this with the importance of the children having the freedom to set their own pace;
- supervising to ensure health and safety of children;
- giving encouragement and support to extend and develop activities;
- ensuring all children have equality of opportunity and equal access to the play opportunities, resources and activities;
- being prepared to do what you are asking the children to do – they may need a role model before trying a new activity;
- joining in when asked.

Meeting changing needs

You may already be clear about what works and what doesn't for the children in your playsetting, and their range of interests, and likes and dislikes. But children change and develop, new children will come and no playsetting should be static in the opportunities it provides for play. Here are some ways you can refresh your ideas:

- actively involve the children in ongoing planning;
- share ideas with other playworkers;
- use the activity/programme planning checklist regularly;

- use the numerous activity ideas books now available (see Further reading at end of this section);
- attend training courses.

Ideas for materials resources and equipment

There are now many good publications with ideas and instructions for a whole range of play activities. Each focuses on a particular theme or type of activity (games, craft or music) in far more depth than can be done here. Some of the books which I have found useful are included at the end of this section. This section looks, rather, at a range of activities and play materials which might be included in your programme of activities. It should not be seen as a complete list of ideas: it is for you and the children you work with to decide which are appropriate for your needs.

Games

- Games which need no equipment (indoor and outdoor) – guessing games, circle games, quizzes, hiding games, traditional children's games, singing games, chasing games, co-operative games, mime games such as charades or 'Give Us a Clue'.
- Board games (mostly indoor) – snakes and ladders, draughts, Ludo, chess, Monopoly, Cows and Leopards, chequers, Lotto, Trivial Pursuit.
- Other games: card games, jacks, Mencala, Twister, Jenga, Connect 4; games with pen and paper such as noughts and crosses; table-top games such as table tennis, Karrom, bar football, pool.
- More active games, indoor and outdoor – games using balls and bats, footballs (ordinary outdoor and sponge indoor), skittles, bowls, boules, hopscotch and team games such as rounders, cricket, football and Unihoc.

  Sporting activities are often of great interest to children and can be a valuable part of what a playsetting has to offer. In a setting where providing opportunities for play is the main aim, the focus should not be on competition. Many games encourage co-operative play, building relationships and developing trust as well as being great fun. They include parachute games, trust games and games where the players invent or change the rules (see Further reading at the end of this section).

EXAMPLE Parachute game

I once participated in a parachute games session with a large group of children aged between 4 and 14. Each child held the edge of the parachute closest to himself. The playworker led us through a series of games, the parachute being transformed from a mushroom to a sea full of sharks, to a pan full of popcorn (lightweight plastic balls), each child participating at his own level of ability. It was necessary for each player to be aware of the others to avoid collision and catastrophe, and to ensure that play could continue. There was lots of laughter.

In the final game we all sat inside the parachute which domed igloo-fashion over our heads as we sat on the edges of the fabric in a closely knit circle. The playworker told us we were in a spaceship which was about to take off. As we swayed from side to side we began to hum. As our humming got louder the movement of the spaceship became more vigorous. Drumming of feet and other improvisations were added to the sound of the spaceship's engines, and the parachute felt like it was spinning into take-off. After few minutes the process was reversed and we wound down back to a slow and steady hum.

ACTIVITY 3.12

1 Choose three games which are new to your playsetting – perhaps from the books listed at the end of this section.

2 Describe why you like them, and what developmental opportunities they could offer.

3 Carry them out with the children in your playsetting. Ask them for their views. Would they wish to change any of the rules?

Small-scale toys and construction (mostly indoors)

Toys such as jigsaws, cars, boats, trains, farm and zoo animals, commercial construction and small play equipment such as Lego, Duplo, Mobilo and Meccano have their place within a programme of activities. Your programme can provide opportunities for children to move through different activities, without losing continuity in their play. They should be able to get the materials they need without losing momentum. Play with toys can stimulate ideas for other play activities.

CASE STUDY 3.2: TOYS AS A STARTING POINT

The children had been spending a lot of time playing with a box of trucks, cars and trains. One day I showed them a book about tunnels and bridges and suggested they might like to make some constructions to use with the cars. A mixed group of boys and girls went enthusiastically to the craft area where there were a lot of flattened cardboard boxes, paint, glue, tape and other bits and pieces. The children did not refer to the book again but eagerly began trying out their own ideas. They divided themselves into groups – three boys aged between six and ten years and two girls both aged eight. One five-year-old boy began to experiment on his own but was soon joined by an older child, who asked if he could help. I was able to relish observing co-operative play in all its glory. Each group demonstrated their ability to be creative, developing their social skills by listening and discussing their ideas.

The three boys Jo, Paul and Dominic made a long rectangular tunnel with road signs and traffic lights. Erin and Emma made a triangular construction. They used mosaic pieces of Sparkle Art as cats' eyes on their road. Ian and Richard made a drawbridge kind of construction using string to pull up a sort of 'car chute' or slide. Very little adult input was necessary or required. I was reminded of how rich is the variety of children's play and how a simple activity can give opportunities for all-round development and fun. The different constructions produced were quite simply brilliant and were used for several weeks in a variety of ways by all the children at PAWS in their play.

Karen King, playworker at PAWS afterschool care scheme

Toys and construction for large-scale active play (mostly outdoors)

Equipment which can encourage active play is limited only by space available, cost, safety and your imagination. Think about using boxes of all shapes and sizes, barrels, tubes, climbing-frames, planks, tyres, slides and chutes, see-saws, rocking boats, trampolines, skipping ropes and materials for making dens, ramps, jumps, tunnels and hidey-holes. Large wheeled toys are often very popular – roller-skates, bikes, scooters, skateboards, go-karts and trucks.

Soft play equipment made of large cut-out shapes of covered foam can offer wonderful possibilities for play. A soft play area or room is often particularly attractive to younger children, and to children with mobility difficulties or sensory impairment, as it can open up new ways of moving and sensory experience. Commercially produced soft play equipment is expensive, but even one or two pieces can be a great addition to your range of play equipment. Think also about using soft mats and cushions which can be homemade.

An adventure playground will have more elaborate construction materials for building changing structures for climbing on, swinging off, sliding down or playing in. (See section 4.1 for safety considerations.)

Environmental play

> The unutterable beauty of a blossom. The grace of a high-flying bird. The roar of the wind in the trees: at one time or another in our lives, nature touches you and me . . . and all of us in some personal special way.
>
> Cornell 1979

Environmental play can take place in cities as well as rural areas. Nature trails, treasure hunts, collecting things, observing wildlife – ants and woodlice, as well as rabbits and pigeons – can provide good starting-points for further exploration and games. They can lead to art, craft and drama activities, as well as special themes and projects. As with all play opportunities, children will approach environmental play with different cultural and social experience and expectations. Sensitivity is required in encouraging some children to get their hands dirty (in digging or planting in soil for example), or approaching or handling insects or other animals.

Environmental play

Using natural materials

A lot can be made of natural materials in creating play opportunities. Sand, water, mud, fir cones, stones, shells and pebbles have dozens of possibilities, from simple tactile, sensory experiences of digging in sand, pouring water, sorting shells, to the elaborate construction of miniature fantasy worlds, complex scientific or technological experiments (making a watermill) or cultivating your own garden, allotment or windowboxes.

Recycling

Environmental awareness can also be encouraged through using recyled materials for play. Egg boxes, scraps of fabric or paper, carpet, wool, cardboard, plastic, cotton-reels, old blankets, tyres and timber which are considered junk by others, can be transformed into dens, games and creative art and craft projects with a little creative thought and action from children and their playworkers.

Stories, books and drama

Stories and books provide a starting-point for many kinds of play. A book corner with an attractive display of books reflecting different themes, cultures and lifestyles and covering a wide range of subjects, and with comfortable seating can also be attractive for children wishing to relax or rest away from the more energetic activities. Stories and books can be the inspiration for imaginative play, drama, dance and music.

These activities can be encouraged by providing other materials: face paints, dressing-up clothes, play wigs, mirrors, puppets and additional props near or around the book corner.

For younger children imaginative play can also be fostered through a home corner with small tables, chairs, pretend cooking equipment, dolls, prams and telephones. This can be varied by setting up a shop, café or fantasy play spaces such as a space-station or treasure island, using whatever interest and materials

A starting-point for drama?

ACTIVITY 3.13

What would you include in your art and craft materials cupboard?

Write a list or draw up a basic stock of materials which you can use for a variety of activities such as mask making, puppet making, printing, weaving, collage, model making, frieze, printing (paper, teeshirt, fabric), hat making, painting, construction and much more.

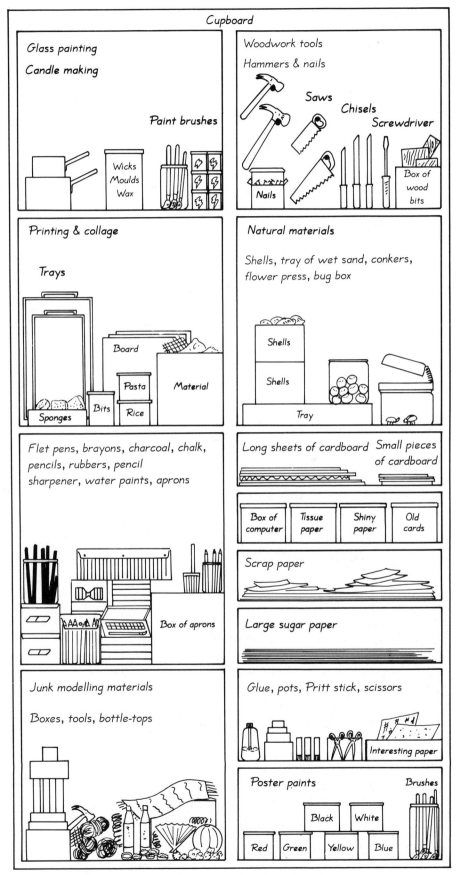

What would you include in your basic art and crafts cupboard?

you have available. All such activities provide good opportunities to promote positive images of different cultures and of children with disabilities in different roles which counter negative stereotypes (see section 1.2).

Music

For music, remember the range of instruments available from other countries that are now available: African skin drums, Chinese bars, Indian bells, maracas, as well as triangles, tambourines, recorders, whistles, cymbals and even a piano if available. Home made percussion instruments can be made from beans, rice, containers of all kinds, wool spools, bottles, teaspoons, combs, papers, plastic or cardboard tubing, hub-caps, string and much more at little or no cost. Simply experimenting with different sounds can be fun in itself, or you can help the children to create their own band or orchestra to accompany a drama, story or game.

A tape-player and range of styles of recorded music is also useful for dancing, listening and relaxation, or stimulating and accompanying imaginative play. The children can also record their own stories and music.

Woodwork

For woodwork you need a workbench and safe devices for clamping as well as a range of timber offcuts in different shapes and sizes. Use real (not toy) tools and make sure they are properly used, stored maintained and supervised by a playworker who knows how to use them. Blunt, ineffective or broken tools can lead to frustration and improper use which is a safety hazard.

Modelling

For modelling materials consider using various types of modelling and potter's clay – both red and gray. Unless you have access to a kiln for firing, the end product will not be very satisfactory as it will crumble and break easily. If children want to make, paint and keep model figures or dishes, you can use clay with nylon fibres which enable it to harden without firing. Alternative modelling materials include Play-doh, saltdough, Plasticine, wax, pastry and Fimo.

Themes

It may be helpful to choose a theme around which to plan activities. All or some activities can be linked to a theme lasting a day, a week or the whole summer or school term. A theme can extend children's knowledge and interest in the world around them. Stories, games, art and craft activities, outings and cooking can all be chosen around a theme such as 'Water', 'Animals' or 'Ourselves'.

ACTIVITY 3.14

1 Ask the children in your playsetting to think of a theme or subject which they would like to use to plan the next week's activities.

2 Using large sheets of paper and coloured pens and crayons, encourage them to write down as many different games, activities (perhaps including visits, outings or inviting visitors) and types of play as they can which relate in some way to their chosen theme.

3 Make a theme chart or collate the children's ideas and drawings into a collage. Involve your colleagues in deciding which of the ideas are feasible

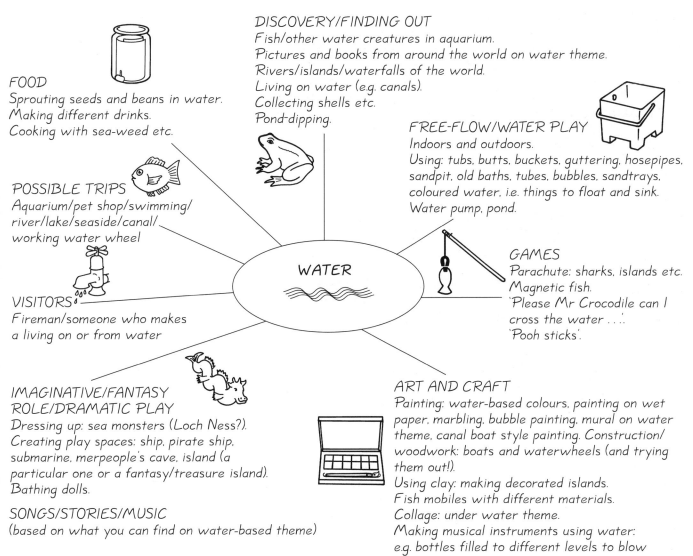

Planning play opportunities around the theme of water . . . What would you add to these suggestions?

ACTIVITY 3.15

Plan a series of activities on the theme of food to carry out in your place of work over a week.

What you can include will depend on what facilities you have available.

Food is more than eating

Food plays a large part in our lives other than providing nutrition. Meals or snack times can be ideal opportunities for social interaction in the playsetting. The time spent sharing a meal can be a time to get to know one another, share information about likes and dislikes or customs and habits, or plan what to do in the next week, day or half-hour.

What children are used to eating will be influenced by family and cultural background. Dietary requirements need to be observed (such as offering vegetarian, kosher, halal or non-dairy alternatives). Children can share information about what they eat at home, and preparing and offering snacks which originate from a range of different cultures can be fun and an interesting way to introduce children to aspects of a culture other than their own.

The activities you might include in a week's programme should provide opportunities for all-round development. Enhance the play environment with displays of fruits and vegetables from different countries, which children can touch and taste. Try a tasting session where children taste different foods without looking at them and guess what they are.

Cooking on an open fire

Have a quiz or use reference books to help children to discover where these fruits and vegetables are grown. Collect pictures of positive images of families of different cultures at mealtimes. The children could draw or paint their favourite foods. Have an international food celebration and serve dishes (perhaps prepared by parents/carers at home) from around the world, or compile an international recipe book for use within the playsetting or to be reproduced for sale to parents, carers and others – the children could illustrate it.

Whether you can cook with children and what you can cook will depend on your playsetting's facilities. On one adventure playground I know, children cooked blackberry jam on an open fire with berries they had picked from their periphery hedge. They also regularly baked potatoes in the hot ashes. Even if you don't have a fire or a kitchen you can involve the children in cold food preparation: fruit salad, other salads, sandwiches and sweets (as an occasional treat). Children of all ages enjoy cooking. It offers endless possibilities for learning skills, independence and lots of fun. Children's imaginative play often revolves around food, and they can make pretend food from clay or saltdough baked hard in the oven and painted as props for a café, shop, picnic or tea party. Before cooking with children, talk to them about good hygiene practices and the reasons for them, and ensure you can provide supervision before the children use a kitchen or a fire outside.

Checklist of points covered in other chapters

1　*Health and safety.* See Chapter 4. Bought toys and equipment should comply with British or European Safety Standards.
2　*Child development.* A rich variety of materials and activities should be introduced which encourage all aspects of child development: see sections 2.1 and 2.2. Cater for all ages involved. Don't be surprised if older children still enjoy dressing up and playing in the sandpit and younger children want to attempt complex craft activities, team games and puzzles.
3　*Choose resources which promote positive images and avoid negative stereotypes.* Do the activities make every child feel good about herself or himself? Do the resources which include images of people (books,

pictures, dolls, puppets) depict different racial and ethnic features in an accurate and uncaricatured way? In the resources and images you provide you can counterbalance stereotypes which marginalise or ridicule people because of the way they look or their family background.

Do your resources encourage children to extend their views about the possibilities open to them – by giving them images and examples of people in active and important roles: girls as well as boys, black people as well as white, people with disabilities as well as able-bodied people? (See also section 1.2.)

4 *Involving others.* Discuss your ideas and plans with colleagues at regular staff planning meetings (section 5.1). Involve children in decisions about what activities to offer (sections 1.2 and 2.3). Involve parents and carers (section 5.2). Make a written programme of activities available to them. Get new ideas, support and advice from local libraries, resource centres and national organisations or visit other similar facilities in your area (section 5.3).

5 *Keeping records.* Records of activities and equipment available are particularly important for new staff and in places where there may be a high turnover of staff (e.g. some summer playschemes). They are useful when for one reason or another the planned programme of activities cannot go ahead. Develop a 'resource file' (see section 3.3). A diary, logbook or scrapbook (involving the children) with pictures and photographs can record activities which have been successful (section 3.4). This can also be useful for publicity for your playsetting and as evidence for your personal portfolio if you are working towards an NVQ in playwork (see Foreword and Endword).

6 *Review and evaluate.* Review your activities regularly. What has worked well? What has not? Why? How might you do things differently? Use the activity sections throughout this book to help evaluate.

7 *Developing resources.* Not all play materials cost a lot of money (see section 3.3).

Using a written plan

Use the planning sheet (below) to plan a week's programme. How many of these activities can you do out of doors? Remember children need:

	Monday	Tuesday	Wednesday	Thursday	Friday
Special activity – theme?					
Opportunities for energetic play					
Art and craft Natural materials					
Building things					
Stories Music Quiet games					
Opportunities for fantasy play/drama					
Food Outings					

Planning sheet

- Social interaction
- Physical activity
- Intellectual stimulation
- Creative achievement
- Emotional stability

Add any other headings you need to suit the activities you are planning. Some activities will be ongoing throughout the week, others will change daily. There are some activities which are always available, such as games, puzzles and toys.

Don't be too rigid about sticking to your plan. It is the overall play environment which creates good play opportunities (section 3.1).

References

Cornell, Joseph Bharat 1979: *Sharing Nature with Children*. Exley.
Rumi, *trans*. Barks, Coleman 1991: *Shouldering the Lion*. Threshold Books.

Further reading

There are many good publications containing ideas and instructions for different types of activities to do with children in the playsetting.

This is just a very small sample of the ones I have found useful:

Blakely, Nancy 1994: *The Mudpies Activity Book* and *More Mudpies – 101 Alternatives to Television*. Tricycle Press (highly recommended).

The following two books contain a wealth of play ideas suitable for a range of playsettings for children aged 5 to 15. They are tried and tested and developed by people directly involved in playwork.

1. National Playing Fields Association 1989: *National Play Ideas Bank*. PLAY-TRAIN.
2. Manchester Play Development Unit National Play Information Centre 1990: *Playwork That Works*.

Activity books with seasonal themes

Fitzjohn, S, Weston, M, and Large, J 1993: *Festivals Together*. Hawthorne Press. (Packed with information and ideas for celebrating festivals originating from around the world – stories, legends, customs rituals, crafts, games and food.)
Petrash, Carol 1993: *Earthwise – environmental crafts and activities with young children*. Floris Books.
West, Shirley 1991: *Open Sez Me – the Magic of Pleasant Discoveries*. (Four books with a range of clear, illustrated ideas for multi-cultural activities and play ideas for winter, spring, summer and autumn care.)

Working with adolescents

Greenaway, Roger 1990: *More than Activities*. The Save the Children Fund.

See also section 1.1 for books on games.

3.3 Ideas and inspirations – a playworker's resource file

The trust and quest for adventure which makes playing (and living) exciting and meaningful

Compared with what we ought to be, we are only half awake. Our fires are dampened, our drafts are checked, we are making use of only a small part of our mental and physical resources.

William James, as quoted in Siegel 1991

This section considers some of the less tangible factors which can make or break a play opportunity: the enthusiasm, resourcefulness and flexibility which are required of playworkers. These are the qualities which enable you to plan, provide and engage in play which is life enhancing for the children and young people with whom you work.

No matter how well planned and resourced, a play opportunity can fall flat if the playworkers lack imagination, sensitivity and humour. This section celebrates these qualities in the playworker and looks at ways in which you can build on your resourcefulness as a playworker.

The child in you

Being and working with children can be a privilege, a joy or a chore. A worker who can enter into the playsetting with a child's eye view and who can bring out the child that is within each of us, gains great insight into human development. If you observe babies and very young children you cannot fail to notice their qualities of openness, wonder, receptivity, and interest and enthusiasm for life. A few rare and gifted souls seem able to carry these qualities with them into adulthood. These are the exceptional playworkers (although they may work in other professions). In many children these qualities are buried from a very early age, for some or all of the their waking hours. Most of us need to build our wall of defence against every day life: disappointments, pain, illness, loss, the need to make a living – endless small and large responsibilities and expectations to fulfil or to fail. We can lose the ability to engage actively with others and our surroundings – the desire to dream, discover and explore. We become cautious, inhibited, often frightened and insecure.

A good playworker needs to find ways of cutting through these defences in himself and in others, to rediscover and maintain the spontaneity, the trust, the adventurousness which makes playing (and living) exciting and meaningful.

ACTIVITY 3.16

1 Look back at Activity 2.1 on page 31. Think again about what and who helped you to develop the knowledge, skills and understanding you have now. When and how did you develop the skills you now use as a playworker?

2 Write or draw a picture or chart of this information. This is sometimes called a lifeline, and can be done in any way you wish. One group of playwork students chose to depict their lifelines in many different ways: a flower, a river, a key, a spider's web (see page 94 for one example).

3 Write down three of your major strengths or skills as a playworker. Think about what helped you develop them.

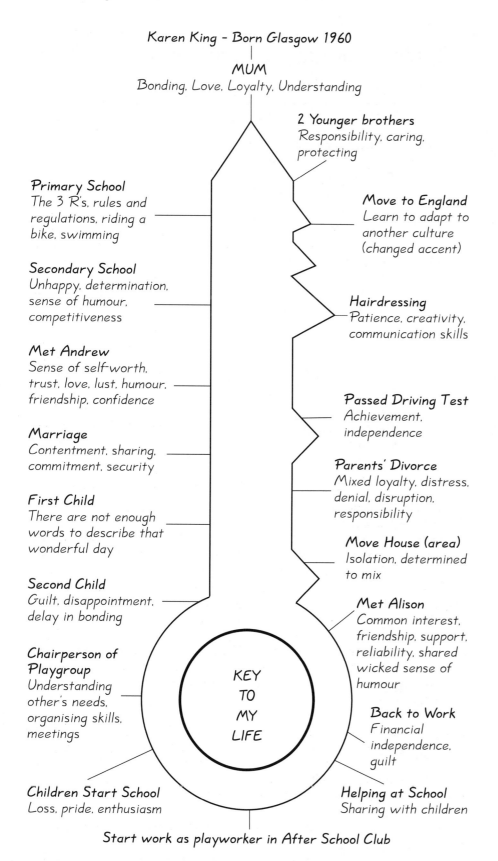

Karen King – Born Glasgow 1960

MUM
Bonding, Love, Loyalty, Understanding

2 Younger brothers
Responsibility, caring, protecting

Primary School
The 3 R's, rules and regulations, riding a bike, swimming

Move to England
Learn to adapt to another culture (changed accent)

Secondary School
Unhappy, determination, sense of humour, competitiveness

Hairdressing
Patience, creativity, communication skills

Met Andrew
Sense of self-worth, trust, love, lust, humour, friendship, confidence

Passed Driving Test
Achievement, independence

Marriage
Contentment, sharing, commitment, security

Parents' Divorce
Mixed loyalty, distress, denial, disruption, responsibility

First Child
There are not enough words to describe that wonderful day

Move House (area)
Isolation, determined to mix

Second Child
Guilt, disappointment, delay in bonding

Met Alison
Common interest, friendship, support, reliability, shared wicked sense of humour

KEY TO MY LIFE

Chairperson of Playgroup
Understanding other's needs, organising skills, meetings

Back to Work
Financial independence, guilt

Children Start School
Loss, pride, enthusiasm

Helping at School
Sharing with children

Start work as playworker in After School Club

PLAYWORKER'S LIFELINE. Karen represented her life and the skills she acquired as a key

You can use your lifeline in many ways. It can help you to:

- recognise that many things influence development;
- clarify and affirm your strengths and skills;
- identify gaps and what areas you need to develop further;
- as a starting-point for a personal profile or curriculum vitae.

Beginnings

The first time I became involved in playwork I attended a one-weeks training course before the summer playscheme season. A group of 25 of us, mostly students, new to playwork and very unsure what to expect, arrived on a sunny morning outside a rather dour college of further education. The leader of the first session (whom I will call Sue) gathered us into a circle. In a clear and friendly voice she called: 'My name's Sue. Do as I do.' She jumped into the circle, arms outstretched, repeating her name, 'Sue! Sue! Sue, Sue, Sue!' Each time she said her name she jumped. We all copied her, some of us giggling a bit nervously. Sue then stood in front of another person in the circle. 'What's your name? Make a movement to express it.' 'Raj', he bowed to the rest of us. 'Raj! Raj! Raj, Raj, Raj', we dutifully copied his bow and intonation five times. Sue then hooked on behind Raj and they went to another course member, Naida, chosen by Raj. By the end of this name game we were all in a chain, one behind the other. We had learned each other's names; we had broken the ice; but more than that we were infected with Sue's enthusiasm, her lack of inhibition and her ability to play. The course went well. Lots of shared knowledge, ideas, skills, understanding and laughter. The mood of that course, and particularly the inspiration provided by Sue, lasted throughout my first, often difficult summer working on an adventure playground, and long beyond.

Beginnings are important. They can set the tone for what is to come. The first day at a playsetting for a child. The first day of a holiday playscheme. The beginning of the day. The start of a new activity. Each beginning is a new opportunity to engage with others. The energy, enthusiasm and ideas you bring can set the tone for what is to follow. There are many ways to start the day.

TO THINK ABOUT

In what circumstances might you use with children a similar start to the day as the one described opposite?

What age group do you think would enjoy such an activity?

CASE STUDY 3.3: SPONTANEOUS PLAY

'At one afterschool club, the playworker put considerable time and effort into planning each session. She would ensure that each session had organised activities that the children liked to do: cooking, making things to take home and outdoor games. Nevertheless four of the children (aged between five and nine) would always bring their own teddies, dolls, dolls clothes, feeding bottles and carry cases. They would use a small side room which had a door which could be closed for privacy, and create their own world of play. It had upright chairs with throw-over covers which provided perfect screens for hiding. The tables had wheels and every object in that room was used in their play. Sometimes they would put the dolls to sleep so that they could join the other children for a drink and a biscuit or to participate in an activity, and then go directly back to their own play. These children came directly from school and the kinds of spontaneous, child-centred play that they wanted to engage in were not possible at school: it could be seen as childish or babyish, the kinds of things you do in a playgroup.'

Dolcie Obhiozele, Play Development Officer, Oxford City Council

In deciding on how you start each session you need to consider where the children are coming from. Do they know each other? Are they likely to be tired, shy or restless and needing to be energetic? The Case study 3.3 above shows how one playworker met the different needs of the children in her group. There were structured activities for those who wanted them, but the freedom and space for others to withdraw into their own world of play, and set their own pace for joining in.

A playworker's tool-kit

Each one of us has our sources of support and inspiration. For you this might come from a friend, a colleague, a teacher, a book, an experience of nature or a piece of music, your family or your work. More often forgotten is the well-spring of resourcefulness that each of has has within ourselves.

On one playwork course the students were asked to bring with them something which was important to them in their work: their 'essential tool'. The first student to present their essential tool to the group said, 'I bring with me first and foremost my imagination and sense of humour'. It was so obvious. Everyone revised their presentations of the very practical tools they had brought – tools which were practical but perhaps not essential.

One essential item in my own playworker's tool-kit is a bundle of different-coloured muslin cloths of all shapes and sizes. They are very lightweight

Using lightweight cloths to create varied play opportunities

ACTIVITY 3.17

Develop your own personal playworker's tool-kit. You can write a list or draw pictures or diagrams.

You could assemble ideas and practical items in a special tool-box.

Things you might want to include:

- personal qualities and skills;
- your sources of support and inspiration;
- essential pieces of equipment which you would bring with you if you were going to work with a group of children where there were no material resources on site – a ball?; paper and crayons?; a pack of cards?; a ball of string?; your favourite book of co-operative games?; balloons?; facepaints?

Include only items which you could easily carry with you. Think about how many different play opportunities you could create with each item.

and can be folded into a small bag or basket, but when spread out they cover a very wide area. They can be used in endless activities with a wide age-range:

- for dressing up – cloaks, belts, hats, scarves, saris, belts and more;
- spread over tables and chairs to form tents, houses and dens;
- knotted into simple puppets or dolls;
- as blankets, table-cloths and curtains (when the sun is too hot or bright)
- as colourful and quick backdrops to displays of artwork, puppet shows or drama;
- knotted into tight rings to be used in a variety of throwing and catching games or for juggling practice.

Another major consideration in developing your tool-kit will be cost. A playworker's tool kit need not be costly. The muslin cost me less than £1.00 per metre, undyed. Another tool-kit might contain recipes for home-made face-paint and modelling materials.

Learning from others

Because playsettings are so diverse and run by so many different organisations they can easily operate in isolation. Try to make time and opportunities to meet other playworkers and, if possible, visit other playsettings. Each playsetting will have particular strengths. Some will develop a particular area of expertise. Look for opportunities where you can share what you do with others. One such opportunity is 'Playday' which has happened every August since its small London-based beginnings in 1987. In recent years people have joined together in towns and villages throughout the UK to organise their own joint play events on this day, bringing people together and raising the profile of the importance of play. Alternatively you could make contact and arrange exchange visits of staff and children with other playsettings.

The following are two examples from people who have specialised in an area of playwork, and have inspired me about the possibilities within playwork.

EXAMPLE 1 Project Sparrowhawk – an environmental playscheme

'We aim to give city children the opportunity to experience how the woodlands can be used in a fun and practical way. A flavour of the "Bodgers" camp with some extras thrown in.

Every day is different depending on the individual children and their interests. However, it would be true to say that each day has a similar rhythm and pattern. Here is a typical day in camp.

After collecting the children we lead them through the forest, stopping only to collect ferns (for den building), and for each of the children to select themselves a walking stick. The children choose strong, straight pieces of hazel and at the same time learn something about woodland management and coppicing.

We lead the children into camp blindfolded – after all, it is a secret camp deep in the woodlands! The blindfolds make them more conscious of sounds, smells and textures. They remove their blindfolds once they are all round the campfire.

Some children sit around the fire and use penknives to whittle their walking sticks with a variety of patterns and markings. (There are sharp tools all around camp and it is vital that the children learn to use all of them safely in order for them to participate in the camp's activities).

A group of children immediately get involved in making charcoal and artist's charcoal. They work in pairs, splitting the logs with large axes

Activities in the wood

and sawing them to length using old-fashioned double-handed saws. These pieces they pack tightly into an oil drum. The artist's charcoal is made by cutting willow withies and wedging them into a tin to be included in the oil drum. The children carry fire from the main camp fire and get a fire blazing at the top of the oil drum before placing the hinged lid and turning the whole drum over to burn for up to eight hours.

Another group of children are using the shaving horses and pole lathes. With supervision and guidance they go through the whole process from sawing the log from the tree to splitting the green wood into usable sections. Using double-handled draw knives they make a section of the wood round and place it on the pole lathe. Then using a variety of chisels they turn the wood into a paper knife, a candle stick, a stool leg ... One child makes a tombstone cross for her guinea pig which died that morning.

Other children are involved in living den building. These are mostly dome-shaped 'benders', decorated with ferns, heather and sheep's wool. Others are making wood sculptures and totem poles. At the end of the day there is also a 'spiders web' of forest life, and the beginnings of a forest 'tunnel' using willow and hazel. For some of the children that come, just being in the woodland is enough, and they spend all day poking and feeding the fire or gazing at the sky though the woodland canopy as they swing in the several hammocks we have slung between the trees.

We end each day round the fire toasting marshmallows, sharing stories and swapping ideas. The children are happy, exhausted and very dirty. Over the years we have also experimented with cooking in underground ovens, making paper from pulped-down bark and woodland plants and flowers, making rope ladders to climb trees and tree houses.

Example from Sharon Crockett, playworker on Project Sparrowhawk, an annual environmental playscheme run for 8- to 14-year-olds by Oxford City Council.

EXAMPLE 2 Journeying – an example of integrated play

Journeying is an idea which I borrowed from a teacher of children with profound and multiple disabilities. The activity was developed with the needs of these children in mind. Journeying is a way of telling a story, or rather going on an adventure, which activates the use of all five senses in the unfolding of the story. Because some children's ability to receive information is impaired through disability, it is necessary to find other ways to communicate the story to them. This can be achieved through the use of touch, taste and smell as well as audio and visual stimulation. The combination of the exciting story and the novelty of other sensory surprises makes this an activity which is accessible and enjoyable for all children. Journeying offers children with more ability the opportunity to understand the experience of children with less ability. Understanding lays the foundation for tolerance and enhanced social skills in adulthood.

An example of a journey

'Monkeying around' is a journey which was inspired by the green theme of Playday 1994. On this occasion the journey was evolved and prepared by playworkers, who invited groups of children to enter into the play experience with them. Given more time within a playsetting, journeying can involve the children from an earlier stage: in inventing and telling the story, and developing the sensory stimuli and 'special effects' to be used. This one was very ambitious. It could be simplified or adapted.

Telling the story

As the children came into the marquee out of a wet rainy day they were invited to step into another world and into the experience of monkeyhood by having a monkey tail pinned on to them. We gave them a brief description of how the journey would happen.

A group of monkeys escape from the zoo and decide to find their way home, even though they are not completely sure of where home is. As the story unfolded, the monkeys journeyed through the city, the ocean, the desert, and eventually found their way home to the jungle. Key phrases were repeated throughout the journey: 'Where are we going?' 'We want to go home' 'Where's home?' 'The jungle'. 'Hold on to your tail'.

As the monkeys progressed through their journey the different environments were communicated in different 'scenes'.

Scene 1. A bus ride through the city

The bus eventually delivers the monkeys to the port and the bus driver tells them that the way to the jungle is over the ocean on a ship.
The sensory effects included:

- city lights and noise;
- dry ice;
- pedestrian crossing,
- port and market;
- noises – car horns and shouting.

Characters included:

- bus driver;
- old lady crossing;
- fish sellers with real fish (smelly!).

Pretend experience included:

- bumpy bus ride;
- stop, start;
- old lady nearly run over;
- finding the ship;
- all aboard.

Other scenes had similar characterisations, pretend experiences and props providing sensory stimulation. Scene 2 is on the ship. The captain falls overboard. He swims and is eaten by a shark. The ship capsizes and the monkeys swim under the sea. In Scene 3 the monkeys are washed ashore on to a beach. Walking, tired, hot, thirsty, they come to an oasis. They are met by Arab people with food and drink, who tell them the way to get to the jungle. In Scene 4 the monkeys reach their destination and party in the jungle.

Guidelines for going on a journey
- Choose a storyline that can be adapted and which lends itself to a variety of sensory experiences.
- The journey should gently invite the participant into the story without being invasive (intruding or persisting when the child indicates he or she is unwilling or uncomfortable). Be creative and flexible in the telling of the story and the use of sensory experiences, but also be safe and sensitive to the needs of individual children.
- Setting up a journey requires some preparation (eg music, props and a run through for the helpers). The number of helpers required depends on the nature and complexity of the journey. In the journey described above there were approximately 15–20 child participants (and adults where appropriate), who remained seated throughout most of the journey. There were six helpers/actors.
- You may find it necessary to explain a few (flexible) ground-rules, especially for more able children, before the start of the journey, such as the need to stay seated for much of the time and (for some children) that the journey requires a willingness to pretend. This can be achieved as part of the story or creating the mood.
- It is useful to have an adult planted among the children in order to encourage children to participate fully.
- As with all integrated play experiences, be flexible in your expectations of how much a child with disabilities can understand, participate in and enjoy a story. Central to the experience of shared play are the warm fuzzy feelings it can cultivate – fun, laughter, understanding and wonder.

ACTIVITY 3.18

1 In Examples 1 and 2 above, try to identify what it was that made the activities good play – the environment, the activities, the materials, the way the children were involved, the sense of achievement?

What can you learn from this which is relevant to your work?

2 Think of a play opportunity either from your own work, from your childhood, or which you have observed which you consider gave the children involved a stimulating and enriching play experience.

3 Write down and try out at least one way of finding out what inspires the children in your playsetting – what makes them feel that they have had a good play experience?

Example from Tracy Collins, co-ordinator of PARASOL, a project which supports children with disabilities or other difficulties in becoming integrated in community playschemes.

Resourcefulness

Resourcefulness is a skill which you can develop. You need to evaluate, change and build on your tool-kit in the light of your own experience and the shared experience of others. Many playworkers become adept at begging and borrowing ideas, skills, expertise, transport, materials, (offcuts, scraps, end of lines, advertising give aways) from a range of sources. Get to know:

- local traders and businesses;
- resource centres, schools and community groups;
- parents and children
- other playworkers

A resource file

Your resource file could include photographs, comments, notes and evaluation of particular activities.

ACTIVITY 3.19

Develop a resource file either for yourself or with colleagues for your playsetting. Use a large loose-leaf folder, so that you can continuously add and update information. Divide it into sections which might include:

- games of all kinds;
- art and craft activities (with instructions);
- essential materials and good sources of materials;

- 'fillers' – five-minute activities to use as contingency plans, at the end of a session, or while waiting for a bus;
- useful contacts;
- tried-and-tested ideas for local visits and trips.

Are there other sections which might be useful to your particular worksetting?

Developing resourcefulness

There will be times when you need to refresh yourself, your ideas and your ability to play. Some things which can help you do this are:

- attending good playwork training;
- staff development work within your team (that is, opportunities to discuss your ideas or a particular aspect of your work, or to share skills);
- networking with other play organisations in your area;
- simple things such as having a good laugh.

Consider Activity 3.20. You can make up your own variations of this game. Change the categories. Assume you are marooned on a desert island. Specify that the pieces of equipment are everyday objects not necessarily obviously suited for play. Get each group to present their ideas to the others as a mini roleplay or drama production or drawing.

Developing your resourcefulness is important. Playwork, like life itself, is often a serious and exhausting business. You need resilience to cope with physical and mental demands made in your work. You have huge responsibilities, and perhaps insufficient funds, support and recognition of what your

ACTIVITY 3.20

This is a game to help you become aware of and develop your resourcefulness. You can play with as few as four people but it is better in larger groups. Play with friends, colleagues or with older children in your play-setting. You will need:

- pens or pencils;
- pieces of coloured paper or card (four colours);
- four bowls, hats or other containers.

Instructions
1 Divide into at least two groups of between two and six people.
2 Allow five minutes for all groups to write down as many ideas as they can in the categories listed below. Each category should be written on small pieces of a different-coloured paper or card. Only one item from each category should go on each piece of paper or card, for example:

- *play environments* such as a classroom, a forest. a beach, a park – one idea per piece of green card;
- *numbers of children* in a group for example, think of numbers between 8 and 200 – one number per piece of yellow card;
- *ages of children* in a group for example, 5- to 7-year-olds, 5- to 15-year-olds, 12- to 15-year-olds – one age group per piece of orange card;

- *description of groups* for example, girls only, boys only, mixed gender, an integrated group of children with a range of disabilities and able-bodied children, children from Asian Muslim families, travellers' children – one description per piece of blue card;
- *play materials* (only one per card) – use the play-worker's tool-kit Activity 3.17 for ideas – one item of equipment per piece of red card.

4 Put all the pieces of paper of the same colour from all groups into a hat or bowl and mix well.
5 Each group draws out one piece of paper from each coloured category.
6 As a group, think of as many kinds of play opportunities you could create or initiate with what you have on the cards you have drawn. You must include all factors on the cards. You cannot include any unspecified materials or equipment. You must consider the likely needs and interests of the age group and description of the group. You need to consider the practical implications of the number of children involved, but can assume you have adequate staffing and supervision.

role entails. You may have to cope with the practical and business sides of running a play facility: shopping, budgeting, meetings, planning, liaising with others, dealing with the concerns and complaints of the users. Yet you cannot afford to lose sight of the intrinsic value of play itself, for the children, for yourselves, and for human development and society at large. You need to look at ways of gaining support and constantly rejuvenating your ability to look at things afresh, to play and to celebrate your work.

RESOURCEFUL RECIPES

Playdough
This recipe is for a soft pliable dough which will last for weeks if kept in a plastic bag or container.

Ingredients

2 cups plain flour	1 cup salt
3 tablespoons cooking oil	2 teaspoons cream of tartar
1½ cups water	food colouring

Instructions
Bring the water, oil and food colouring to boil in a saucepan. Add all remaining ingredients and stir well. Allow to cool. Knead to a soft pliable consistency.

Saltdough

This dough can be modelled into shapes which can be baked in the oven, painted and varnished to keep. You can also add food colouring or concentrated cold water dye to the dough before modelling with it. It works as well as expensive brand-named modelling materials for making beads, jewellery, badges, gifts, decorations and so on.

Ingredients
6 cups plain flour
1 ½ cups salt
2 ½ cups water

Instructions
Mix all ingredients together. Knead well. When models are ready, place on an oiled baking tray and bake for about 1 hour at 325°F (gas mark 3). Paint and varnish when cool.
(*Note:* bulky items will need to be cooked for longer.)

Paint
A simple quick paint can be made from thin flour-and-water paste (1 tablespoon of flour to 2 tablespoons water) with a few drops of food colouring. Make it thicker if it is to be used for papier mâché or finger paints.

Such coloured paste can also be used to spread thickly on pieces of card (a cut-up cardboard box?). Make pictures using different tools (sticks, toothbrushes, etc.) for scraping patterns, and decorate with small items such as shells, lentils, glitter . . .

Reference

James, William, in Siegel, B. 1991: *Peace, love and Healing*. Arrow Books.

Further reading

Scholastic publish a series of 'Bright Ideas' books. Although geared at the classroom many of the activities contained in these books are suitable for adapting in playsettings.

For more information about 'Playday', contact: National Voluntary Council for Children's Play, National Play Information Centre, 359–361 Euston Road, London NW1 3AL.

For more information about Journeying, contact: Resources for Learning (The Consortium), Jack Tizard School, Finlay Street, London SW6 6HB; Tel: 0171 610 3755.

3.4 Keeping records

A quality club administers its business efficiently.
                        Kids' Clubs Network Quality Assurance Workbook 1994

Record keeping is important for many reasons. Many records, such as accounts and records of children, are legal requirements. Each play setting will have a different system of record keeping. The kind of records you keep in your playsetting will depend on its aims, organisation, resourcing and legal status.

This section covers the essential records which need to be kept in any play facility registered by the local authority under the Children Act 1989. It also looks at aspects of dealing with money as required for N/SVQ assessment at level 3.

ACTIVITY 3.21

1 Think about: how do written records contribute to the quality of your playsetting?

2 List all the records you think are essential to maintaining high standards in your playsetting.

Who is responsible?

What records you keep and how you keep them must be agreed with your managers. This should include what forms must be filled in, when they should be filled in and who is responsible for making sure they are satisfactorily completed, updated, maintained and stored. In some voluntary organisations a member of the management committee will have responsibility for completing and maintaining some of the records. For example, the treasurer may deal with all aspects relating to money and insurance and the secretary or waiting list organiser with admissions. In a large organisation or business the playsetting may have paid administrators.

Whatever your situation, as playworker you need to know what records are kept and who keeps them so that you can pass on, record or retrieve information when you need to.

ACTIVITY 3.22

Consider the following situations:

1 You and another playworker take 20 children on a trip to the seaside. One child cuts herself badly on a broken glass bottle and needs to go to hospital to have the wound stitched.
2 While involved in a collage activity with a group of children, you use the last of the glue.
3 A father brings a new child to your playsetting for the first time.
4 A small fire breaks out in the kitchen and you need to evacuate the building.

5 You arrive at work to find that your playsetting has been burgled and all the play materials are strewn around the floor.

In each case decide:

● what documents or records would need to be completed or referred to in dealing with the situation;
● what action needs to be taken and what records would need to be completed;
● who would be responsible for completing any such records in a similar situation in your playsetting.

Documents to be displayed

For reasons of safety, and to comply with legislation, certain documents need to be displayed during opening times of the playsetting. The documents and the issues they raise are dealt with in separate chapters. The following check-list summarises the sections where you will find further information.

Document	Where to display	Section for further information
Certificate of Registration (Children Act 1989 local authority)	Noticeboard, reception or office	1.2, 4.2
Certificate of employer's liability insurance cover	As above	4.2
Fire/evacuation procedure	In every room	4.1
Emergency procedure and numbers of emergency services	Accessible close to telephone	4.1
Information about health and safety at work	Given to all employees	4.2

Documents to be displayed at the playsetting

Children's records
Initial registration form

One person in the playsetting should respond to enquiries from prospective new children or their parents and handle the waiting list if there is one. If you are that person, you will need to have copies of any written information about the playsetting to give to them. (This is dealt with more fully in sections 2.3 and 5.2 on new children settling in.)

In any playsetting which offers childcare, an initial registration form will need to be completed and signed by the child's parent or carer and given to the senior playworker or supervisor before the child can be enrolled. See page 106 for the kind of information to include on this form. The section on who is to collect the child would not be relevant in an open access or drop-in play-setting. Some playsettings may require different or additional information.

If you are not responsible for dealing with initial enquiries you need to know who is so that you can direct interested visitors appropriately.

Check that you can read all the details on the form and that you under-stand them fully before you file it. Files should be organised alphabetically and kept up to date. Files of children no longer attending the playsetting should be removed and stored.

Monitoring children's progress

Playsettings are unlikely to require formal monitoring of children's progress in the way in which health or education agencies do, but there may be occa-sions where you need to observe and record a child's behaviour, either because of particular concerns about the child (see sections 2.4 and 4.3) or because you want to discover how you can best meet his or her needs. There are many informal ways of involving children in recording their own progress. These have been discussed in section 2.3.

HILLTOP PLAYSCHEME
REGISTRATION FORM

All children who attend must be registered.

Children remain at the playscheme until collected by a named adult.

Please contact the playscheme co-ordinator if you have any questions about the form or need help filling it in.

All records are kept in a secure place and no parent or member of the general public will be given access to records other than those of their own child.

Child's full name: *Steffan Voigt*

Name by which the child likes to be known: *Steff*

Address: *20a Green Street, Oldstone, Oxon*

Date of Birth: *26.10.86*

Parents'/guardians' names: *Ms B Voigt*

Mr J Mann

Telephone Numbers: Daytime: *Mother: 22266 Father: 11333* ...... Evening: *60022*
(Please give both parents' numbers if appropriate)

Name by which parent is known at work (and job title if relevant):
Bee Voigt/Jay Mann

Child's dietary requirements: food to be excluded from diet, known food allergies etc:
Allergies to peanuts and dairy produce

Any known medical problems or needs (including allergies): ....
Occasional asthma

Any other special needs or information you want to give: ....
Close friends with Tipu Singh

Name and address of person collecting child from playscheme if different from above:
Mrs Singh, 6 Brown Close, Oldstone ..... Telephone: *77722*

Details of a second contact who may be able to collect the child in an emergency:
Mr R Voigt, 42 Greyfriars, Oldstone ..... Telephone: *882233*

Please Note: Any changes to the person/people who are to collect the child must be notified in advance, in writing to the playscheme co-ordinator. We will only let the child leave with a named person.

Name of Child's Doctor *Dr Elliot*

Address: *The Surgery, Elm Rise,*

...... *Oldstone* .... Telephone Number: *525252*

Example of a child's registration form

Confidentiality

Children's records must be kept in a safe place, but you must be able to get access to them quickly in the event of an accident or other emergency. They should not, in normal circumstances, be accessible to anyone who does not have responsibility for the care and well-being of the child.

A local authority registration officer will need to know that you are keeping appropriate records and may ask to see them as part of your setting's annual inspection. Parents have the right to see records containing information about themselves or their children (but see section 4.3 for children's protection issues). If you store information about people on computer you may need to be registered under the Data Protection Act. This may not apply to some playsettings if they come under the auspices of a larger organisation such as a local authority. There are some circumstances in which you can apply for an exemption. You can find out more from the Data Protection Registrar (see Further reading at end of this section).

Records for health and safety
Consent forms

You need parental consent to take children on off-site trips and activities and outings. Some playsettings ask parents to complete a consent form giving them permission to take the child on local trips – the park, swimming, to buy cooking ingredients – at any time during the opening hours of the playsetting. This can be included on the initial registration form.

A separate consent form is usually required for longer individual trips such as an outing to the seaside or overnight camp, particularly if the trip involves leaving or returning outside the normal opening hours of the session. A consent form which has to be signed and returned helps to ensure that parents receive and are aware of the necessary information, such as leaving and arrival times and what to bring.

It is helpful if parents give you permission to sign emergency medical treatment consent forms in their absence, if they themselves cannot be contacted and the doctor advises that treatment is urgently required. Asking parents to complete such a form also gives them the opportunity to let you know if they have objections to particular treatments.

Who is here?

It must always be clear who is working in the playsetting on any particular day. This may mean staff rotas or schedules, a copy of which should be displayed in the office and on the noticeboard. Playworkers' and managers' names, addresses and contact numbers should also be kept near the the telephone, together with names and contact numbers of anyone who can cover in the event of staff sickness or emergency.

In a playcare setting a daily register will be maintained for marking children present. If children leave at different times you will also need a system to ensure that you know who is in the building at any time. Some caresettings ask parents and carers collecting their children to use a signing-out book.

In drop-in and open-access settings, such as many adventure playgrounds, daily registration may not be appropriate or even possible as children come and go throughout the session. In these cases particular attention needs to given to supervision of the premises and how evacuation procedures (fire drills) are carried out. Overall numbers of children using the setting need to be monitored. Playworkers need to identify new children quickly and obtain the necessary information for admission – including emergency contacts and any signed parental consent forms required.

The accident book

All accidents and injuries which take place in the playsetting should be recorded. In most cases this will be in an accident book. Some larger organisations have their own accident report forms. The accident book can be kept together with the first-aid kit. See section 4.1 for information regarding legislation and reporting accidents and dangerous diseases (RIDDOR).

The visitors' book

This records all visitors to the playsetting. They should sign in on arrival and sign out on leaving.

This is useful for safety reasons, but can also be an interesting way to remember visitors. Get feedback about how they experienced your playsetting by including a column for their comments on leaving.

HILLTOP PLAYSCHEME

ACCIDENT REPORT FORM

Date and time: *7-7-95   2.30 pm*

Name of injured person: *Millicent Stevens (Millie)*

How and where the incident occurred:
Fell off bench playing tig in outside area.

Nature of the incident/injury sustained: (be specific – r or l limb etc.)

Bumped head (grazed forehead), slight swelling. No signs of concussion. Twisted right arm. No swelling but painful.

Witnesses to the incident:
Mari S and Lou G (playworkers)

Action taken by staff: (include name of staff member dealing with incident/administering first aid etc.)

Mari cleaned graze with cold water. Mari monitored situation during afternoon. Millie continued to complain of painful arm. Mari informed her mother on collection and suggested she take her to casualty if pain continued.

Sarah Stevens

Parent/Carer informed: (signature of parent/carer)

Example accident report

ACTIVITY 3.23

Marion is the playworker supervising outside one afternoon when two girls collide during a game of 'Stuck in the Mud'. Lucy appears to have twisted her left ankle and Min has bumped her head on the concrete. It is bleeding slightly and a lump is appearing, but Min did not lose consciousness. While comforting the children, Marion sends another child indoors to fetch Aislin, the senior worker, who is also the first-aider. Aislin determines that the ankle does not appear to be broken and helps both girls indoors in order to clean Min's head and bandage Lucy's ankle.

1 Decide who should fill in the accident report.

2 Fill in an accident report or entry into an accident book as if you were the responsible playworker in the above situation, including all relevant details.

Equipment list

Keep an updated list or inventory of equipment in the playsetting. This is important for insurance purposes, and a copy should be held by the person responsible for dealing with insurance matters (see section 4.2). Keep separate lists for consumables, such as craft materials, and longer-lasting equipment which will be replaced only when it becomes too worn or broken. The inventory is useful for playworkers to keep a record of materials bought and when reordering. Add details of new equipment to the inventory as soon as possible after you receive them, and remove obsolete items immediately.

				Page: 3
Item (equipment)	**Supplier**	**Date ordered**	**Cost/price**	**Date received**
Music Gato Drum	Local music shop	3.8.95	£58.60	3.8.95
6 x hand bells	NES Arnold	10.8.95	£3 each	28.8.95

				Page: 5
Item (consumables)	**Supplier**	**Date ordered**	**Cost/price**	**Date received**
Finger paints x 8 pots	Early Learning Centre	29.7.95	£2 per pot	29.7.95
Paper (newsprint roll)	Collect from local newspaper printers	1.8.95	free	1.8.95

Example of an inventory of equipment

Other records

There are occasions when other records are useful or necessary. Some are dealt with in other sections. Records kept in your playsetting might include:

- notes or minutes of meetings (section 5.1);
- health and safety checklists (section 4.2);
- forms for recording formal complaints (section 5.2);
- records of contact with other agencies (for example social services with reference to concern about safety or well-being of a child – see section 4.3);
- policies, monitoring and evaluation forms, reports and development plans (section 5.3);
- programme of activities and planning notes (section 3.2);
- resource file (section 3.3);
- playworker's observations (throughout the book);
- records of financial transactions (see Working with money, overleaf).

There will also be personnel records relating to staff employment.

> Wednesday 1st March 1995
> I lic my uftsl club
> I lic guk moolin I mada woolt
> Angus loves fot bool and sosrs cavds
> today i dt coocin
>
> by Pany ♡♡♡xx
> oooo

I like my afterschool club.
I like junk modelling. I made a wallet.
Angus loves football and sorcerer's cave.
Today I did cooking.

You can involve the children in record keeping

Working with money

Many tasks within the playsetting require dealing with money. These may include:

- collecting fees;
- budgeting;
- buying large equipment and restocking supplies of materials;
- buying day-to-day purchases like fruit for snacks;
- keeping accounts and other financial records;
- paying bills, rent, salaries, insurance costs;
- paying volunteer's expenses;
- fundraising – including applying for grants.

Who does what?

Managers will be responsible for overall financial planning. They will set the budget and decide how many staff can be employed and how much can be spent on play materials and other needs. In voluntary organisations, management committee members may also take on many other tasks. Some large organisations or businesses may have a paid member of staff to keep the financial records. Everyone must be clear about who does what. This should be written down, and your responsibilities should form part of your job description.

Budgeting. Overall budgeting is the responsibility of managers. But you may be involved in setting priorities about what is most needed – deciding whether to use money for paying more volunteers' expenses or buying a large piece of equipment, for example. You may have sole responsibility for a part of the budget such as the money which has been allocated for purchasing play materials and other frequently used goods such as food, cleaning materials and paints.

If you have responsibility for all or part of a budget you need to know how much money is in it and for how long it has to last. You will need to plan ahead to work out what should be spent when. It is a good idea not to plan every penny but to set aside a contingency fund for unexpected or spontaneous events. If you find you are running out of money well before time you need to inform the person responsible for the overall budget as early as possible. This will allow them to assess the reason for this and, if necessary, re-prioritise or fundraise to allocate more to meet continuing needs.

Petty cash. You will probably need a regular amount of cash for small purchases. For this you will need a lockable petty cash box and a system for recording what you spend and getting the cash you need. The Imprest system for petty cash works by allowing you a weekly float – an agreed sum of £50, for example. Record your receipt of this cash in the petty cash book.

Record details of everything you spend and attach the relevant receipts. Each week the float is then topped up to its original amount. So if £50 is put in the cash box on Monday, and you spend £48.50 during the week, the £48.50 will be transferred to the petty cash box the following Monday, so you start off with £50 again. Of course you can operate this system fortnightly or at any other agreed interval.

Whenever money is taken out of the petty cash box a petty cash voucher (available from stationery shops) should be made out recording who has taken the money and what for. Once the purchase has been made the total section should be filled in, recording what has been spent. Pin the receipt of the purchase to this voucher.

Keeping accounts. For N/SVQ levels 2 and 3 you are not expected to be responsible for keeping the overall accounts of the playsetting. At level 3 it is assumed you are required to keep accounts of your own budget.

Keep updated and accurate records of all money received and all money spent, and what it is spent on. This is essential so that the overall accounts of the playsetting can be accurately audited (a legal requirement) and so that you can be accountable for any money for which you are responsible. Keeping accurate and up-to-date records also helps in budgeting, forward planning and protects you from any misunderstandings or accusations of mishandling money.

The accounts should record details of all payments made and all money received. Use an analysed account book with lots of columns (available from stationary shops) whether you are keeping records of a petty cash account, a goods and materials budget, or casual staff wages and expenses. The example on page 112 shows you what an analysed petty cash book might look like. If you are required to keep more complicated accounts or need to 'reconcile' or balance accounts with bank statements, you may need to attend a basic book-keeping course. (See also suggested further reading at the end of this section).

Petty Cash Voucher	Folio	24	
	Date	21/4/95	
For what required	AMOUNT	£	p
Cooking ingredients		5	00
Change returned (receipt attached)			26
Amount spent		4	74
Signature	*Samantha Creaner*		
Passed by	*J Whistle*		

A petty cash voucher should be completed for all money taken from the petty cash box

		RECEIPTS				EXPENSES								
Date	Descrip.	Amount		Date	Description	Total Payout		Post		Refresh-ments		Travel		Craft materials		Sundries	

CLIENT
SUBJECT Analysed Accounts (Petty Cash) 1995
ACCOUNT RECEIPTS FROM / / TO / /   EXPENSES

Date	Descrip.	Amount		Date	Description	Total Payout		Post		Refresh-ments		Travel		Craft materials		Sundries	
4.4. 1	Cash	50	-	4/4	Stamps	5	30	5	30								
2				7/4	Milk	1	75			1	75						
3				10/4	Volunteer bus fares	3	-					3	-				
4				21/4	Food for snacks	17	50			17	50						
5				24/4	Paints	6	20							6	20		
4.5. 6	Cash	33	75		Total	33	75										
7																	
8																	
9																	

Keeping careful record of what money is received and how it is spent is essential for budgeting, planning and accountability

Record enough detail so that you or anyone else may clearly see how much was spent by whom and how much was received from whom and what for. Invoice and cheque numbers should be recorded.

Collection of fees. If you are collecting fees you will need a receipt book to issue a receipt each time you receive any money. The receipt will give the date, amount received, from whom, and will have space for your signature. Keep a copy of these receipts for your own records. If you bank the fees yourself, keep a copy of who you have received the money from and the bank counterfoil to give to the treasurer, your manager or accountant. If you do not bank the income from fees yourself, as soon as you hand the money over get a receipt for the full amount from the person (usually the treasurer) who takes the money from you and deposits it in the bank. Make sure you have somewhere secure for keeping cash. Follow the procedures of your workplace with regard to how the fees are collected and the amount of money each family must pay. If you have any difficulty with collecting fees, report this to a senior staff member and the person responsible for banking the fees. Keep all money received from fees separate from petty cash and other income.

Ordering equipment. New equipment may be bought from local shops or suppliers or ordered from specialist or general mail-order companies. If you are the person responsible for ordering and re-ordering play materials and equipment, you need to be clear about the funds available for this. Make sure you have checked with the person authorised to make the payments that the money is available, before making a commitment to new purchases.

How are decisions made concerning what to buy? This will depend on play opportunities planned and the resources already available. All involved in planning for play within the setting can help decide what is needed. They must know how much money is available and realise the consequences of particular choices: 'If we buy glitter paints we can't get sequins as well'; or 'If we replace the slide we will not have enough money left to buy more skipping ropes this time'.

Get quotes or price lists from more than one supplier so that you can compare and ensure you are getting value for money. You may be able to borrow or lease equipment: some local authorities have equipment they will loan or lease to voluntary organisations. You may have a toy library or play association which you can join and from whom you can borrow equipment. Some areas have resource centres or 'scrapstores' which collect waste materials –

ACTIVITY 3.24

1 Make a list of all the sources of play material and equipment you use or might need in your playsetting (you can use your inventory).

2 Divide the list into:

● things to buy; and
● things which you can maybe borrow, lease or hire (contact your local authority for advice on what can be loaned, or look in the telephone directory).

3 Get price lists and mail-order catalogues. Do you know how to fill in the order forms? If this is not a job you usually do, ask if you can be involved in completing the next order.

4 Find out the procedures, including paperwork and deposits required for any materials which can be borrowed.

from paper, cardboard tubes and wool, to industrial spare parts, nettings, rope and so on – which are safe to use (with a lot of added imagination) in the playsetting.

Once you have received the goods, check that your order is complete and that you have received what is written on the receipt (if you have paid) or the invoice (if you have not yet paid). If the order is incorrect, deal with the mistake promptly, in person or in writing. If this is not your responsibility, inform the appropriate person. Ideally the person responsible for ordering will check the order and invoice and make the payments.

If you do not receive an order within the time stated by your supplier, it should be followed up promptly by the person responsible.

Where possible all purchases should be paid for by cheque, as carrying a cheque book is safer than carrying large amounts of cash. There is also no chance of being short-changed and you will have an additional record of the amount spent on the cheque book stub if you lose the receipt. (Small items such as biscuits or bus fares will be paid for in cash.) Keep a receipt for all these payments and record each transaction in a petty-cash book. Keep cash in a safe place at all times.

Overall points to remember when keeping records

- Know who is responsible for keeping what records.
- Inform the appropriate person of any information relating to records which are not your responsibility to maintain.
- Record all transactions as soon as possible.
- Keep all records up to date.
- Ensure all records are legible.
- Store all records in a secure place.
- Maintain confidentiality.

Reference

1994: Kids' Clubs Network Quality Assurance Pack.

Further reading

Hughes, Vera and Weller, David 1990: *Setting up a business*. 'Teach Yourself' series, Hodder & Stoughton.
Piper, A.G. 1984 reissued 1992: *Book-keeping*. 'Teach Yourself' series, Hodder & Stoughton.

Two useful publications written for voluntary groups, with practical advice and examples about many of the issues raised in this section, are:

Adirondack, Sandra Merrit, Cox, Fardon 1989: *Just About Managing*. Osborne Books (particularly Chapter 13 on money) London Voluntary Service Council.
Forbes, Duncan, Hayes, Ruth, Reason, Jacki 1994: *Voluntary but not Amateur*. London Voluntary Service Council. (Chapter 8 deals with keeping accounts.)
    Both publications are produced by and available from: London Voluntary Service Council, 68 Chalton Street, London NW1 1JR.

For further information about Data Protection contact: Office of the Data Protection Registrar, Wycliffe House, Water Lane, Wilmslow, Cheshire SK9 5AF. Tel: 01625 5335777.

4 Health, safety and well-being

4.1 Health and safety 1 – children's health needs and emergency procedures

We can't give our children the future, strive though we may to make it secure. But we can give them the present.

Kathleen Norris (1880–1966), *Hands Full of Living*

The first part of this section looks at factors which can improve or endanger children's health and how these might relate to playwork. The second part looks at dealing with emergency situations and the importance of clear emergency procedures and first-aid qualifications.

The role of the playworker regarding children's health

As a playworker you have a responsibility to:

- be aware of what can affect children's health;
- get information regarding individual children's health needs;
- act on information regarding individual health needs;
- provide an environment within the playsetting which promotes healthy development;
- encourage children to take responsibility for their own health, in and outside the play setting.

What affects children's health?

Just about everything! Some diseases are inherited, as are the chances of getting certain diseases later in life. The environment into which we are born and live can affect our health in many ways. Babies and children need food, shelter, responsive adults and opportunities to explore and develop skills, knowledge and understanding for healthy all-round development. A lack of any of these, such as poor nourishment, inadequate housing, neglect or abuse by parents or other carers, will have ill effects on healthy development. Other factors which can affect the health of the child include environmental hazards (pollution, constant loud noise), infection, accidents and poor hygiene. Economic and social factors affect the ability to provide a healthy environment.

They include where the family lives, type of housing, money, access to healthcare and the awareness of parents and carers of health issues.

The Health Service places considerable importance on preventive health-care in the child's early years. Doctors and health visitors give advice and support on issues relating to children's nutrition and general healthcare and have programmes for monitoring children's development and giving immunisations against some diseases.

Health issues within the playsetting

Your playsetting should have a general policy on health which includes:

- information on child's health required on registration;
- information for parents and carers about when not to send a child to the playsetting for health reasons;
- policy on storing and administering medication;
- emergency procedures.

Initial information

Ensure that parents or carers have included any important health informa-tion on the registration form. This is particularly important if the child needs to take medicines or has a condition which might need prompt medical treat-ment (allergies to wasp stings or peanuts, for example) or has other allergies or dietary requirements (see Keeping records, section 3.4).

Communicable diseases

Communicable diseases are those which can be passed on to another person, and including colds and influenza. Children suffering from communicable diseases are usually better off at home, and may be a particular risk to other children – for example, to those who have a non-infectious illness such as leukaemia or sickle-cell disease, or who need to take medication which makes it harder for them to fight off common infections. Staff should follow the same guidelines with regard to staying away from the playsetting if they have a communicable illness.

It is helpful if you refer to your health policy in a general information leaflet or prospectus for parents and carers of children who are new to the playsetting. This might include: 'A child suffering from a communicable disease, other than HIV or Hepatitis B, should not be brought to the playsetting until he is no longer infectious'.

Children with Human Immunodeficiency Virus (HIV) or Hepatitis B are not normally excluded as these illnesses are only transmitted through exchange of body fluids and are not a risk if good hygiene practices are observed within the setting (see below under Foods, health and hygiene). HIV and AIDS have had a lot of scare-story publicity in the press. Contact an expert or attend training for the most up to date research findings into the causes and spread of any illness you are concerned about or if you need information. (Your area health authority should be able to give you contacts, or try the Useful contacts section at the end of the book.)

Where a child becomes ill within the playsetting, playworkers need to reassure and comfort the child, ensure that she has somewhere to rest, and contact the parent/carer or emergency contact on the child's registration form to ask them to collect the child.

Disease and incubation period	Period when infectious	Period of exclusion of infected person	Period of exclusion of contacts
Bronchiolitis 5–8 days	During acute stage of illness	Until the person feels well	None
Chickenpox and shingles 13–21 days	1–2 days before to 5 days after spots develop	Until the spots have crusted over *and* the child feels well	If contact is a woman in last 3 weeks of pregnancy, seek advice from GP/obstetrician
Conjunctivitis 12–72 hours	During active infection	Until eye no longer appears infected	None
Diarrhoea and vomiting (*Campylobacter Cryptosporidiosis Dysentery Food poisoning Gastro-enteritis Giardiasis Salmonellosis*) Varies, few hours to few days	While having symptoms of diarrhoea and vomiting	Until symptom free for 48 hours and the person feels well. In some circumstances you may need to seek advice from a consultant in communicable disease control (CCDC)	None
Fifth disease (*Parvovirus or 'Slapped cheek syndrome'*) Variable 4–20 days	Infectious before onset of the rash	Until the child feels well	None
Glandular fever Probably 4–6 weeks	While virus present in saliva	Until the person feels well	None
Hand, foot and mouth disease 3–5 days	During acute stage of illness	Until the person feels well	None
Head and body lice (*Pediculosis*) Eggs hatch in 1 week	As long as eggs or lice remain alive	None if treated	None. (Household contacts should be treated at same time)
Hepatitis A (*Epidemic Jaundice*) 2–6 weeks	Several days before first symptom until 7 days after onset of jaundice	Until 7 days after onset of jaundice *and* the person feels well	None. (Household contacts should seek advice from their GP)
Hepatitis B 6 weeks–6 months	Not infectious under normal school conditions	Until the person feels well	None
Herpes simplex (*Cold sore*) 2–21 days	During infection	None	None
HIV Infection Variable	Not infectious under normal school conditions	None	None

Guide to communicable diseases. Always ask for expert medical advice when you need further information

Disease and incubation period	Period when infectious	Period of exclusion of infected person	Period of exclusion of contacts
Impetigo Commonly 4–10 days	As long as septic spots are discharging pus	Until responding to treatment *and* the spots have dried up	None
Measles 7–14 days	1 day before first symptom until 4 days after onset of rash	Until 4 days after onset of rash *and* the person feels well	None
Meningitis 2–10 days depending on cause	Clinical cases are rarely infectious	Until the person feels well	None. (Household contacts may be given antibiotic treatment)
Mumps 12–25 days, commonly 18 days	7 days before and up to 9 days after onset of swelling	Until the person feels well	None
Ringworm on body *(Tinea corporis)* 4–10 days	As long as rash is present	None once under treatment	None
Rubella *(German measles)* 16–18 days	1 week before and at least 4 days after onset of rash	Until the person feels well	None. (If contact is pregnant woman, seek advice from GP)
Scabies Few days to 6 weeks	Until mites and eggs are destroyed by treatment	Until day after treatment	None. (Household contacts should be treated at same time)
Scarlet fever and Streptococcal Infection 1–3 days	Day sore throat starts until 24 hours after antibiotics started	Until the person feels well	None
Threadworms 2–6 weeks for life cycle to complete	When eggs are shed in the faeces (stools)	None after the treatment has started	None. (Household contacts should be treated at same time)
Tuberculosis *(TB)* Usually 4–6 weeks	Only when sputum contains the bacteria	Until the person feels well	None. (Close contacts may need screening)
Verrucae *(Plantar warts)* 2–3 months	As long as wart is present	None	None
Whooping cough *(Pertussis)* 7–10 days	2–4 days before until 21 days after start of coughing. If treated with antibiotic, 5 days after starting course	Until the person feels well	None

Note: Treatment offered to household contacts may be extended to other close contacts

Non-transmittable diseases

There are many chronic illnesses and conditions which cannot be passed on from one child to another. These include asthma, eczema, sickle-cell disease, cancers, thalassaemia, epilepsy, hay fever and all kinds of allergic reactions. Of these asthma is the most common, with one in ten children suffering from it at some time. About one in 400 African Carribean people in Britain have sickle-cell disease.

A good, up-to-date, healthcare book (see Further reading at the end of this section) is essential for your playsetting and can give you full information about all such illnesses and conditions. Remember, too, that each child can be affected to a different degree. Some may feel ill nearly all the time, while others are affected severely only when they have a crisis in their illness.

Talk to the parents and the children about their illness and what you can do to support them. Are there any observable warning signs for the onset of a crisis or attack? What medical intervention or support might be needed? Is the child more susceptible to common infections? Does he need to be kept warm or to avoid specific foods or other substances or conditions?

Support children in dealing with their feelings about their illness or condition, and encourage them to take the lead in choosing and pacing their play to meet their needs and wishes. Encourage discussions within the playsetting about the nature of different conditions. Give accurate information, in language appropriate to the age and development of the children. Focus on what each child can do rather than what they cannot.

Medication

In most cases playworkers will not be expected to give medicines to children. If children are admitted who require ongoing medication, playworkers should have written permission and instructions from the child's parent or usual carer as to how and when it should be given to the child. The parent or carer should also demonstrate to the playworker how it should be given. Many older children will take responsibility for their own medication, but you will need to discuss this with the playworkers to agree storage arrangements for medicines and emergency procedures. Medicines must be stored in a secure place inaccessible to other children. Some medicines need to be stored in the fridge. Check the expiry date of all medicines before use.

Food, health and hygiene

Your playsetting may provide the children with a drink and a snack or, a full-scale meal, or the children may bring packed lunches. You may also undertake activities involving food as part of your play provision. In all cases, where food is consumed aspects of hygiene must be considered (see further on in this section).

Food for health

Health experts agree that we should cut down on fats and sugars and increase our intake of fibre, fresh fruits and vegetables. Where possible fresh unprocessed foods are better for children's health than processed or refined ones.

Catering for different needs

Some children in your group will have specific dietary requirements, and information on this should be obtained as part of the initial registration process

---

ACTIVITY 4.1

1 If you offer snacks or meals can you offer:

- wholemeal flour rather than white;
- fresh fruit rather than sweets, crisps or biscuits;
- water, diluted fruit juice or milk instead of sweetened drinks with additives.

2 Invite a healthcare expert into your playsetting to talk to the children about the nutritional value of different foods and why a healthy diet is important.

3 Involve the children in planning a week's menu of interesting and healthy snacks.

ACTIVITY 4.2

1 Observe two children involved in food preparation, cooking food, or serving food. Record their language and behaviour. After the observation ask yourself:

What evidence did these children show about their knowledge, skills and understanding of:

- food hygiene
- awareness of their own needs and those of others?

2 Think of three ways to build on each of these two areas; either with the two children already observed, if this is appropriate to their interests and needs, or within the playsetting as a whole.

(see section 3.4). Many cultures have religious grounds for not eating certain foods. Others avoid certain foods for moral, ethical or health reasons. It is important to respect individual and family beliefs and choices and to cater for specific requirements where possible. Vegetarian dishes are usually acceptable in a greater range of diets than meat dishes, as many diets specify avoidance of certain meat products. Bear this in mind when catering for a large group or in advance for a group whose dietary requirements are not known to you.

Children with co-ordination or mobility difficulties may need their own adaptations to equipment to enable them to feed themselves and join the group for snacks or meal-times. Such equipment – cutlery with especially thick handles for example – should be obtained with the advice of parents, carers and specialists such as the child's occupational therapist, physiotherapist or special needs support worker.

Involving children in food activities

Whatever part food plays within your playsetting, children should where possible have the opportunity to be involved in the planning, preparation and serving. By joining in these activities children can:

- make their likes and dislikes known;
- know that their needs and wishes are listened to;
- develop skills, knowledge and understanding;
- gain awareness of the needs of others;
- learn about healthy eating;
- develop hygiene awareness and good hygiene practice.

Legislation

If you prepare or provide any food in your playsetting, whether a snack or a full-scale hot meal, you must comply with the Food Safety Act 1990, The Food Hygiene (General) Regulations 1970 and the Food Hygiene (Amendment) Regulations 1990 and 1991. All people involved in providing food for others need to comply.

Your local authority environmental health department is responsible for enforcing this legislation. They will be able to give advice and guidance on how this legislation affects your playsetting and where to get training in food hygiene, and will inspect your facilities.

Any illness which might have been caused by consumption of food eaten or prepared within the playsetting should be reported to your local environmental health department.

Cleaning

All surfaces need to be cleaned regularly, in particular those used for food preparation, using an appropriate cleaning agent (see COSHH regulations, see page 120). Use a food preparation board or plates which can be washed and disinfected. Wash fresh fruit and vegetables thoroughly before consumption. You will need somewhere to do the washing up which has hot water and is not the same washbasin used for washing hands after going to the toilet. Paper towels or hot-air dryers are more hygienic than fabric towels for drying hands.

Storage

Some foods (meat, fish, dairy produce, precooked foods, sauces) need to be kept in the refrigerator at less than 5°C. These and some other foods such as eggs, which are not fully cooked until hard, are particularly good breeding grounds for harmful bacteria such as salmonella. They are best avoided in the playsetting unless you have access to a refrigerator. Even then, you will need to be rigorous in your hygiene practices (washing hands and cleaning food preparation boards) and methods of storage to avoid contamination passing from one kind of food to another – meat juices dripping in the refrigerator, for example. Other foods (flour, rice, cereal, sugar, biscuits) should be labelled and stored in a container or plastic bag, separately from other materials.

Other hygiene matters

All playsettings need to develop and maintain good hygiene practices. Poor hygiene is a major factor in the spread of disease. Children might need to be reminded to wash their hands after using the toilet, blowing their nose, touching pets or handling waste. Before handling food they need to wash their hands and to wear aprons to protect their clothes, and to protect the food from fibres, dirt or loose buttons. Adults need to provide good role-models.

Body fluids – in particular blood and faeces – can carry infection. Some serious diseases such as HIV and Hepatitis B are only contagious through direct contact with body fluids – through sexual intercourse or if infected blood gets into an open cut or sore of an uninfected person. You cannot catch these diseases by kissing, touching or sharing cups and crockery.

Cleaning of spillages of body fluids needs particular attention to hygiene, to protect the playworkers and the children, even if you believe there is no risk of yourself or anyone in your playsetting carrying or becoming infected with these viruses. Where possible spillages should be covered with paper towels and then cleaned with an appropriate cleaning fluid (see COSHH regulations note, below). Staff dealing with the spillage must wear disposable gloves.

Cover any cuts, grazes or spots on your or the children's hands with a waterproof plaster before cooking or cleaning spillages. Dispose of all waste materials in a safe, secure manner – double wrap in leak-proof bags and mark as waste materials. Your local authority may supply specially marked bags for the disposal of contaminated waste materials.

Help with personal hygiene

Some children need help with regard to personal hygiene. Access to toilets and handwashing facilities need to be considered for children with mobility difficulties. For an older child with continence difficulties, particular washing or changing facilities may be required. Every opportunity for the child to be independently responsible for their own hygiene requirements should be encouraged. Again, individual children's needs should be assessed involving the child and the child's parents or carers. Specialist help – in making adaptations to equipment, for example – should be sought where required.

Legislation: COSHH regulations

The COSHH (The Control of Substances Hazardous to Health) Regulations require employers to assess the use of all hazardous substances in the workplace, from paint to paraffin, from bleach to hair dye. In some cases this may mean that large organisations have a restricted list of cleaning materials allowed. Some prohibit the use of bleach, for example, but must recommend brand-name alternatives. This may be particularly significant if you share a

ACTIVITY 4.3

Look at the hygiene practices within your workplace. Can you think of any ways of improving them?

Example

One playworker I know found that the same cloth was often inadvertently used for different cleaning purposes. She introduced different-coloured clothes for different cleaning purposes – white for before and after food preparation, blue for art and craft, red for cleaning the floor.

Cooking in the playsetting

ACTIVITY 4.4

Find out whether your facility has restrictions on what cleaning materials can be used under COSHH regulations. What is the recommended cleaning agent for dealing with body fluid spillages? (Your local authority health and safety officer should be able to help if you are unsure.)

premises (of a school, for example) and some cleaning agents are not allowed. In all cases the use of substances hazardous to health needs to be assessed and control measures taken:

- replace with a less hazardous alternatives;
- store safely;
- follow instructions for use;
- wear protective clothing

Health promotion

You may see health education as the responsibility of schools, health service and the local authority. But children of all ages will ask questions about issues relating to health – from smoking, drugs and alcohol to sexual health, illness and disability. They will need honest and informed answers from adults whom they trust. Even a five-year-old may ask 'What is AIDS?' after seeing a television programme or advert. Playworkers need to consider how to answer these questions appropriately, without breaching the trust of the child and carers. (See section 2.3 on answering children's questions.)

Older children and teenagers will almost certainly know someone who has had personal experience of some of these issues, if they have not had first-hand experience themselves. You need to be informed in order to give accurate information. If you feel unable to answer a question fully or accurately on the spot, you should know where to get the information from, or where to refer the child who is doing the asking. Management and staff should agree on appropriate ways of dealing with these issues when they arise. They may decide on active health promotion within the playsetting, including inviting visitors with specialist knowledge. In the case of five- and six-year-olds this may be a 'Look after your teeth' campaign, for 14- and 15-year-olds it might be 'HIV and AIDS awareness'.

It is important to involve your managers, the children's parents and carers, and your health authority or other recognised health advisory agency

ACTIVITY 4.5

Ask the children in your play-setting if they would like to design posters on why good hygiene practices are important – and the possible consequences of not following good practice.

in planning such activities, and to have have their support. There may be legal implications if you are perceived to be encouraging illegal acts, such as under-age heterosexual or homosexual sex, through discussion or distribution of materials relating to contraception and safe sex.

Smoking

The effects of smoking and secondary or passive smoking are well documented. Smoking increases the risks of developing a range of diseases including: chronic bronchitis, lung cancer and cardiovascular disease. A No smoking policy should be maintained within the playsetting.

First aid

An adolescent boy was playing 'Sardines' with a group of younger children. He was eventually found in a shed, unconscious and blue having suffered a major heart attack. The two responsible adults gave resuscitation for 25 minutes until the ambulance arrived, keeping him breathing and saving his life. What would happen if a similar incident occurred in your playsetting?

Knowledge of and training in first aid saves lives in those vital minutes before the emergency services arrive. Ideally all playworkers should have a working knowledge of first aid. At least one worker should hold a first aid certificate from a nationally recognised organisation such as the Red Cross or St John's Ambulance. These certificates are usually valid for three years, when they need to be updated through further training. As first aid is a skill best developed through such practical training, this book does not cover first aid knowledge and skills; instead practical experience and further reading is recommended.

All playsettings require a properly equipped first-aid kit. One person should be responsible for making sure the first aid-kit is always fully stocked. Keep a list of contents within the first-aid kit. The first-aid kit should be stored in a safe place which is easily accessible to staff. The box or cupboard in which it is stored should be marked with the first-aid symbol – a white cross on green background.

Kids' Clubs Network recommends the following contents for a first-aid box for 30 children between the ages of 5 and 12:

- Card or leaflet giving general guidance
- Sterile triangular bandages (4);
- Non allergic adhesive plasters;
- Sterile eye pad with attachment (2);
- Assorted dressings (medium) (12);
- Assorted dressings (large) (6);
- Assorted dressings (extra large) (3);
- Assorted adhesive dressings (plasters) (30);
- Safety pins;
- Paper tissues;
- Plastic disposable gloves;
- Disposable bag for soiled material.

Do not keep medicines or antiseptic creams and liquids. Medicines should be given only with proper consent and instructions, and should be stored separately. Creams, liquids and sprays can cause allergic reactions. Plasters can also cause reactions, so use hypoallergenic brands, and ask a question about allergies, including allergies to plasters, on your enrolment or registration form.

ACTIVITY 4.6

Make a list of helpful sources of information and advice on health issues in your local area – including names, addresses and telephone numbers. You might include your local health visitor, community health unit, health education and voluntary organisations. Use the local library, telephone book (look under 'Regional Health Authority' and 'Local Authority' district/city/ county council) and the list of national organisations in Appendix 2 of this book. Many national organisations have local contacts. Next to each contact make a note of when you think you would need the advice or support of that particular organisation.

EXAMPLE

Local health visitor: Mrs June Fisher, tel: – (come and talk about nutrition)
Police, tel: – (road safety issues)

Discuss your list with the senior worker and colleagues. If they agree, contact two or three people on your list. Ask them what advice and support they can offer your playsetting. Can they suggest other useful contacts?

Emergency procedures
Dealing with accidents and injuries

Each playsetting will need to have its own emergency procedures written down and displayed so that all staff, including temporary staff and volunteers, are aware of them. They should include named first-aider, location of first aid box and local emergency telephone contacts.

The following is a sample 'code of practice' for dealing with accidents and injuries. (*Note:* this is a suggested code of practice only. Actions will not necessarily be carried out in this order, or by one individual only):

- keep calm;
- reassure and comfort injured child;
- assess injury without moving the child;
- diffuse the situation – explain the situation and reassure or distract non-injured children;
- get cover to supervise children;
- refer to appropriate staff member, named first-aider, emergency services, or administer first aid as appropriate and according to agreed procedures of your setting
- contact injured child's parent or carer;
- if parent not contactable, accompany child to hospital in ambulance if necessary;
- record accident in accident book;
- explain accident to parent/carer;
- report accident to appropriate authority (see under 'Legislation reporting accidents' below).

Legislation: reporting accidents

All accidents should be reported to parents or carers. Any accident involving injury from part of the premises, materials or equipment should be reported to the manager and employer. Any accident requiring medical treatment should be reported to the employers. Employers are required by law to report any accidents that stop a person working for more than three days to the Health and Safety Executive or environmental health department, within seven days (form F2508). Some injuries such as broken bones and unconsciousness must be reported immediately. If in doubt, phone anyway. (See section 4.2 on Health and safety legislation.)

In case of fire

The fire drill procedures should be displayed. They will include what action to take and the assembly point for calling the register. Staff should know who will check the building (including toilets) and who will collect the register and children's records. Your local fire department can give advice. Ideally, alternative premises should be identified locally where children can wait in bad weather while parents are contacted or until the premises are made safe.

Looking after yourself

As well as looking after the health needs of the children in your care you will need to consider your own health needs. There are many factors which may affect your health outside the playsetting. Part of working as a member of a team is giving and receiving support from other team members (see section 5.2).

Examples of conditions within the playsetting which could adversely affect your own as well as the children's health include:

- light and ventilation;
- moving heavy play equipment;
- stress;
- use correct lifting techniques before moving heavy equipment:
- assess the weight of the load;
- assess centre of gravity of load;
- check for sharp edges;
- get help/use a trolley;
- follow correct lifting technique.

Stress

Stress can lead to depression and is one of the most common reasons for people taking time off work. If you are experiencing stress at work it may be because you are feeling unsupported – whether in dealing with the behaviour of a child, parent or colleague, having unrealistic demands made on your time, skills or energy, or simply feeling put-upon or unappreciated. It is important to communicate the reasons clearly to colleagues and management as early as possible, so that you and they can take all possible steps to maintain a healthy working environment for all.

Reference

Norris, Kathleen (1880–1966), *Hands Full of Living*

Further reading

Leach, Penelope 1991: *The Parents' A to Z – A guide to children's health, growth and happiness.* Penguin.
Mayall, Berry 1986: *Keeping Children Healthy.* Allen & Unwin.
Whiting, Mary, and Lobstein, Tim 1992: *The Nursery Food Book.* Edward Arnold. (Nutritional information, food activities and multicultural recipes easy to adapt for older children.)

As reference books for the playsetting:
British Red Cross 1994: *First Aid for Children Fast.* Dorling Kindersley.
Smith, Tony 1992: *The Macmillan Guide to Family Health.* Macmillan.

Assess the weight

Use mechanical aids where possible

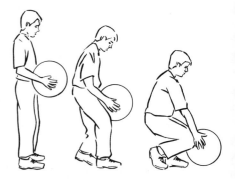

Get help and work as a team

Lift in stages, taking the load on your knees first, and then to the carrying position. The middle of the load should be level with your waist

Use correct lifting technique

4.2 Health and safety 2 – safe space for play

TO THINK ABOUT

The role of risk taking in children's play.

Risk taking is a part of everyday life. Without taking risks we are not challenged and do not have the opportunities to develop new skills, explore what is possible or discover our potential. Almost every decision we take involves some level of risk.

Questions
1 How can you provide opportunities within your playsetting which enable children to take risks, and make choices about these risks which develop their skills of judgement and give them personal responsibility?
2 How do such opportunities differ from unacceptable risks in the playsetting?

The fishermen know that the sea is dangerous and the storm terrible, but they never found these dangers sufficient reason for remaining ashore
from *Dear Theo*, An autobiography of Vincent Van Gogh

There are potential dangers all around us. Fishermen learn how to assess how hazardous the sea is in different conditions and take precautionary measures – a sound boat, skilled crew and lifesaving equipment – to minimise the risks to their safety.

An awareness of health and safety issues belongs to all aspects of play-work, and there are references to health and safety throughout this book. This section looks more closely at how playworkers can ensure the safety of children in the day-to-day activities and use of the playsetting, and summarises relevant legislation.

Children need to feel secure about their playsetting. They have the right to expect that those who are responsible for their care will make sure that the premises, activities and play materials are safe and suitable.

Children also must learn how to become responsible for their own safety, and need opportunities to develop the skills and judgement to do this. Through play children try out their skills and gain understanding of their own achievements and limitations.

Preventing accidents

Every year an estimated 1.8 million children visit a hospital accident and emergency department in the UK following an accident away from home (the *Dettol Report*, 1994). Children aged 5–14 have 85 per cent of non-home child accidents, and sport and general play account for 72 per cent of accidents in this age-group. Transport areas (streets and car parks especially) are the main danger areas for young children away from home. Every year several hundred children are killed in road accidents, and they are at greatest risk as pedestrians.

Playworkers need to be aware of safety issues in their setting and have a commonsense approach to accident prevention. Accidents are nearly always avoidable. A definition of an accident in a playsetting is 'an unplanned and

ACTIVITY 4.7

What immediate action would you take in the following situations?

1 You are in the outside area of your playsetting before the children arrive and you find broken glass bottles near the perimeter fence.

2 You are chatting to some children playing on a tyre swing and you notice the rope is frayed and thin.

3 As you are looking around the playsetting before leaving, you find that two sharp woodwork tools have been left on the floor.

4 A child brings in a glass painting kit which used to belong to his sister, but which he has said can be donated to your playsetting. The instructions are lost, but the child knows what to do and asks, 'Can we do some today?'

What follow-up action would you take in each situation to try to ensure it was not repeated?

uncontrolled event which has led to or could have caused injury to persons, damage to premises, equipment or other loss'.

To prevent accidents you must identify what is likely to cause them. Safety issues need to be discussed within your team so that you can reach agreement on what are acceptable and unacceptable risks and the roles and responsibilities of individuals for health and safety matters.

Hazards and risks

When looking at the safety of your own playsetting you will need to decide what might be a danger to the safety of the children and what to do about it. Initially you should identify the hazards and assess the risks.

A hazard is something which could cause harm to someone. A risk is how likely it is that a hazard will cause actual harm. Your playsetting will probably contain lots of hazards, and what you and your colleagues should decide is whether the risk involved is acceptable or not.

A British or European Safety Standard label on bought equipment ensures that it has been subject to testing and assessment for safety, but you must still follow instructions and ensure it is properly used, stored and maintained.

The BSI Kitemark means that the product has been tested by the British Standards Institution and will be regularly checked by qualified inspectors to ensure it reaches the agreed standards for safety

$C\epsilon$

The CE mark means that the manufacturer claims that the products meet the standards of the relevant Community Directives

Identified hazard	Risk assessment
Climbing frame	While there is always the possibility that a child could fall from the climbing frame, everything has been done to minimise the risk. The structure complies with health safety standards, it is checked regularly for signs of wear and tear or vandalism, it is mounted on an approved surface, children are supervised appropriately and know and understand what is acceptable and unacceptable (dangerous) behaviour. If the climbing frame were removed it would limit the opportunity for childrens play. In these conditions the climbing frame is an acceptable hazard and should stay.
Broken glass in outside play area	Obvious hazard with unacceptable risk. It limits children's play opportunities and is a danger to them. Outside area should be checked before every session, and broken glass and other rubbish removed.
Frayed rope on tyre swing	Danger to children. Unacceptable risk – needs to be replaced immediately.
Matches	Potential danger to children. Necessary in playsetting for cooking, and maybe candles or bonfires? Need to consider when can children use matches themselves and what supervision is required. Secure storage so that children cannot get hold of and use matches inappropriately. Acceptable risk given the above points.
Cleaning materials	Cleaning materials will be necessary, but need to consider safe storage and who will have access to them (see COSHH Regulation section 4.1).
Woodwork tools	Can cause injury but can also encourage and extend children's play opportunities. Need to consider age and ability of children using the tools, supervision, safe behaviour, appropriate use, and storage and maintenance of tools

Who is responsible?

Children have the right to expect that the playworkers have taken steps to prevent them from coming to any harm in the playsetting. Playworkers' views on what these steps are will vary from one worker to another. You will have your own views on what is an 'acceptable risk'.

ACTIVITY 4.8

Identifying hazards and assessing risks

1 Walk around your play facility. Look at the buildings, from floor to ceiling. What things in the building might cause harm to children? How might this occur? Make a list.

2 Discuss with your colleagues and managers which things on your list present an acceptable risk and which need to be removed or replaced. (See examples above.)

3 Do the same in your outside play area and with your play equipment.

ACTIVITY 4.9

Who is responsible?
Write down who is responsible in your playsetting for:

- carrying out checks of premises and play materials;
- ensuring buildings and materials are properly maintained and in a good state of repair;
- reporting breakages or replacing worn items;
- monitoring that health and safety policies are being followed by all concerned;
- reviewing health and safety policies if they are not working?

By law the employers are responsible for making the workplace a healthy and safe place to work. Employees have the duty to take reasonable care of themselves and others affected by their work, and to co-operate with their employers on all matters relating to health and safety. If you share the premises, and occupy a building owned by another group, you are also legally bound to have regard for the safety of yourselves and others using the premises.

If your playsetting is run or managed by a large organisation such as a local authority you will have your own health and safety representative who can be called on for advice. A large organisation will also have health and safety policies and procedures which you must follow. In a smaller organisation, such as a voluntary community playscheme, it is important that clear health and safety guidelines and procedures are drawn up by management and staff and given to all those who are affected. Such guidelines and procedures should make clear who is responsible for doing what.

Consider Activity 4.9. If you do not know the answers to the questions in this activity, discuss them with your senior colleague or manager. While you yourself may not be responsible for most of these activities, you need to know who is so that you can report any problems, breakages, hazards or concerns promptly to the right person. The following activity will help you identify clearly who is responsible and what your own responsibilities are. You can use a grid or checksheet as illustrated on page 128.

ACTIVITY 4.10

Planning activity – safety checklists

1 Make a check-list of all aspects of your premises and equipment which need checking for reasons of safety – daily, weekly, once a term or once a year. You can use Activity 4.8 to decide what needs checking together with your list or inventory of materials and equipment (see section 3.4).

2 Write on the list who should check each item and what you should do if you find a problem with any of the items on the list.

3 Where it is your responsibility to check a particular item, write down how often you should check and how you will check each time (see example on page 128).

Arrivals and departures

The times when children arrive at and leave the playsetting are often those during which accidents are most likely to occur. This is because there are frequently many other people on the premises, such as parents and carers collecting or delivering children. You and your colleagues are busy with setting out or tidying up play materials or giving or receiving information about

ACTIVITY 4.11

Observation exercise

1 Spend 20 minutes at the beginning and at the end of a session observing the arrivals to and departures from your place of work.

2 Ask yourself:
- Is the supervision of children adequate at all times?
- Do children know where to collect their coats?
- Are there opportunities for playworkers to

communicate with parent or carers on urgent matters?
- Do children know what they can do if they have to wait for their parents or carers to collect them or to talk to the playworkers?
- Are there any problems with traffic congestion or road safety outside the setting?

3 Discuss your observations with colleagues. Is there any way arrival and departure time should be changed to improve safety?

E X A M P L E

NAME OF GROUP:

DATE:

Safety Checklist

What needs checking	Who will check	How to check	How often to check	Action if faulty/ who to report to
Building				
Floors (trip hazards etc.)	Supervisor	Visual check	Daily	Remove hazard
Windows	Supervisor	Test	Daily	Report to Caretaker
Doors	Supervisor	Test	Daily	School Head Management Committee
Outside Areas				
Perimeter fence and gates	Assistant 1	Visual	Daily	Remove hazard –
Ground area (for rubbish etc.)	Assistant 1	Visual	Daily	Report to:
Structures/Fixed equipment.	Health & Safety Officer – City council	Detailed survey	Monthly	Report to Health & Safety Report to Repairs Section
Equipment				
Play materials out:	Assistant 2	Visual/	Daily	Remove/replace
Tools	Assistant 2	Test	before use	Report to supervisor
Electrical	Whoever uses it	Test before use	Before use	Send for repair Report to:
Fire prevention				
Procedures displayed	Supervisor	Visual		Report to: Management
Fire exits	Supervisor	Visual	Daily	Get advice from
Extinguishers	Supervisor	Visual		Fire Department
Fire blanket	Supervisor	Visual		
Fire drills	Supervisor	Carry out	3 x a year	Repeat drill
Emergencies				
First-aid box	Named first aider	Visual	Once a week	Replace used items
Procedures displayed		Visual	Daily	Ensure new procedures displayed
Other Items				
Storage shed	Assistant 1	Check secure	Daily	Report to Management Committee
Toilets	Assistant 2	Visual	Daily	
Cleaning materials	Supervisor	check complete & store correctly.	Daily	Replace as required
Heating	Supervisor	Check comfortable temperature Fire guards etc.	Daily/as required	

Supervisor: Sarah   Contact for Health & Safety - Local authority: Gill. Tel. 07777
Assistant 1:   Paul   Fire Department: Tel. 006644
Assistant 2:   Brenda   Caretaker: Tel 11113
Named First Aider: Paul   Management Rep for Safety: Bill. Tel. 36666

children or other concerns. Points of access and departure can in themselves be hazardous if, for example, people are able to leave prams or buggies in narrow entrance halls, or if the playsetting is close to a busy road or car park.

If you work in a playcare setting you need to know who has permission to collect each child at the end of the session. You must not let the child go with any other person unless you have authorisation in advance from the child's usual carer. You also need to know who to contact if a child does not arrive when expected or is not collected.

Do not take the child to your home. As a final resort, if no contact can be made with the carer, call the duty social worker at your local social services department.

Off-site activities

Many play facilities will include outings and visits such as a trip to the park, to the swimming pool, to the nearest bit of woodland or a day trip to the seaside.

Off-site activities demand particular attention to health and safety. While you would regularly check your outside play area, you cannot check the whole of your local park for hazards such as discarded syringes. Once again it is important that you encourage children to take responsibility for their own safety. The ground-rules for going offsite need to be agreed and clearly understood by workers and children. They include when not to run ahead or cross the road and what to do if a child gets lost. Children should be made aware of any hazards they might come across during the outing such as waste materials, poisonous plants or deep water.

Other safety points you should consider when planning an off-site activity include:

- Insurance – does your insurance cover off site activities?
- Consent – have you got parents'/carers' written consent?
- Supervision – what supervision (staff–child ratios) will you need? This will depend on the age and abilities of the children, the type of activity and, in some cases, your insurance policy. It is a good idea to divide children into small groups, each with a responsible adult.
- Transport – are you fully insured, is the vehicle roadworthy (MOT certificate?), and are seatbelts fitted?
- Children's records – who will be responsible for taking a register and keeping count of children? It is useful to take a duplicate set of children's registration forms with you on trips. This means you will have all the relevant details and contacts in the event of an accident but a copy will remain in the playsetting in case of loss or damage.
- Contact – take the number of someone to contact in the event of a delay so that they can inform and reassure parents and carers when they come to collect the children
- First Aid – take a first-aid kit and someone with emergency first aid training.

Children need to become responsible for their own safety

Children do not grow up or live in totally safe environments. Through play, children can learn how to cope with dangers in everyday life, from crossing the road to handling tools, from understanding what can cause harm to being

Using a two-handled blade

able to protect themselves. It is not the aim of any playsetting to provide a totally accident-proof, sterile setting, different and apart from the world in which the children live. Even if this were possible it would severely limit the opportunities for play it could offer.

Use your knowledge of child development and the needs, interests and abilities of the children in your care to plan appropriate activities. Use your knowledge of health and safety issues to enable children to develop independence in taking responsibility for their own safety. If children know where things are kept and how to put them away safely when they have finished with them, and are involved in making the rules and decisions of the setting, they will be better able and more willing to take on this responsibility.

Children learn through imitation and example. You can provide good role models for safe behaviour and handling materials and equipment in a safe way. You could also plan activities specifically around health and safety topics or invite experts in to give talks or lead activities on topics such as fire, road safety and first aid.

Health and safety law

Health and Safety legislation which may have a bearing on your work within the playsetting includes:

- The Health and Safety at Work Act 1974;
- Health and Safety (First Aid) Regulations 1981;
- The Control of Substances Hazardous to Health Regulations 1988;
- The Electricity at Work Regulations 1989;
- The Health and Safety (Information to Employees) Regulations 1989;
- The Reporting of Injuries, Diseases and Dangerous Occurrences Regulations 1985.

Legislation relating to food preparation is covered in section 4.1.

Health and safety law is enforced by one of two agencies: your nearest health and safety executive or your local authority Environmental Health Department. You should have a Health and Safety at Work Act information

---

ACTIVITY 4.12

Find out who is responsible for enforcing health and safety law within your setting.

Ensure that you have a poster or leaflets giving basic health and safety law information.

Obtain the following free leaflets from your supervisor, your managers or your nearest health and safety executive office:

- Health and Safety at Work etc. Act 1974: The Act outlined (HSC2)
- Health and Safety at Work etc. Act 1974: Advice to Employees (HSC5)
- Reporting under 'RIDDOR' (Reporting of Injuries, Diseases and Dangerous Occurrences Regulations 1985)(HSC24)
- COSHH (Control of Substances Hazardous to Health Regulations 1988) a brief guide for employers (INDG 136) First Aid in Small workplaces (INDG 3)

What are the health and safety considerations of this activity?

poster (published by HMSO and available from large bookstores) displayed where staff can see it. Alternatively employees can be given leaflets covering the same information. On the poster there is a space for filling in the address and contact number of your health and safety enforcement office. If there are more than five people employed in your organisation you must by law, have your own health and safety policy for the setting.

Fire

There are two main acts on fire safety: The Fire Services Act 1947 and the Fire Precautions Act 1971 as amended by the Fire Safety and Safety of Places of Sport Act 1987. Fire departments are required to give advice free of charge to any person or regulatory authority who requests it. Certain premises require a fire certificate. Some local authorities will ask the fire officer to inspect your premises as part of the registration process under the Children Act. The main points of concern are:

- the means of escape (easily accessible and kept clear);
- the fire-fighting equipment (extinguishers and fire blanket);
- means of warning in the event of fire heating and fire guards;
- electrical safety;
- storage of flammable materials;
- staff awareness of procedures and practice of fire drills.

Insurance and transport

All playsettings employing staff must be insured against employers liability and a copy of the Employer's Liability Certificate must be displayed – in the office if you have one (Employer's Liability (Compulsory Insurance) Act 1969). The Children Act recommends that all playsettings have public liability insurance. Some local authorities make this a condition of grant aid or registration. Buildings should also be insured, although this will probably be the responsibility of whoever owns the building. Additional insurance may be needed to cover materials and equipment (contents), personal effects and special events such as overnight stays.

   If you use a minibus to transport children on trips you will have to comply with the Transport Act 1985. Your minibus requires a permit, the driver must be over 21 years with full driving licence and insurance, and you must carry appropriate fire extinguishers and first aid equipment. Some insurance policies insist that the driver is over 25 years old. Currently the law requires seatbelts to be fitted in front seats only, but new legislation may shortly require seatbelts for rear seats also. New minibuses are mostly already following good practice by fitting these belts in advance of the the legislation. All passengers must be able to open all door locks from the inside. Contact the Department of Transport or your local traffic commissioner for further information.

The role of the playworker

Look at the following check-list of the aspects of your role which relate to health and safety. Do you:

- provide a safe space in which children can, through play, develop skills to enable them to take responsibility for their own safety?
- identify hazards and assess risks to prevent accidents?
- give consistent information to children, parents and other users of the playsetting?

ACTIVITY 4.13

Health and safety quiz

1 Does you workplace have a health and safety policy? What does it include?
2 Is your playsetting registered under the Children Act? If so, where is the registration certificate displayed and are there any special conditions? If not, what are the reasons for this? (for example does it fall outside of the registration criteria – see section 1.2.)
3 Has the fire officer inspected the premises and made any recommendation?
4 Are emergency procedures and procedures for evacuating the building on display?

5 Do you know where the fire extinguishers and fire blanket are to be found and how and when to use them?
6 When and how often are fire drills carried out?
7 Are you aware of who supervises which play area at any time?
8 Are there procedures for ensuring the safe arrival and departure of children from the setting?
9 Who has responsibility for checking safety of premises and equipment on a day-to-day basis. When and how do they carry this out?
10 Do bought toys and equipment comply to British or European health and safety standards?

- agree and understand procedures which ensure that safety checks are regularly carried out?
- help to review these procedures regularly to ensure they remain effective?
- work within the law?

Are you clear about what are the roles and responsibilities – your own and those of others – in each of these areas? You can get further information and advice from the organisations listed under Health and safety in Appendix 2. Your telephone directory will have numbers for your local authority, fire, social services, education and leisure departments

Reference

The Dettol Report 1994: *Child Accidents in the UK*. Dettol Care Network in association with the Child Accident Prevention Trust (CAPT).

Further reading

Child Accident Prevention Trust 1992: *Accident prevention in day care and playsettings: a practical guide*. Child Accident Prevention Trust (jointly distributed by CAPT and NES Arnold).
Cohen, Kilham and Oates 1989, 1993: *Child Safety*. Impact Books.
Crown/NCPRU 1992: *Play Ground Safety Guidelines*. Available from National Children's Play and Recreation Unit/Department for Education, or National Play Information Centre.
1984: *Toward a Safer Adventure Playground*. National Playing Fields Association, currently being updated by Playlink.

4.3 Child protection

> There is danger in this world we live in, and we only increase our jeopardy by dealing in illusions – by pretending that only strangers are dangerous, that the danger is 'out there' somewhere, not here close to home where we live, love work and play.
>
> Peg Flandreau West 1989

Child abuse is a complex and distressing subject. You may have to deal with suspected or actual cases of child abuse in your work. You may be asked to be involved in monitoring a child on the child protection register. This is why you should have the opportunity to consider the issue in depth before you are in the position of having to deal with it first hand. Probably the best way for you to do this is to attend training where you can examine your own feelings and share thoughts with other playworkers as well as get essential information about referral procedures and what happens after a referral has been made.

The approach taken throughout this book has been that children should not be viewed as objects of concern. They are individuals with rights and expectations and a developing understanding of themselves and the world around them. But children are also often in a vulnerable position within their families and society at large. They are usually physically weaker than adults and do not have the same level of experience or the range of knowledge, understanding or independence. They are not normally granted the same rights or access to decision making about their lives.

The children within your care are individuals. You as playworker should recognise and respect their needs, skills, understanding and experience, and encourage their active participation in decision making and taking responsibility for themselves. You have a responsibility to ensure that the children in your care can play and develop to their full potential within the playsetting. This sometimes involves protecting them from abuse from those against whom they have little power to protect themselves. Section 2.4 has looked at this issue in relation to behaviour within the playsetting, for example bullying. This section looks at child protection and the responsibilities of playworkers in the wider context of children suffering abuse or likely to suffer abuse from anyone within and outside the playsetting.

The role of the playworker

Your playsetting has a particular place within the life of each child who attends. As the playworker you are one of the adults who provide a role model for each child and you are a potential source of trusted support. A child might confide in you that he is or has been suffering abuse (disclosed abuse); you may observe symptoms such as unexplained injuries or changes in behaviour which give cause for concern (suspected abuse); someone may tell you that a child is being abused or that they are abusing a child themselves (reported abuse).

You have a duty to discuss your concerns if you have reason to believe that a child has been or is being abused. To carry out this duty, you need to know about:

- the possible associated features (sometimes called signs and symptoms) of different types of abuse;
- your playsetting's procedures for dealing with suspected, reported or disclosed child abuse – your own responsibilities; the responsibilities of others and the action to be taken;

- the procedures of your local authority for investigating possible abuse – what action they will take when you or another member of staff make a referral? In some areas your local NSPCC team can also take referrals. Both NSPCC and social services will work with specially trained police officers if a criminal offence may have been committed.
- sources of help, advice and support.

Dealing with personal feelings about abuse

Attitudes to different kinds of abuse vary and are affected by individuals' own experiences (including perhaps first-hand experience of abuse as a child) and cultural and family values. One person may see public humiliation or shaming as more abusive than a private beating. Another may see sexual abuse as far worse than neglect. What disgusts one may seem tolerable to another.

It is not the role of the playworker to judge, assess or investigate suspected abuse. However, if and when you have to respond to an incident or suspected incident within your worksetting, you may need personal support to help you deal with the feelings it brings out in you.

Kinds of abuse: what you might observe

Child abuse is difficult to define. Any definition will be subject to change as thinking and practice develops. Abuse has been categorised into four different types: physical, sexual, emotional and neglect, but these are not mutually exclusive – an abused child may well be suffering more than one type. The categories are useful in coming to a working definition and identifying particular features – physical or behavioural – which may be associated with abuse. Many of the symptoms described below, in particular the behaviours, can be caused by a variety of other factors which are not related to child abuse.

Physical abuse

This is any form of actual injury inflicted (or knowingly not prevented) by a person having custody or care of the child. Sometimes called non-accidental injury, it includes bruises, cuts, fractures, burns, scalds, scratches, bites or administration of poisonous substances. The symptoms of physical abuse are often the most easily recognisable – though you should remember that children frequently bruise and injure themselves accidentally.

Bruises which may signify abuse are:

- those in places unlikely to be caused by falls – inside thighs, behind ears, groin area;
- bruises with an unusual shape – finger marks caused by violent gripping or slapping;
- weals caused by straps or other implements

Cigarette burns may also be symptoms of abuse.

You should also be concerned if the explanation of how the injury occurred given by a child or adult is inconsistent, or unlikely given the appearance of the injury, or if there has been a delay in seeking medical treatment. A child who is suffering physical abuse may appear fearful of adult reactions, have poor concentration or be unwilling to undress (for swimming for example) and expose marks hidden beneath clothing.

ACTIVITY 4.14

If you have not been on any child protection training, find out whether there is such training available in your area (ask your local social services department or NSPCC). Find out if your local authority produces any guidelines on child protection issues for day-care/play providers. All local authorities should have guidelines outlining the procedures for child abuse referral and investigation in their area even if they do not provide guidelines specifically for daycare/play providers

Sexual abuse

Sexual abuse is the exploitation of children to meet the sexual demands of adults. Exploitation is the key word here as sexual abuse is also about power and control. In many cases abusers are the ones who have been abused themselves as children. Direct sexual abuse can involve genital contact, oral, anal or vaginal penetration, masturbation or ejaculation on to the child's skin.

Indirect sexual abuse includes genital exposure ('flashing') using children in, or exposing children to, pornographic material, or encouraging two children to have sex. While sex between adolescents under 16 years of age or between an older person and a child under 16 is unlawful, it is not considered to be abuse if exploitation is not an issue, that is, if both parties were consenting, force was not used, and there has been no misuse of power based on age difference (five years or more) or other form of authority.

Signs of sexual abuse can include bruising on breasts, inner thighs or buttocks, stained underclothes, genital injuries, soreness or rashes, urinary tract infections or frequent headaches and stomach pains. The playworker should be concerned if a child has difficulty walking or sitting, shows sexually explicit behaviour (including compulsive masturbation) or if they have inappropriate sexual knowledge for their age. Other behaviour which may indicate sexual abuse includes terror of particular people or one person, anxiety, feelings of worthlessness and over-compliant behaviour.

Emotional abuse

Children need love, attention and stimulation as well as physical care if they are to develop into healthy adolescents and adults. They gain their cues on how to behave from adult role models around them. Verbal attacks, isolation, humiliation, extremes of inconsistent care or over protectiveness lead to loss of self-confidence and the ability to form relationships with others. Such psychological damage can be as harmful to children as some physical abuse in that it can permanently damage the child's ability to form relationships and take part in social activities. Symptoms of emotional abuse can include communication difficulties, lethargy, stunted growth, constant wetting or soiling, poor self-esteem, rocking back and forth, aggression, unresponsiveness and complete withdrawal from activities in the playsetting.

Neglect

Neglect is the denial of children's right to food, warmth, medical care or other aspects of care including supervision to ensure that they are not exposed to dangers such as heaters or traffic before they are old enough to cope with them. Neglect can result in the child suffering preventable injuries or being unable to thrive due to poor nutrition, lack of essential medical care and lack of adult attention, stimulation and support. Symptoms of neglect may include low weight, voracious appetite, unclean appearance or smells and inappropriate dressing such as sandals in winter. The child may show a lack of interest in what is going on in the playsetting or the carer may show a lack of interest in the child.

Notice that the same symptoms may appear in different categories of abuse. Be aware, too, that abuse may be occurring when there are no outward signs to observe. If you notice any of the above symptoms in a child, remember that there may be a reasonable explanation which is not related to abuse. But never ignore any observation which suggests that there may be something wrong, particularly if a number of symptoms are noticed or there is a marked change in behaviour. It is your responsibility as an adult and as a playworker to share your concerns with the appropriate person, following the procedures of your setting.

Child protection procedures in the playsetting

Procedures for the playsetting should be in line with the procedures of the agency responsible for investigating child abuse in your area (NSPCC or Social Services Department, or an inter-agency organisation). The local procedures will have been drawn up in consultation with representatives from health and education, and playworkers should be included in this process.

Within your playsetting the most senior worker should have the responsibility for making referrals. If the senior worker is not present, and the situation is potentially life-threatening or the child is severely injured, another worker will need to know how to contact the hospital or duty social worker, preferably in consultation with a member of the management of your playsetting. If the situation is not life threatening, and you or your senior worker think that it is unlikely that the symptoms giving cause for concern are caused by abuse, it may be appropriate to take one or all of the following courses of action:

- Share concerns with other members of staff. Have they any observations or insights?
- Make notes of your observations which have given rise to concern, including dates, times and what you have seen or heard. Do not record personal judgements or opinions. All such records are strictly confidential and must be kept in a safe place which cannot be accessed by anyone other than yourself or a senior colleague. You may need to share them with the appropriate authority if there is an investigation.
- Ask for an informal discussion with your contact in Social Services or NSPCC to help decide whether you need to make an immediate referral.
- Share your concerns with the parents or carers of the child concerned (but see below).

Sharing your concerns with parents

A senior worker may decide to share concerns with the parents of the child. This will require a great deal of sensitivity. If you notice bruises or injuries it would be useful to ask the child and parent how the injury happened. There is likely to be a reasonable explanation. If a child is displaying aggressive, withdrawn or over-compliant behaviour, again the parent or child may be able to suggest reasons – conflict at home or a bereavement, say. However, it is important not to take on the role of an investigator. Do not question the replies you receive, or attempt to probe or cross-examine. It may be that the parent is the abuser, or a close relative or partner of the abuser. There may be a risk that the child will be blamed for your concerns, or that additional pressure will be placed on the child 'not to tell.' In extreme cases it could put the child's life in danger. If in any doubt, make the referral immediately, but stay calm and do not panic.

If a child tells you that he or she is being abused, stay calm. Your reaction to such disclosure is very important. Listen to what the child says, without probing or rushing. Reassure the child that he or she was right to talk to you. Do not promise confidentiality; explain that you will need to share the information with others who can help. Refer the information to the senior colleague responsible or to Social Services or the NSPCC as soon as you can.

ACTIVITY 4.16

Find out

- how you make a referral;
- what happens after a referral has been made;
- (if you are the senior worker) who can you talk to informally within social services or the NSPCC to get informal advice and support if you are concerned.

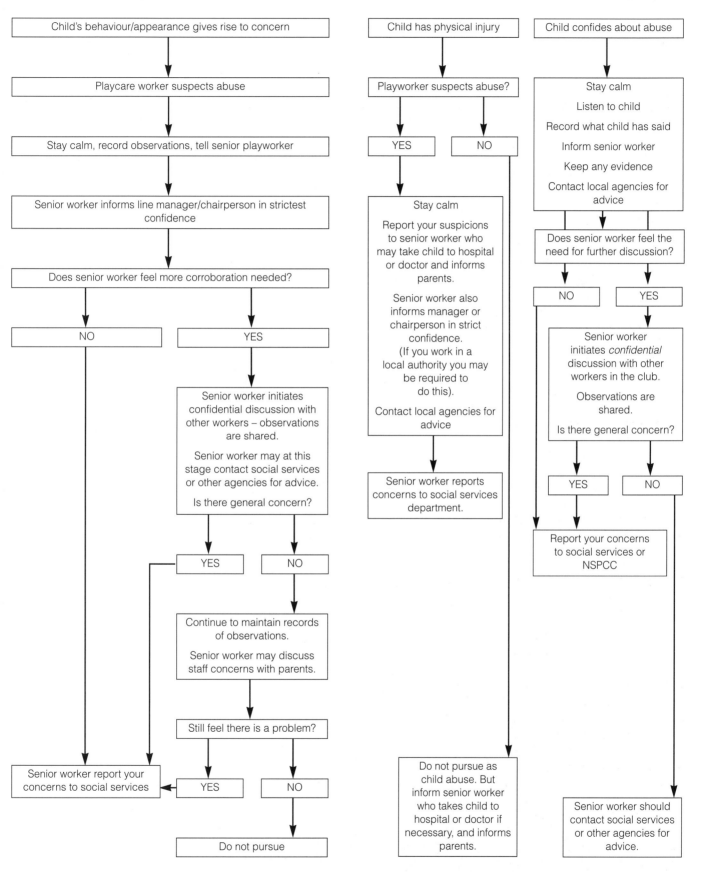

Taking action relating to an incident or possible incident of child abuse (from Kids' Clubs Network: The role of playcare workers in the protection of children from abuse)

Record the information as factually as possible, including the date and time it was given to you.

Remember that it is not the playworker's responsibility to investigate. You should not physically examine the child or ask leading questions. A leading question is one which suggests to the child that you suspect or expect a particular answer. Examples of such questions are: 'Did someone do this to you?'; 'Are you frightened of so and so?'; 'Have they been hurting you?'; 'Did you burn yourself when you were alone in the house?'. This could intimidate the child further and complicate and undermine the role of Social Services or the NSPCC team if a referral is made.

Making a referral
Initial contact

The senior playworker should know the contact number of the child protection agency (Social Services or NSPCC), and will usually be the person who makes the referral. Out of hours, or if the child protection workers are not available, the duty social worker will be able to take the referral. If you cannot speak to the person you want, ask to speak to his or her senior. Keep trying until you speak to an appropriate person. Make sure you have the details (name, address, date of birth) of the child to hand, and that you can give a clear description of the incidents or observations which have led you to make the referral. Ask for the name and the job title of the person to whom you speak, and ask what will happen next. Keep a record of your conversation and the name of your contact.

Investigation

If the incident is very serious or potentially life threatening, the social worker may come to your setting immediately and talk to you and the child. You will need to organise the time and space for this. It is more likely that the investigation team will make other enquiries to help them build up a full picture. This may take some time as they will want to speak to the child's school, health visitor or doctor before approaching the parents or carers and child. They may also need to arrange for the child to be medically examined. Concerns may have been expressed already from other agencies. If you are anxious and have heard nothing you can telephone your contact to find out what is happening.

If anyone telephones you asking for information in connection with a child protection investigation, ask for their name and telephone number and tell them you will call them back. This way you can check that they are who they say they are – and not give out information inappropriately. If you need time to think about what you want to say, take the telephone number and arrange to ring back later. If you are in any doubt, give no information and refer the matter immediately to your supervisor or your contact in Social Services.

Assessment and case conference

When the investigation team have made their assessment they will decide what further action is necessary. They may call a case conference, which you may be asked to attend. The case conference will be conducted with the full knowledge (and if possible participation) of the parents. Other professionals already involved with the child and family will also be invited. Depending on the age of the child she will also be informed and consulted. The case conference (in the context of child protection work) is a forum for exchange of information and discussion about the alleged or suspected abuse. The outcome of the conference will decide if the child should be placed on the child protection register, what support is needed for the child and the family, and what further assessment and review are needed. In some cases criminal proceedings may be initiated against the abuser, or the child may be taken into care. However, the Children Act emphasises the right of the child to have his or her views taken into account and that in many cases what is needed is support from a variety of agencies to help enable the family to stay together.

Anxieties about making a referral and dealing with parents

You may be aware of stories in the national press about children being taken away from their homes in the middle of the night, or about over-zealous social workers taking children into care only for it to emerge that allegations of abuse were unfounded. You may have a good relationship with the parents of the child and be reluctant to discuss you concerns behind their back. You might worry about the consequences of a parent finding out that you have made the referral and even fear for your own safety.

In such situations, remember these points:

- your first responsibility is for the welfare of the child;
- many parents will recognise this and appreciate that you made the referral out of concern;
- it is not your responsibility to make judgements – only to share your concerns;
- if someone else has already expressed concerns about the child to the child protection team your views might be essential additional information in building up a complete picture. But don't wait for or rely on someone else making the referral.

Remember: 'The consequences of reporting suspected abuse and being wrong can be difficult. The consequences of not reporting suspected child abuse could be fatal!' (*Protecting Children*: NSPCC).

It may be helpful if you ensure that parents are aware of your legal responsibilities from the beginning. Include a statement about your child protection procedures in the written information you give to parents when the child first comes to your playsetting, alongside statements on equal opportunities and health and safety. This could read:

- 'Like all childcare workers, we have a responsibility to protect the children in our care, and will share our concerns with Social Services if we fear a child may be suffering abuse or neglect'; Or
- 'The staff are always ready to discuss with you any concerns you have about your child. Our first responsibility is to the children in our care. If we have any concerns about the welfare or safety of a child, we have a duty to share these concerns with the appropriate authority.'

The role of the playsetting in preventing abuse
Support for families

Playsettings can provide a vital role as part of the support which can be offered to families or children under stress. Within the playsetting parents know that their children are well cared for and receive the stimulation and support from peers and adults which may not always be possible at home. Parents whose children are cared for within a playsetting may be gaining time to pursue other work, training, rest or support. This may be essential for their own personal development and self-esteem and necessary for them to be able to continue their parenting role in a way which encourages the healthy development of their children.

Support for children

You may have children in your playsetting who have been abused or who are on the child protection register. The role of the playworker as an important and caring professional in the lives of such children is increasingly recognised.

Play itself can be very therapeutic in enabling a child to come to terms with all kinds of traumatic or distressing experiences, but play therapy is a specialist area and you should not attempt to become an amateur psychologist in setting up or interpreting a child's play for therapeutic purposes without training, help and support.

Protective behaviour for children and playworkers
Relationships based on openness and trust

All children need to learn about human relationships, trust, affection and love. What is appropriate physical touching depends on the nature of the relationship – mother and baby, father and daughter, brother and sister, teacher and pupil, doctor and patient, two toddler friends or adolescent lovers. Children who are abused are made part of relationships which are distorted from those considered acceptable by the rest of society. This damages the trust built up within the relationship of the child and someone more powerful than themselves, and they may find it difficult to establish the ground-rules for future relationships.

In your playsetting you can encourage relationships based on openness, honesty and trust, where keeping secrets is not given positive value and telling tales is not penalised. You can discuss the difference between happy secrets or surprises and secrets which make children uncomfortable or unhappy. You cannot agree to keep what a child says confidential until you know what it is about. Explain that you may need to talk to someone else in order to help.

Personal safety

Help children recognise situations which make them feel uncomfortable and learn that it is alright to say 'No'. This applies to any activity within the play-setting which makes them feel uncomfortable or unhappy but should not prevent you from finding ways to gently encourage the child to participate in activities which are challenging. Peg Flandreau West of Protective Behaviours Inc. links concepts of personal safety with adventurousness:

> We cannot promise ourselves, or make a promise to others, that we can be safe all the time. We can promise that we can act to feel safe all the time. The extension of this attitude is that we can feel safe and empowered even while dealing with physically dangerous situations.
>
> Peg Flandreau West 1989

Through play children can test and challenge their fears and anxieties. They can develop strategies and get support to overcome their anxieties and know when to say 'Yes' as well as when to say 'No'. Play opportunities which give

Relationships of trust

children choices and empower them to make decisions and take the lead can enable them to recognise and express their feelings. With support, they can develop strategies to face challenges, overcome fears, and develop confidence and adventurousness.

If you feel it is important to undertake work with the children which is specifically related to child protection – due to questions from the children or disclosure of abuse, for example – plan it carefully in consultation with other staff. You will need prior training, support and expert advice. You should inform and involve the parents and liaise with local schools to find out what the children are getting there.

Looking at your own behaviour

Male playworkers in particular are often anxious about how their behaviour might be perceived. Physical contact when playing with and caring for children is important. However, publicity has often been given to cases of male careworkers abusing children in childcare settings. Some groups have even questioned whether male workers should be allowed in settings caring for young children. Good recruitment procedures of staff *and volunteers* can include some safeguards against appointing abusers.

Children may demand physical affection beyond what you feel is appropriate. An older child or adolescent may develop a 'crush' on a you, want to hold your hand all the time or to sit on your lap or be kissed. A younger child may want to sit on your lap for a story or on a swing, or constantly involve you in rough and tumble play. It is your responsibility to set clear boundaries in your relationships with the children and to deal with any inappropriate advances assertively, without rejecting the child. Explain to the child clearly what is or is not appropriate and why. For example, you might say: 'I don't want you to sit on my lap, it is not comfortable for me and stops me from talking to the others. Would you like to sit next to me here?'; or 'I'm glad that you like my company and I've enjoyed our game. I am going to work with some other children now but I think Terry might like a game.' You may need support from other team members in this, to back you up, or to ensure that children who need physical contact are not rejected.

Matters of personal hygiene – taking a child with special needs to the toilet, for example, or changing for swimming – may also be an issue. Some daycare and play facilities have a policy that there should always be two workers present in these situations or that the door should always be left open. However, the child's right to privacy must also be considered. You could have a policy of always letting another member of staff know when you need to accompany a child to the toilet and of making sure that this is not always left to the same member of staff. When taking children on trips it is important to have both male and female playworkers or volunteers so that the children can be escorted to public toilets or helped with changing for swimming.

Discuss any concerns you might have about the expectations of others and your own role. The procedures of your playsetting should protect against the possibility of child abuse within the playsetting and protect you from being open to false accusations.

Reference

Barrett et al., 1989 (1994): *Protecting Children – A Guide for Teachers on Child Abuse*. NSPCC.

West, Peg Flandreau 1989: *The Basic Essentials* Protective Behaviours, Inc. (US), Essence Training and Publication PTY Ltd, Australia.

Further reading

Elliot, Michele 1986: *Keeping Safe, a Practical Guide to Talking with Children.* (3rd Edn.) New English Library.

Kids' Clubs Network 1990: *The Role of Playcare Workers in the Protection of Children from Abuse.* Kids' Clubs Network.

Working Together HMSO.

Other publications suitable for children and those working with children of different ages are available from Kidscape and NSPCC.

5 Working with adults

5.1 Teamwork

When a group of people get together to work towards specific aims and objectives they are a team. Teams can be effective or not effective in achieving their aims, depending on how well they work together.

Playworkers usually work as part of a team. Someone once told me that a manager's job is like that of a conductor of an orchestra. A playwork team could be compared to that of a group of musicians making music. The 'music' is the whole of the play service you provide. The musicians (or playworkers) need to agree on what tune they are playing. Each musician needs to know his or her part, although sometimes they produce excellent music by improvisation. If one member plays too loud, the music is distorted. If one member plays out of tune or out of rhythm with the others, the music is spoilt. They must listen to each other. Each musician has particular skills and knows his or her instrument. Some instruments emphasise the rhythm, others the melody. In a larger team such as an orchestra, the conductor helps the musicians work together. The conductor knows the music well, understands what each musician can contribute and what can be achieved out of each instrument even when she or he can't play it. It takes practice to play together well, but the music which can be created by playing together is far greater than the sum of its individual parts.

Whatever your role you need to know how the team works so that you can carry out your job as an effective part of it. This section will help you:

- look at how your team works;
- be clear about roles and responsibilities within the team;
- understand the importance of good communication;
- identify sources of support;
- contribute to meetings and evaluate your own work;
- consider ways of dealing with conflict in the team.

Identifying your team

In this section your team will be the group of adults you work with in order to carry out the day-to-day tasks and overall delivery of the service your playsetting aims to provide. Your team may consist of a manager, a supervisor, three paid playworkers and two permanent volunteers. Alternatively you may have a management committee, including representatives from your main funders or the local authority, or you may operate as a collective with no managers or supervisors.

ACTIVITY 5.1

Draw a plan of all the people within your team. If you work with a management committee you may identify a 'team within a team'; that is, you and any other playworkers may work as a smaller, staff-only team when it comes to day-to-day work with children, planning and organising the play environment and activities. The larger team, including the whole committee, would meet over some issues – policy making, funding, overall planning, marketing, reviewing procedures and dealing with complaints or grievances.

1. Brushbury Park Leisure Centre

Centre
manager

Permanent
staff members

Casual workers

2. Summer Playscheme

Naida   Tessa   Sasha

Chris

17-year-old volunteers

3. Kridlinton Kids' Club

The committee

Jordan   Violet the   Dean   Mary
co-ordinator

Three team structures

URGENTLY NEEDED PLAYWORKER

Do you have the following skills: manager, cook, counsellor, sports and games player, artist, referee, first-aider, craftsperson, singer, dramatist and arbitrator? Above all you need to have imagination, a sense of humour and enjoy being with children.

If you have the above skills and qualities please contact: Kridlinton Kids' Club
Tel

It takes a lot to be a playworker

Shared aims

The main purpose of your team will be to ensure that you provide the best play or playcare possible. Exactly what you aim to provide and how you judge what is 'the best possible' will depend on the type of playsetting you work in. Each member of your team should be clear about what you wish to provide and the aims and objectives of your playsetting. This is looked at in more detail in section 5.3.

Defining roles and responsibilities

Once you have clear aims and objectives you need to know how to meet them. What skills do they demand and how are responsibilities divided?

Procedures

You need clear guidelines or procedures for the action needed in particular situations. Such procedures must include who is responsible for taking the appropriate action and how referral of information to that person should be made. You need to know about:

- dealing with difficult behaviour (see section 2.4)
- admissions procedure (see section 5.2)
- complaints procedures (see section 5.2)
- accident procedure (see section 4.1)
- emergency evacuation procedure (see section 4.1)
- dealing with unwell children (see section 4.1).

Job descriptions

These describe the tasks of the playworkers and other staff members.

> *EXAMPLE* Job description – Playworker
>
> To be responsible to: the Centre Manager and the Management Committee
>
> Duties and responsibilities
>
> 1 To work with other members of the team to provide a safe, stimulating environment for play, including the preparation of a range of interesting, challenging and fun activities appropriate to the ages and stages of development of the children.
> 2 To work towards providing equal opportunities in all aspects of the work and to abide by agreed policies of the playsetting.
> 3 To act in a responsible manner towards children at all times.
> 4 To respond to their needs and interests in planning and entering into play opportunities, with due regard to safety.
> 5 To be responsible with other team members for ensuring that play materials and equipment are properly used, maintained and stored and for reporting any worn or damaged materials to the centre manager.
> 6 To attend weekly meetings as appropriate and contribute to planning, monitoring and evaluation of the work of the playsetting.
> 7 To liaise with parents over the needs and interests of individual children and encourage parents' active involvement and support within the playsetting.
> 8 To work with volunteers and individuals or organisations involved in play- or childcare-related professions as requested by the centre manager.

9 To administer first aid as appropriate.
10 To undertake any other reasonable duties as directed by the centre manager or the management committee.

The range of duties in your job description will depend on your type of play-setting, and the aims and objectives of your setting.

All staff members, whether paid or volunteers, should be clear about what is expected of them.

ACTIVITY 5.2

Have you got a job description? If you have, go to section 2.

1 Write your own job description. List all the tasks you undertake in the course of your work and any others which you might be required to undertake in particular circumstances.

2 Consider each task within your job description in turn. Ask yourself:

● Do I have the skills required to successfully undertake these tasks?

● Are all the tasks reasonable and in line with the overall aims and objectives of this playsetting?
● Do I frequently have to undertake tasks which are not in my job description?

If you lack confidence or are unclear about any of the tasks, discuss this with your supervisor or manager. Should your job description be amended? Do you need training to enable you to fulfil all the requirements of your job description?

Working with a committee

If you work with a management committee you may have a change of management every year. It is therefore particularly important that the responsibilities of the various committee roles (chairperson, treasurer or secretary) as well as those of the playworkers, are written down, clearly understood and regularly reviewed.

ACTIVITY 5.3

How clear are you about who should do what in your playsetting?
Write the name of the person or people within your playsetting responsible for carrying out the following tasks:

● collecting fees (if fees are payable);
● preparing the play environment, including setting up particular activities every day;
● showing visitors or new children around;
● dealing with accidents;
● carrying out safety checks on equipment;
● dealing with complaints from parents;
● ensuring all equipment is safely stored at the end of the session;
● supervising children during the session;

● dealing with a child's unacceptable behaviour;
● banking money;
● preparing a programme of activities;
● dealing with wages;
● attending planning meetings;
● dealing with disclosed, reported or suspected child abuse;
● ensuring children's records are complete and up to date.

If you are unsure about who is responsible for any of these tasks, find out from the rest of the team. You might wish to refer to other sections in this book (for example, sections 4.1 and 4.2 on health and safety and section 4.3 on child protection) to help clarify possible roles and responsibilities.

Working together

A team is one particular type of group. Groups function in different ways in terms of how individual members interact and communicate, how they assume power or influence the group and how they form relationships and create change. This is called 'group dynamics'. Groups function as entities in their own right and individuals' behaviour and ability to perform their tasks well or less well will be affected by the group. A group's efforts will be more than the sum of its parts – a group which works well together will be more effective than if its members work individually.

In a good team:

- there is good communication between its members;
- team members share and understand common aims and co-operate to achieve them;
- there are clearly defined tasks and responsibilities within the team;
- work planned can be achieved within the limitations of time and money;
- work is fairly distributed according to skills and abilities of team members;
- work is shared within the limits of individual roles and responsibilities;
- individual team members' strengths and weaknesses are acknowledged and team members support each other in times of stress;
- team members respect each other's views, beliefs, family background, individual circumstances and needs;
- all members are encouraged to contribute to planning, evaluation and making suggestions for new working methods.

If a team does not work well together it is unlikely to achieve its aims. Unresolved conflict or breakdown in communication can lead to sniping about or between team members, the formation of opposing cliques and subgroups or the development of fantasies or paranoia about other team members. This can lead to stress, dissatisfaction, absenteeism and unreliability by individual team members, and an inability by the group as a whole to focus on providing good play experiences for children.

ACTIVITY 5.4

You can do this activity on your own, but it is better if you do it with the other members of your team and share your views and possible solutions for working better together.

1   Give at least five answers to questions a and b.

   a   What does your team do well? For example, 'We all attend meetings'; 'We share workloads in times of stress'; 'We are clear about what we each have to do'.

   b   What does your team do not so well? For example, 'Some members turn up late'; 'We sometimes complain about colleagues behind their backs'.

You could also give your team marks out of ten for each point on the 'specification for a good team' list above.

2   Think about:

- how you can build on the positive aspects;
- what are the causes of the negative aspects;
- what you can do to improve them.

Communication within the team

Communication takes many forms: verbal or non-verbal (body language, sign language, written), formal or informal. Different patterns of communication can emerge within a group, which will affect the way people work together (see page 148). Many of the principles of good communication raised in

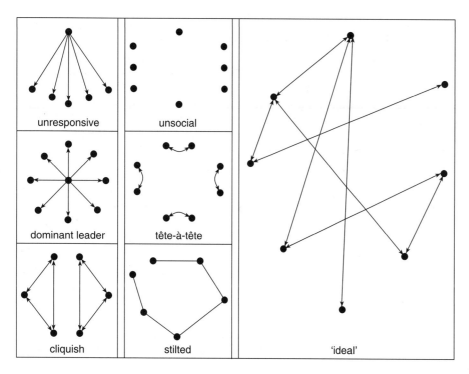

Different patterns of group communication

section 2.3 on forming relationships with children apply equally to working with adults.

Ideally all team members should have plenty of opportunities for face-to-face communication so that ideas can be shared, concerns aired, and a cross-fertilisation of new ideas can take place. This may mean allowing time at the beginning and end of work to talk informally, as well as regular meetings with a set agenda.

So what is meant by 'good' communication'? Think about the following points:

- listening;
- body language;
- expressing yourself clearly;
- giving and receiving feedback and criticism;
- written communication.

Listening

At work, try and listen to what is actually said rather than what you think is said. Check that you have understood what is being said by summarising what you have heard in your own words, and asking if you have got it right. Don't be too quick to agree or disagree. Good listening is a skill which can be developed. It forms a large part of many counselling courses.

Body language

Take note of body language. If you are fidgeting, looking at your watch or slumped in a chair with your eyes half closed you will not appear to be listening, even if you are, and this will not encourage communication. Is the speaker's body language consistent with what they are saying? Inconsistent

---

ACTIVITY 5.5

Try this exercise with a friend or team member.

1 Your colleague spends five minutes (timed) talking about something which is important to him or her. You are the listener and should not interrupt. Listen only to what you are told without interpreting, judging, or putting yourself into the speaker's shoes. If the speaker comes to a stop, you can show that you are attending by keeping eye contact, nodding or smiling. Interjecting words such as 'Yes', 'Mm', 'Right', 'I see' or 'I know' in pauses can also show that you are attending. If necessary ask questions relating to what you have just heard.

2 Once the five minutes is up summarise what you have heard, without adding any of your own thoughts or interpretations. Ask the speaker how close the summary is to what he or she actually said.

3 Listener and speaker then swap roles and repeat the exercise.

Note: Many people do not find it easy to listen to someone even for five minutes without wanting to add their own thoughts or give examples of agreement from their own experience. If this is the case in your role play, discuss possible reasons.

body language could be saying 'Yes that's great news' while having a downcast facial expression and posture; or 'I don't mind staying on to help' while looking at watch, or edging towards the door. Take account of the fact that different cultures give different meaning to body language. Maintaining eye contact can be a sign of insolence rather than attentiveness in some cultures, for example, and nodding does not always signify agreement.

Expressing yourself clearly

Even very good listeners are not mind readers. If you do not say what you think or feel, you cannot blame others for not understanding you. For example, if you have health problems or a domestic crisis which affects your work, you should explain this, without necessarily going into any details. Otherwise your sudden need to leave punctually or to take time off could be interpreted as loss of interest, unreliability or taken as a personal slight. If you frequently find that you are doing things you don't really want or have time to do, think twice before agreeing quite so readily next time. If you are constantly pressured into doing things out of your own feelings of guilt, fear or the need to be popular, you will not do them as well as if they are the things you choose to do. It is better to say 'No' or even 'Maybe' to a request for help, than 'Yes' now and then have to find an excuse as to why you are unable to see it through. Give honest responses to requests. Try using phrases such as 'I choose to' rather than 'I have to'. Say 'I don't want to' rather than 'I ought to'.

> *EXAMPLE* Responding honestly
>
> 'I choose to work late because I achieve better play opportunities within the playsetting if I put in more preparation', not, 'I have to work late because otherwise the work doesn't get done.' (The second part of this sentence may be true but no one can *make* you work above your contracted hours. If you do not choose to stay late, rather than remaining resentful, raise the issue of the need for greater shared responsibility for the workload between the team, or suggest the need for setting more achieveable goals within the time and resources available.)

If you feel you are constantly misunderstood or exploited, or that you cannot express yourself clearly, it may help to attend an assertiveness course.

Giving criticism

There will be times when you feel critical about the words or actions of another team member within the worksetting. This may be:

- minor irritation (you don't like the way C always opens all the windows without asking whether anyone else finds it too warm – in fact you often get cold);
- something more serious relating to a colleague's work practice (you think B is discriminating against an individual child, or that she shouts too often and inappropriately).

In either case it is important that you raise the issue with the person concerned, either informally between yourselves or at a team meeting if extra support or arbitration is needed. Try not to be condemning. Criticise the action or incident, not the person.

Be specific. Say, 'I feel cold with the windows open. Would you check with the other staff members before opening them next time?' instead of 'You're so insensitive, just opening the windows whenever it suits you'. Try to use a moderate tone of voice and stand in a relaxed way. Give the person to whom you are making the criticism the opportunity to respond.

Behaviour which involves discrimination or inappropriate childcare practices should always be challenged. It may also need to be referred to the person responsible for dealing with grievances according to the policies and procedures of your playsetting.

Receiving criticism

If someone criticises you, you must first listen to what they say. Ask for clarification or specific examples – 'What exactly did I say or do to a parent that you felt was rude?'. Decide whether the criticism is wholly or partially valid. Accept any facts, but not personal judgements or interpretations – 'Yes, I did ask Mrs B to come and see me another time, but I do not agree that my manner was rude. Her question was not urgent and I explained that I was very busy and would see her at the end of the session.' Be prepared to accept valid criticism and admit mistakes.

Written communication

A daily logbook or diary can also be useful in keeping team members, particularly part-time workers, informed and in touch.

Meetings

A meeting is an opportunity for you to spend time with other team members away from the day to day work situation, to share ideas and make decisions about your playsetting. Meetings can have different purposes and be formal or informal.

An agenda and a facilitator

All meetings should have a purpose and an agenda – a list of things which need to be discussed. All team members should be able to put items on to the agenda before the meeting. The meeting will need a chairperson or facilitator – someone who:

- ensures the meeting starts and ends on time;
- introduces the meeting;
- makes sure all items on the agenda are discussed;
- gives everyone a chance to talk and ensures that no one dominates the discussion.

A management committee will have a formally appointed chairperson: in other situations it may be the manager or the supervisor. In some cases team members take turns at facilitating meetings. This enables all team members to develop facilitation skills and prevents fixed patterns of communication developing, such as one or two people doing all the talking or always having the final say. However, meetings led by an unskilled or inexperienced facilitator or chairperson can be very frustrating, particularly if there is a lot of business to get through or major decisions must be made when there is no agreement.

> **TO THINK ABOUT**
>
> What meetings do you attend in your playsetting?
>
> Is there more than one kind of meeting, involving different people and with different objectives?

CASE STUDY 5.1: MEETINGS AT KRIDLINTON KIDS' CLUB

Weekly staff and children planning meetings

The co-ordinator (who is also a playworker) and the three other playworkers of Kridlinton Kids' Club meet every Friday. All the workers make notes of things they want to bring up at the next meeting during the week and write them down in the team diary.

Issues discussed every week include:

- review of the week – what went well, what did not?
- planning for the following week.

Other issues which are discussed as they arise may include:

- individual children's achievements or needs;
- gripes or grievances between colleagues;
- sharing information about local community or other events or concerns relevant to playwork or the playsetting.

The first part of the meeting about reviewing and planning involves the children. They participate either personally or by writing down, or asking someone else to write down, suggestions/ideas to go in the box for discussion.

The second part of the meeting, involving discussions about individual children, concerns or grievances, happens after club hours when the children have left.

Bi-monthly team meeting with managers

Once every other month the playworkers meet with the management committee to discuss issues of finance or policy. The co-ordinator meets informally with the chairperson of the committee at other times.

Quarterly staff development and training meetings

Four times a year the playworkers have a staff development day. Half of this day is used for forward planning of play opportunities within the setting. The playworkers share ideas for themes to be explored, aspects of the play environment they would like to develop, training they wish to attend, equipment needed and so on. They sometimes invite other people to join them – for example, a musician who is going to help run some music sessions in the playsetting at the request of a group of children who want to form a band. The second half of the day is spent either looking at how they work as a team – practicing their groupwork and communication skills, or looking at a particular aspect of playwork they want to develop. Topics for these sessions have included equal opportunities (gender, race, disability) within the playsetting, observing children and encouraging different kinds of play – co-operative, solitary, exploratory and so on. Again they sometimes invite someone from outside the team with special skills, knowledge or understanding to lead the session.

These are the regular team meetings at Kridlinton Kids' Club. The co-ordinator also meets individually with the playworkers for supervision sessions and there is an Annual General Meeting and social.

Notes and minutes

All meetings should be recorded in the form of notes or minutes, and one person will do this. Records of the meetings should include the main points discussed, any decisions taken, action which needs to be taken as a result of these decisions, whose responsibility it is to take such action, and when it should be completed by. Enough detail should be recorded to enable the person responsible to be clear about what needs to be done. All team members should receive a copy of the minutes in time to carry out any action specified.

Small working groups

If the team is small – a dozen people or less – meetings can be a useful forum for sharing ideas, planning and evaluating the work. In a larger team, it may be better for these activities to be undertaken in smaller groups, with full meetings being used only to make final decisions, fulfil legal and business requirements and take votes.

Dealing with conflict

All teams have their share of disagreements and conflict. It is healthy for a team to contain different and sometimes opposing views if it leads to a new and better understanding or improved ways of working. This requires good communication between team members. Solving conflict often calls for negotiation – a willingness to compromise or meet halfway, so that both sides feel that their views have been taken into account. Some conflicts cannot be resolved in this way and need to be referred to someone with the authority to decide what course of action should be taken.

Conflicts should not be allowed to drag on, but be dealt with promptly to avoid individuals becoming unduly stressed or debilitated. It is particularly important that conflicts between team members are not allowed to disrupt the work of the playsetting. Disagreements between colleagues which arise during a working session should be dealt with after the session and/or during the next team meeting. Remember to approach conflict by stressing your disagreement with the idea, not the individual who advances it.

Your rights

Your conditions of service should be clearly laid down in your contract of employment. You should know about the hours you will be expected to work, your pay and any notice required if you wish to leave, or notice due to you if you are asked to leave. Your playsetting should have a grievance procedure with clear guidelines on who is the person responsible for dealing with it. Any decisions taken should be in line with legislation and the overall policies of the organisation.

All play facilities which employ staff must comply with employment law in terms of the recruitment and selection, conditions of service and employees' payment and rights. You can get more information about how these laws relate to you and your rights as an employee from your local Department of Employment Office, Citizens' Advice Bureau or neighbourhood advice centre if you have one.

Giving and receiving support

Every member of the team has the right to respect from their colleagues. It is important to recognise the skills, cultural and religious practices and

---

ACTIVITY 5.6

1 On your own answer these questions as honestly as possible.

- what areas of work do you do particularly well?
- what areas of your work need clarification, more attention?
- do you need training in a particular area?
- do you want to develop new skills or particular areas of your work?

2 Share your answers with a trusted colleague and ask for their assessment of your answers. Is that how they would have answered on your behalf?

3 What opportunities do you have to give and receive comments on your strengths and weaknesses and areas for development as a member of the team? What other opportunities would you like?

---

contributions of others and to have your own contributions and needs recognised and understood. It helps if there is a formal way of doing this – such as individual supervision sessions between a manager or supervisor and less senior members of staff – as well as informal praise being given when it is deserved.

As team members it is important that you are able to help each other reach your full potential within the worksetting. Make opportunities to increase your self-confidence and find any other sources of help or support required. Challenge any evidence of discrimination against another team member and give support to the person discriminated against to help them to assert their rights and sustain their confidence and self-esteem.

For the team to be effective you need to communicate and co-operate with a positive attitude, valuing each other's contributions. Individual team members need to support each other within their roles and responsibilities. All team members should have the opportunity to make suggestions for change in working practice and to be part of the process of evaluating and reviewing the work of the team (see section 5.3).

Further reading

Adirondack, S. M. 1989: *Just About Managing*. London Voluntary Service Council. A practical booklet aimed at voluntary organisations, including sections on teamwork, stress and conflict.

Bennet R. 1994: *Organisational Behaviour*. M&E Business Handbook, Longman. (A more theoretical approach to organisations and group dynamics.)

Gawlinski, G. and Graessle, L. 1988: *Planning Together – The art of effective teamwork*. National Council for Voluntary Organisations. (A workbook to help team building.)

Henderson, Penny and Foster, G. 1991: *Groupwork – The Effective Trainer* a series by National Extension College Trust. A pack which includes a booklet for trainers and information for students.

Scottish Council for Voluntary Organisations. *Committees Training Workpack*. (For information about roles and responsibilities within committees.)

Walmsley, Claire 1991: *Assertiveness – the right to be you*. BBC.

A useful reference for those working with volunteers in a playsetting is:

Buck, Donne 1987: *Involving Volunteers in Children's Play*. The Volunteer Centre (UK) and Play Board.

5.2 Working with parents and carers

In recent years teachers, health workers and social workers, daycare and play-care workers have moved increasingly towards 'shared care'. This means understanding and respecting that the parents are the main carers of their children. This section looks at what this can mean in your playsetting: how parents can be involved and the importance of good communication.

What do we mean by parent?

Throughout this section, where the word 'parents' is used it is taken to mean the adult or adults who has or have the main responsibility for the child at home. In some cases I have used parent or carer to emphasise this point, but in other cases this became impossibly clumsy. The person or persons who take the parenting role will not necessarily be the biological parents. Children may live with a lone parent, a grandparent or other relative, gay or lesbian parents, adoptive parents, step-parents, a foster parent or social workers in a children's home.

Children first

It is the children who are the focus of playwork, and the users of the play-setting. Section 2.3 looked at the importance of good communication with children, and there are references and activities about involving children throughout this book. Meeting their needs, and holding their interests at heart should be your priority.

Parents also have an interest in ensuring that the playsetting meets the needs of their children and will usually have the final say in whether their child attends or stays. The parents give permission and often pay the fees where fees are payable. They can also provide your strongest support. While you, as playworker, have much to contribute to the well-being of the children in your care, you need to communicate with parents, respect their rights, and work in partnership with them.

Open access and older children

If your playsetting is an open-access facility, or caters only for older children, it may be that you rarely, if ever, see the parents of the children. Communication with the parents will then be indirect through the children, but consent forms for trips and so on will still need the signature of a parent. Information about the setting, its policies and practice should be made available whenever and however possible – on notice-boards (within the playsetting and in the wider community), in leaflets for children to take home and through good publicity.

Equal opportunities

Children live in different types of families. They may have one parent, absent parents, a gay parent, a disabled parent. They may live in a small family unit of just one adult and one child, a nuclear family of mother, father and children, or an extended family of relations and inlaws. Many children have more than one home if their parents are separated. Parents have different religious beliefs, cultural backgrounds, customs or lifestyles. It is important for the children that their own and other families' values are respected within the playsetting. As far as possible all parents should have the same opportunities for communicating with you and becoming involved. This may mean that you need to get written information translated into another language, arrange for an interpreter for a consultation meeting or, in the case of a housebound parent, do a home visit or send a child home with a diary to share – a notebook or scrapbook which the child takes between home and playsetting in which she can record (draw, stick, write) things which she wants to remember to tell or discuss with her parent or her playworkers.

'This is my sister Nafeesa who looks after me' (Loren, aged 8)

ACTIVITY 5.7

Find out in your playsetting:

- how parents get information about the setting;
- how they can express their views on what goes on there;
- ways in which the parents can alter what goes on in the playsetting;
- what opportunities there are for a parent to discuss a child's progress in the playsetting and be involved in planning future play opportunities.

How can parents be involved?
Legislation

The Children Act 1989 (Guidance and Regulations Vol. 2) stresses the importance of involving parents and states:

> Providers should make sure that there are sufficient opportunities for parents and the people who work with the child to discuss his progress and plan for future activities (para 6.12).
>
> Certain parental rights should be considered as part of a definition of quality of care because this enables parents to influence the nature of their children's care environments. To this end the following opportunities for parents should be considered:
>
> - to acquire information about the care environment
> - to express their view on the care environment
> - to alter the care environment of their child
> - to choose between alternative childcare environments. (para 6.29).

Settling a child into the playsetting

Parents have known their children a lot longer than you have. Parents know their child's cultural, medical and social history, her likes and dislikes and past experiences, good and bad. If they are able to share some of this knowledge with you it can help you to get to know the child more quickly, smooth the settling in time and avoid the pitfalls which can come from making incorrect assumptions.

Communicating with parents from the beginning

Communicate with parents right from the start and let them know how and when they can communicate with you at work. When a new child visits the playsetting for the first time a friendly welcome to the parents as well as the child makes a good start. It is also important that you provide a welcoming atmosphere at the start of each session. Parents may drop in unexpectedly to get information or view the playsetting when you do not have the time to show them around. In this situation you could invite them to look around by themselves and ask questions later, refer them to someone who can show them around or arrange an alternative time for them to visit. Be polite and have some written information for them to take away.

Make time for communication with parents.

Communication with parents is equally important after the child has settled and throughout the time he remains in your playsetting. Parents need to know when you can discuss any issues or concerns which require more than a minute or two. Communication is important both ways. Only you and your colleagues know how the child is getting on within the playsetting as seen from an adult point of view, and you may spend more time with him during his waking hours than the parent does.

Not all parents will ask about how their child is getting on, even if they do have questions, because they recognise that you are busy and have many children in your care. They may see you as a professional (however friendly) and believe they do not have the right to take up your time.

Sharing the care

Good communication can help you to plan better for individual needs and circumstances, and to share any achievements or concerns.

If you keep records of the children's development or activities, make time to share your observations with the parents of the child concerned. Draw the parents attention to particular achievements – 'Have you seen Sunita's puppet? It took her three days to make it. The children want to use it in a puppet show next week'; or 'Sam braved the aerial swing today – it took a lot of courage';

ACTIVITY 5.8

1 Each playsetting is different. Make sure you know who has responsibility in your playsetting for welcoming visitors and showing people around, and when and how this takes place.

2 Make a list of the questions you think a parent might ask when visiting a playsetting with a view to enrolling their child. What answers would you give?

TO THINK ABOUT

When are you available to talk to parents about issues which take more than a minute or two? How do parents know when you are available?

ACTIVITY 5.9

Consider the following situations.

1 Liam is six and unhappy. When asked what is wrong he says that his cat got run over.

2 Imran and Rashida are 10 and 11. They have taken a great interest in preparing snacks and cooking in the playsetting. Over several weeks they have also involved the younger children in setting up 'cafés' in which to serve their food.

3 In your playsetting you overhear three or four children aged 13 and 14 talking about joyriding and how their mates want them to join in driving stolen cars.

4 Rosa and Paul are 15. They will soon be too old to come to the playsetting. Recently they have inspired numerous artistic projects within your setting, including airbrushing T-shirts and elaborate face painting with younger children. They are looking for a work experience placement from school.

Now ask yourself:

- As the playworker in each of the situations, what, if anything, would you say to the children's parents? Ask a colleague to take the part of the parent, and practise what you might say.
- What activities would you plan within the playsetting to meet these children's needs?

ACTIVITY 5.10

Make a list of the ways in which you involve parents in your place of work.

List three new ways which you might like to introduce.

or 'Ashley has been particularly helpful in looking after the two new children this week – showing them where things are and involving them in the games'.

The ways in which you involve parents can be very simple, like having a suggestions box in the entrance to your playsetting (and acting on the suggestions – which can be less straight forward). You might have an open diary or logbook (see section 3.4). Make sure it is in a place which is accessible for parents to look at regularly and perhaps add their own comments.

Parents as managers

If you work in a voluntary or community group it is more likely that parents of the children make up most of the management committee and have a major influence on how it is run. Some parents will need help and encouragement to feel confident about taking on management tasks.

If a parent is unwilling or unable to sit on the management committee she may be happy to be part of a small working group to look at a particular aspect of the playsetting which needs development such as fundraising or building new play structures.

Publicising play

Parents who see the benefits to their own children of the play opportunities provided in your setting can give the best word-of-mouth publicity. Such parents may also become involved in campaigning for and supporting play facilities and the rights of children within the local community.

Sharing practical skills

Many parents will have particular skills which they may be willing to share. They may work in healthcare and be able to give a talk or share information with the children on a health-related issue. Perhaps they have practical skills to offer – carpentry, sewing dressing up clothes, art, craft, sport or cookery – or they may have time to help out. Ask for contributions (written, artistic or simply informative) for a newsletter. Parents with computers or access to photocopying or printing facilities may help you to produce it.

Social events

Social events can be a good way to enable parents to get to know you, other staff, other children and their parents. Many playsettings invite parents to barbeques, festival celebrations or social evenings or to accompany them on trips or camps.

Providing information to parents

Information can be passed from you to parents in many forms:

- verbally through the children;
- through notes, letters or newsletters;
- in a prospectus or information sheet;
- by notices on noticeboard;
- more formally during meetings and consultations;
- informally if and when the parent brings or collects the child.

All these are useful opportunities for sharing different kinds of information. Choose the method of communication which seems most suitable for the information you wish to share, the age of the children and your type of play-setting (see Activity 5.11).

You might, for example, decide you could redesign the noticeboard with photographs of staff, programme of activities, important notices and displays of children's work. Alternatively you could involve your colleagues in changing the organisation of the start and end of the session to allow you more time for informal chat with parents.

Remember to consider the needs of parents who do not speak fluent English. You might be able to enlist the help of a bilingual member of the family to interpret, translate some of your written material for wider circulation, or learn key words yourself.

Written information

Sometimes it is important that information is written down. This is the case for all policies and procedures and for information which might need to be regularly referred to by staff, management and parents.

Written information enables parents or carers to:

- have accurate information about the group;
- understand the reasons why the setting operates in the way it does;
- decide whether your setting is likely to be suitable for their child;
- become more involved and share responsibility for the care and the quality of play experience for their child.

Written information for parents helps ensure that management and staff:

- give the same information to all parents;
- have decided what policies are needed for the group and the kind of service they wish to provide;
- know the policies of the group and give accurate information to others;
- take the same line in a given situation.

ACTIVITY 5.11

1 List how your place of work shares information with parents?

2 Discuss with a colleague which of the above methods of communication are best for which kinds of information.

3 Choose one from the above list which you and your colleague think has room for improvement in your playsetting and decide how to improve it.

> **CASE STUDY 5.2: WHAT IS THE PLAYSETTINGS ADMISSIONS POLICY?**
>
> Two mothers come to the playsetting, each wanting to put her child's name on the waiting-list. There is only one place likely to become available during the following six months. The first mother says that her child should have the place because he is older than the other child. Also, they have no garden at home. The second mother says her child should have priority because she is working and needs the childcare.

In Case study 5.2 a worker from a playsetting which has a clear policy about admissions will know on what basis places are awarded and how needs are prioritised. She will know what answer to give. If her playsetting has no admissions policy, the worker responsible for the waiting list will carry sole responsibility for such decisions. She will be open to accusations of favouritism, bias and discrimination, whatever decision she takes.

EXAMPLE Admissions policy

The aim of our playsetting is to provide play opportunities for local children and childcare for working parents.

- Our playsetting takes children between the ages of 5 and 12 in the geographical area of (state catchment area if there is one).
- Places are awarded to children on the waiting-list in order of date of birth.
- To book a place, please contact the waiting-list organiser.
- The waiting-list organiser is: (name of person responsible who may also be a playworker, a management committee member, secretary).
- she can be contacted: (address, telephone number when available in playsetting).
- Priority will be given to siblings of children who attend or have already attended the scheme and children or families with other circumstances which give rise to a referral from another agency (health, education, social services or voluntary support group). (Such referrals must be consistent with the aims of the setting.)
- A number of places are reserved for children in these categories (five for children of parents working for a local employer who has purchased places; three for emergency referrals).
- If your child has special needs, but you do not have contact with a referring agency, please contact the waiting-list organiser who will be able to advise you. (If a child may be entitled to a priority subsidised place, the waiting-list organiser should know the procedure and who to contact in social services if a referral is needed.)
- All questions relating to booking places or the waiting-list should be addressed to the waiting-list organiser, or in writing to: (name and contact address of the chairperson or manager).

This example will not be appropriate for all playsettings. Open access facilities, for example, have particular requirements for their policies and procedures.

If you work in such a playsetting you are likely to have less contact with the parents of the children who attend. Regular children may arrive with a group of new friends one day. You will need to know what to do when more children attend than has been expected: how will you ensure safe and adequate supervision, space, materials and equipment?

Conditions of attendance

Conditions of attendance may form part of an admissions policy. They will include information about any circumstances in which a child could lose his or her place. If fees are payable, information should be be given on any assisted, supported or sponsored places available, concessions or discounts for siblings. Conditions of attendance may include payment in advance, period of notice required on leaving, and arrangements for holidays and sickness. If you work in an open access playsetting you will need to inform children and their parents as appropriate (in information leaflets, on consent forms, or on notice-boards) that it is not a childcare facility, and that children are free to leave when they wish. If the playsetting becomes dangerously full, it may be necessary to refuse admission to more children on a particular day.

All parents and carers should know about the policies of your playsetting

Initial information given to parents about the playsetting should contain statements which summarise the policies. Parents and carers should know how they can obtain copies.

EXAMPLE Statement about equal opportunities policy

(Name of your playsetting) is committed to equality of opportunity and is opposed to any direct and indirect discrimination against its staff, the children attending, their parents, carers or others working with or coming into contact with our organisation.

We are actively working towards ensuring that our activities, recruitment and employment policies give equal access and opportunity to all regardless of gender, race, colour, age, marital status, disability, religion, social class, sexuality, employment status, ethnic or national origin or any other unjustifiable criteria.

Other chapters contain example statements relating to other areas of policy (sections 4.1 and 4.2 health and safety, section 2.4 on behaviour, section 4.3 on child protection).

Section 5.3 looks in more detail at forming and reviewing policies.

Give parents and children clearly presented information to take away with them

---

ACTIVITY 5.12

Draft an initial information sheet or booklet for new parents, to include:

- aims of group – who it serves, what is on offer – activities, care, age of children, where it runs;
- opening hours;
- Fees or cost, if any;
- admissions – how to book a place or get on the waiting-list if there is one;
- staffing and management: who runs the group, staff–child ratios;
- policies and procedures – how can parents find out what approach the group has on equal opportunities, children with special needs, health and safety, behaviour limits set and methods of discipline, child protection issues;

Provide a brief statement on each of these areas (see Example on p. 160) and information about where the fuller policies are held.

What other information do you wish to include?

If you already have an information sheet or booklet, think of improvements which could be made – perhaps including some of the suggestions made above?

Sharing concerns

Parents have the right to expect confidentiality from professionals working with their children. This means that you should not gossip with colleagues or other parents about the private lives of children or their parents. You do have a responsibility, however, to share any concerns about the welfare of the children in your care with other professionals in some circumstances (see section 4.3 on child protection), and should be wary of promising not to tell anyone, either to a child or a parent.

Dealing with complaints

A clear complaints procedure helps define responsibilities and prevents you being drawn into discussions about matters you are not in a position to deal with. Be clear about what kinds of complaints you can deal with yourself and when to pass complaints or concerns on to a senior colleague.

A parent making a complaint needs to know that he or she will be listened to, but should be politely referred to the person who is responsible for dealing with it. An upset parent may need the space and time to calm down and be reassured that their complaint will be taken seriously. This does not mean that the playworker should make false promises or agree to any action beyond the procedures of the setting.

ACTIVITY 5.13

1 Consider the following situations:

- Mr Price is upset that his daughter ripped her coat while playing outside yesterday. He thinks the play-setting should pay for a new one.
- Mrs Ho says her son has been bullied by an older boy. She says if you don't sort it out she will.
- Miss Bellini wants to know why she has to pay for her daughter to attend the playsetting when the Greens get free places. She knows they have got loads of money. 'Have you seen the car they bought last week?' she says.
- Mr Douglas has heard that one of your colleagues is gay. He doesn't think 'such people' should be allowed to work with children.

How would you deal with each situation immediately? How would the complaint be followed up?

2 Discuss with a colleague to check that you are in agreement about appropriate action and who has the responsibility for following the complaint through.

3 Role-play the situation with a colleague to develop your confidence in dealing with situations such as these.

The points about communication made in sections 2.3 and 5.1 about listening, expressing yourself clearly and paying attention to body language and tone of voice apply here too.

It is important for staff, management and children that parents are given accurate and consistent information at all times. Parents and playworkers are partners in the care of the children, and both have the welfare and well-being of the children as their common starting point.

Reference

Her Majesty's Stationery Office 1991: *The Children Act 1989, Guidance and Regulations*, Vol. 2. HMSO

Further reading

Petrie, Pat 1989: *Communicating with Children and Adults*. Edward Arnold.
Siraj-Blatchford, Iram 1994: *The Early Years – Laying the Foundations for Racial Equality*, Trentham Books (Chapter 5 on involving parents).
National Children's Bureau have produced several Partnership Papers on different aspects of professionals and parents working together.

5.3 Promoting play and getting support

CASE STUDY 5.3: VISITORS TO THE PLAYSETTING

Hilltop Leisure Centre provides afterschool and holiday play and care for children aged 5–14. Five people are visiting today:

1   Ms Sheehy, who is looking for childcare for her ten-year-old son.
2   Carl Sheehy, who is visiting with his mother.
3   Mrs Aktar, teacher from the local school, who wants to know more about the centre, which several of the children from her class attend. She also wants to find out if an Asian girls' youth group which she runs after school twice a week can use any of the leisure facilities.
4. Mr Kirk, a social worker, wants to find day-time respite care for a child whose family is under stress.
5   Ms Broom, a local councillor, wants to see how the grant from the council is being spent.

In case study 5.3 what will each of the visitors be looking for? What information will they need? What might each of these people have to offer the playsetting? As the playworker, what might you want to ask them?

Your playsetting does not exist in isolation. The children who come to your setting have families, homes and schools and live in a community. Your playsetting is part of a network of other facilities catering for children and their families. The people or organisations paying for the service will want to know that they are getting value for money – whether you charge fees or are funded by grants. Your playsetting will need to earn its place as a well-used resource which is recognised as valuable both by those who use it and by others who may not fully understand the value of play. They may see playsettings as a low priority compared with other services.

You should be clear about your aims and objectives within your play-setting and translate them into policies which are regularly monitored and evaluated. You need to consult and work with others to ensure that your play-setting continues to meet the needs of the children it is intended to serve. If you successfully promote your playsetting and the values of playwork you will be able to draw on many sources of support in your work with individual children and for playwork as a whole.

What can we offer you – what can you offer us?

In Case study 5.3 Ms Sheehy and Carl will want to know whether the play opportunities of Hilltop Leisure Centre will interest Carl and meet his needs. How welcoming and friendly is the centre? Carl wants to know whether any other children he knows go there and how strict the rules are. Ms Sheehy wants to know whether the opening hours will fit in with her work. She wants to know that Carl will be safe and happy. Are the staff qualified? Is the centre registered with the local authority? Can she afford the fees? Are there concessions for people on low income or lone parents?

Carl and Ms Sheehy are potential customers. They are the people which the leisure centre aims to serve. Without them the leisure centre would not exist.

Mrs Aktar wants to share some concerns she has about a girl in her class who uses the centre, and whose behaviour has recently become withdrawn. How does she behave in the centre? Have the playworkers noticed any changes? Mrs Aktar wants such communication to continue between the school and the centre. Mrs Aktar wants to see the facilities and to find out who can use them. Do they have an equal opportunities policy? Are the facilities used by the Asian community?

Mrs Aktar can provide playworkers with information and understanding of the some of the children who attend (those who are in her class). She might also help to create closer links with the Asian community and suggest changes or improvements to the services offered which would attract more Asian customers.

Mr Kirk wants to know what kind of play opportunities are on offer. Will they meet the needs of his client? What approach is taken by the playworkers? Are they qualified? Are there any places free? If not, are there any priority places for children in need? How much will it cost?

Representing social services, Mr Kirk is a potential customer. He may be able to set up a service contract with the centre which pays for two priority places for use by children referred by social services at all times. He may know about grants or opportunities for staff training (in child protection issues for example). He may be able to help the centre meet its commitment to equal opportunities with advice or by referring further children in need.

As a councillor, Ms Broom wants to know that the centre is meeting its obligations under the terms of the large grant and service agreement with the local authority. How many children attend? Do they fully represent the local community? Is work carried out in accordance with the local authority's health and safety and equal opportunities policies?

If she likes what she sees, Ms Broom can be a very important voice of support – for the leisure centre and for the value of play to the local community – when decisions are made about budgets, grant and cuts. She can put the centre in touch with council officers and others who can support and promote their work and activities. She wants to see last year's accounts and evaluation report. Do the play and care services offered by the leisure centre warrant the money, in the light of resources needed by other services

– for building and for roads, for education, for the sick, the elderly and the unemployed?

All the visitors to Hilltop Leisure Centre want to know about the general approach of the staff and management to their work. Is it a safe place to be? Is it an enjoyable place to be? Who does it aim to serve?

These are the sort of people who will visit your setting. Their questions are those which may be asked by your visitors.

Staff at your playsetting will able to give full and clear answers if you have the following:

- clear aims, shared objectives and policies which are regularly reviewed;
- have a simple information booklet containing essential information for potential customers;
- written policies and evaluation reports available on request.

What are your aims?

Your playsetting came into being because of a need or a demand. It may have been a group of parents who needed childcare, or a headteacher concerned about children going home from school to an empty house, who started things moving. It may have been a a group of representatives from a local community, including parents, who were concerned about the lack of safe spaces for children to play in their area. Perhaps your playsetting was set up by an organisation as a service for its employees and their families, a local authority offering play as part of its recreational services or a leisure company wanting to sell out-of-school care and/or play activities as part of a business.

The reasons behind why it was set up will form the basis of the aims of the setting. As more people become involved – children, staff, parents – it is important that everyone is aware of the aims and shares them, so that you can work together to meet them.

Once a common aim has been agreed, those involved must consider exactly what they are going to provide to meet it – for example, art and craft, games, food, opportunities for unstructured play and experienced workers. You should develop a shared approach to achieving objectives within resources available and current legislation. This will form the basis of the policies of your playsetting.

Aiming for play

ACTIVITY 5.14

Have you got written aims or a statement of purpose for your setting? Do you think all members of your team share the same aims?

If you do not, or if you feel that the current statement of purpose or written aims do not accurately reflect the service you are providing, try the following activity either in a group with all team members or with just one other worker.

1 Each person takes 15–20 minutes to write down one to two sentences that in their view describe the reason for the team's existence. For example: 'providing high quality play opportunities for local children out of school hours'; 'providing childcare for working parents'; 'promoting equal opportunities in play for school-aged children'.

2 One person acts as facilitator and lists everybody's sentences on a flip-chart, and encourages team members to look at:

- Areas of agreement, for example: 'We all agree we should provide quality play opportunities for children out of school hours, and that we want to promote equal opportunities.'
- Areas of apparent disagreement. For example: 'We want to promote equal opportunities, but how can we do this if we are providing a childcare service to working parents?'; 'We shouldn't use the words "high quality" unless we can agree on what we mean by it.'

3 Through discussion try to arrive at a single statement with which everyone can agree. For example: 'We aim to offer play opportunities which are fun and encourage exploration, learning new skills and healthy all-round development, within a safe and caring environment, to local children between the ages of 5 and 15, regardless of the individual circumstances or family background of the child.'

Reflect on the common statement of purpose for several days before coming together to consider whether it still seems acceptable and appropriate to each person involved.

Policies

What policies are needed?

Most playsettings will require the following policies:

- admission and attendance;
- health and safety;
- equal opportunities;
- positive behaviour.

These policies will be interrelated. The equal opportunities policy will have a direct bearing on the admissions policy.

> *EXAMPLE* Admissions policy – equal opportunities
>
> When the playsetting is full, places will be allocated by computerised random selection from the waiting-list of children who are old enough to attend. We strive to ensure that the admissions policy does not discriminate against individual children or groups on any grounds, and that it enables each child to have an equal opportunity to attend.

The behaviour policy will relate to health and safety:

> *EXAMPLE* Behaviour policy – health and safety
>
> We have a rule that the children cannot access fire lighting equipment or other hazardous materials without permission and supervision from staff.

The behaviour policy will also relate to the equal opportunities policy (see section 2.4 for more on behaviour).

ACTIVITY 5.15

What policies do you have in your playsetting? Do they include those mentioned on page 165? If the answer is 'Yes' complete sections (1) and (3). If the answer is 'No' complete sections (1) and (2).

1 Say why policies for the playsetting are important for playworkers.

Give two examples of a situation in which you might need to refer to them.

2 If you do not have policies in your setting, or if you think there are some missing, ask for it to be put on the agenda for discussion at the next team meeting, or discuss it with a senior member of staff.

With the agreement of your colleagues and managers, contact the Kids' Clubs Network, another playsetting or a play association if you have one in your area. Ask for example or model policies to bring to your team as a starting point in developing policies for your playsetting.

3 If you have policies in your playsetting:
- Have you seen them?
- Do you understand them?
- Do they relate to what happens in your playsetting everyday?
- Are the parents and carers aware of the policies?
- Do they know how to get copies?
- When and how are policies reviewed and amended?

If you cannot answer these questions, or if you are unclear about any of the issues, discuss them with a senior staff member or ask for the subject to be put on the agenda for the next team meeting.

EXAMPLE

No child should feel intimidated, or be subjected to discrimination by the behaviour of adults or children within the playsetting: intimidating, racist or sexist language and behaviour will be not be accepted.

How are policies formed?

Each playsetting needs to form its own policies to ensure that they are meaningful to those who work within it. It is the responsibility of the management of the setting to form the policies and ensure that they are implemented.

Policies aim to create and support good quality play opportunities

Your involvement

In many cases the management will wish to involve the playwork staff in forming, reviewing and revising policies. Make sure that you know and understand the policies and what they mean in terms of daily practice. Inform the management if a policy is not clear, or becomes irrelevant or unworkable and needs to be amended.

Forming and reviewing policies takes time. It would be impracticable for everybody concerned to be involved at every stage. You might be asked to be part of a working group of representatives – management members, playworkers, parents and older children – to draw up a draft document. This draft can then be circulated for comments from wider management, older children or staff and parents, and discussed at a team meeting.

Involving children

Older children should be able to play an active part in deciding the policies of the setting through being invited to join discussions, contribute ideas, or through representation on a small working group. Younger children can also be involved in discussions about equal opportunities (what is fair or unfair?) and acceptable and unacceptable behaviour and sanctions within the play-setting (see section 2.4).

Policies can go beyond the law

Policies must be set within the framework of the law, but the law sets out minimum requirements. Many policies will go beyond legal requirements to ensure that the playsetting provides not just lawful and adequate play and care, but good-quality or excellent play and care.

> *EXAMPLE* A policy beyond legal requirements
>
> The law requires that the playsetting does not discriminate against individuals or groups on the grounds of race, colour, nationality or ethnic origin. The policy of the playsetting may go further by:
>
> - requiring all staff to have attended training in equal opportunities;
> - setting up a system for monitoring that the children who actually attend the playsetting are representative of the local area or from the families the playsetting is intended to serve and, if this is not the case, having an admissions policy which gives priority to children from under-represented groups.
> - developing anti-discriminatory childcare practices (see section 1.2).

Using model policies

While it is important for each playsetting to have policies which are relevant to its circumstances, it is not necessary to write them from scratch. Several national organisations have produced good example policies which can be used as a starting-point. Some may need very little amending to meet your needs although it is not a good idea to adopt a policy without considering the issues as a team. The process of asking 'How does each policy affect our work within our playsetting?' is essential in coming to shared understanding of what your policies mean in practice. Kids' Clubs Network, the Pre-school Learning Alliance and the National Council for Voluntary Organisations can provide model policies – see Appendix 2: Useful contacts.

You may also be able to get help from your local authority recreation department, social services or education department or your local play association if you have one. If yours is a relatively new setting you may be able to get help and advice from a more established playsetting in your area, which is more advanced in establishing its policies.

Monitoring and reviewing aims and policies

Some things which you, your co-workers or management may take for granted may not actually be happening in practice. The management of your playsetting need to know that what actually happens is the same as what the policies say should happen. They must also make sure that the playsetting meets the needs it was intended to serve, or that it changes or expands to meet new needs. For this they should have a system for monitoring and review.

Your involvement

You may be involved in various ways such as:

- asking parents and carers to fill in questionnaires;
- contributing to discussions at team meetings;
- alerting managers to matters which you observe in your work and believe to be contrary to the playsetting's policies, such as a safety hazard, a problem with numbers and new admissions, or an example of discriminatory practice.
- giving verbal or written reports.

Monitoring who uses the playsetting

If you ask parents and carers to fill in forms which involve monitoring of ethnicity, gender or other criteria of the user group, such information should be sensitively handled. Always explain why you need information. Confidentiality must be guaranteed, and the forms should be detached and stored away from any other information which could identify those who completed them. Information about the children who use your playsetting, which has been collected in this way, can be compared with publicly available information about the population of particular areas (available from your local authority or

TO THINK ABOUT

Has the service you provide changed or expanded? Are you meeting the needs your playsetting was intended to serve? Have you identified new needs?

How do you know that the policies of the playsetting are being put into practice?

There are often many practical considerations in putting policy into practice

ACTIVITY 5.16

Read the following case studies:

Case study A
A play setting is situated in a geographical area with a population of 20 per cent Asian families. No Asian children attend the setting. There is an equal opportunities policy in place.

Case study B
A child with complex learning and behavioural difficulties is refused a place at a playsetting on the grounds that they do not have the staff to cope. The written information about the playsetting includes a statement that they aim to cater for children with special needs

Case study C
The staff agree with the policy of the playsetting that they value and respect other cultures, but the books on the bookshelves and pictures on the wall contain stories and images of only white children and their families in a European context, apart from one poster of a famous black athlete.

Answer the following questions in respect of each case study:

- How might this gap between policy and practice have occurred?
- What action would you take to ensure that the playsetting puts its policies into practice?

library). If there is an imbalance there are positive steps which can be taken. In a situation such as that in (Activity 5.16, Case study A), you could:

- ask why this situation could have occurred;
- find out how the information about the playsetting can be translated into other languages;
- talk to representatives and spokespeople of the local Asian community (community worker, representative from local temple or mosque?);
- consider whether the opening times or activities should be varied, expanded or changed;
- ask what other reasons there might be.

Perhaps the club is not perceived as catering for the Asian members of the community, that the activities are aimed at the current user group and parents or carers and children would not feel comfortable. If there are no Asian workers or managers and the images and resources of the setting do not reflect different cultures positively, this might also be a barrier. (See Kapasi, 1992.)

In Case study B of Activity 5.16 it is possible that staff and management are unaware of local sources of support and financial assistance, or the possibility of additional staff to support the integration of a child with special needs. Steps should be taken to acquire this knowledge. Contact your local authority, local support groups or national organisations (see Appendix 2). Training may be needed to give existing staff the skills and confidence to provide for the child with special needs, or contact could be made with organisations who train and support volunteers who might help.

Staff development and training

Policies and their implementation can also be monitored through support and supervision for staff. Playworkers should make time to look at broader issues of practice:

- How are resources and materials selected to ensure that they are interesting, informative, enjoyable and reflect the multicultural world in which we live?
- How can stereotyping be avoided – as is not the case in in Case study C Activity 5.16? (See sections 1.2, 2.3, 3.1 and 3.2.)

Too often every meeting is taken up with business or day-to-day planning or organisational issues. A regular staff development meeting or training session, with a prepared programme for looking at a particular area of policy and how it relates to practice – health and safety, equal opportunities, child protection – will ensure that staff continue to look at how the policies of the setting relate to their practice within it (see section 5.1).

External monitoring

Monitoring can take many forms. If your playsetting is registered under the Children Act 1989 your registration and inspection officer will want to see that your policies are within the framework of the law and will also look for evidence of how they are put into practice. If you are funded by a local authority, council officers will need to monitor that you are providing the service intended and that the authority's money is properly spent. They may ask for questionnaires to be completed and reports submitted and may examine your accounts.

Reports

You may be asked to give reports on different aspects of your work. Depending on the kind of playsetting you work in and your level of responsibility this could range from reporting to your team members on a conference or training event you have attended to giving a verbal or short written report to your management committee on the summer playscheme. You might also be responsible for giving a written annual report to your local authority department on how your playsetting has met its aims over the previous year.

Whatever kind of report you have to give there are four main things to remember:

1   What is the purpose of the report?
2   Who is it for?
3   What are the main points you should make?
4   What are your conclusions or recommendations – that is, what should happen as a result of your report?

If you are giving a verbal report, make notes under each of these headings. A more formal written report should be laid out under the following headings:

- Title of report;
- Contents list (for a long report with appendices);
- Introduction (aims and objectives or purpose and scope of report);
- Main body of report (current situation, what happened, your research advantages, disadvantages);
- Conclusions and recommendations (summarise main points and give an opinion).

A written report should have your name, job title and organisation and the date – day, month and year. If you have statistics, results of questionnaires or additional relevant information you should attach them as numbered appendices. Keep the body of your report to the point.

Promoting your playsetting

Visitors

It may not always be convenient to show visitors around and give them information, as it may interfere with your work with the children. Visitors must be welcomed, however, treated politely, and their enquiries dealt with. There are several ways you can minimise the disruption and increase the comfort of the visitor. If the visitor makes an appointment:

- decide as a team which are the best times to have visitors, when someone can be free to show them around and answer questions.

If a visitor drops in:

- discuss as a team how to handle drop-in visits at inconvenient times;
- ask the visitor who they wish to see, and what is the purpose of their visit.
- arrange a comfortable area where visitors can be asked to wait until someone is free to speak to them;
- have some written information available, or a scrapbook of photographs or children's artwork for the visitor to look at while waiting;
- explain to the visitor that you are busy. Ask if he would like to wait until you are free – say approximately how long – or arrange to come back another time.

Whether or not the visitor has an appointment:

- Make sure visitors know how to find you by placing a simple map on any general information sheet or publicity material. Put signposts and welcome posters on the premises.
- If appropriate, involve one or more of the children in showing the visitor some aspects of the playsetting ('Rowena, would you like to show Miss X your green dragon, while I just finish reading this story?').
- Display publicity material, newsletter, information sheets on a noticeboard.

Publicity

How to get good publicity is a specialist area in itself. The identity of the playsetting can be helped by having a catchy name which relates to what the playsetting is about and a good logo for use on posters, newsletters, notices and letter headings. You should also consider:

Your internal noticeboard. This is a very useful way of sharing information and presenting what you do. Make sure your notice-board is located where people will pass by and read it – daily, if possible. Don't let it become a sad affair with out-of-date information, tatty notices and faded posters or pictures.

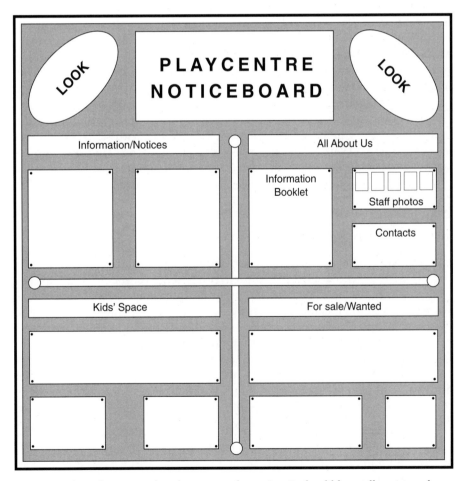

Your noticeboard can say a lot about your playsetting. It should be: well positioned (easily and often seen); well presented (clear and simple); well maintained (frequently updated)

One person should be responsible for maintaining the notice-board and changing displays. Include names and photographs of staff, at least one thing done by the children and ways in which people can get more involved.

Promotional material. If your playsetting has the resources it is well worth having an attractive leaflet or poster printed, preferably in colour and on reasonably good paper. This should give key information only, with advice on where to get further details. Make sure that it reflects the aims of your playsetting and does not contain material which could cause offence. Is there a need to print it in more than one language?

Spreading the word. Use any contacts to spread the word about what you do. You might need to take out advertisements in local newspapers about the service you provide or special fund-raising events. Newspapers, radio and TV are always on the lookout for human-interest stories. Someone in your organisation should be responsible for making contact with the local media. Be sure you tell them in advance if any of your planned activities might present the perfect photo opportunity. You might be able to put up short-term displays in the local library, school or community centre.

Support for play

There are several national organisations which promote the value of play and care, which campaign for children's right to play and provide invaluable ideas and support. Some of these are listed under 'Play' in Appendix 2 of this book. It is often well worth the cost of joining one or more of these organisations for the support you receive in their membership newsletters – practical ideas, ideas for finding funds, information and national initiatives. Locally you may have a play association which brings several organisations together to swap ideas, share common concerns and act as a voice for play in campaigning or applying for resources.

Attending meetings with relevant organisations is time consuming, but it is worth it if you gain useful information, meet people with skills, knowledge and resources you can call upon, and you can promote the value of your playsetting and your own skills, knowledge and understanding.

Supporting children and families
Links with other agencies

Children and their families may have contact with many people outside the playsetting who contribute to their education, well-being and support. There may be teachers, doctors and other healthcare workers, police, social workers, religious leaders and advice centre or ethnic minority and community organisations.

Your playsetting is part of the network of community services in your local area. If all the members of that network know about each other – what each service provides, how to make contact or be referred, what is on offer and who can benefit – they will be in a good position to meet the needs of the children with whom they come into contact:

- A teacher might identify a health problem and refer the child and family to the doctor.
- A community police officer might identify a care need and refer to a playsetting.
- A playworker might hear about a problem a family is having in receiving the right welfare benefits and can refer to an advice centre.

ACTIVITY 5.17

Find out about any other play organisations in your local area. Can you get together to share ideas, resources, social events or perhaps celebrate National Play Day? Do you have a local play association or umbrella group with shared aims and interests? Which of your local authority departments is responsible for supporting or promoting play? Does your local authority have a play policy?

Volunteers

Playwork has a long tradition of involving volunteers. They can be a tremendous source of support in all areas, from working with children to publicity, fundraising, collecting and storing materials, maintenance, staff support or support of an individual child.

Involving volunteers requires planning, supervision, monitoring and support. They need to know what is expected of them and to have the chance to make clear the time and experience they have to offer as well as what they are willing to do. Proper recruitment and selection procedures should be applied to volunteers working with children, including interview, references, checking past history and police and health checks (if these are available to your playsetting). Volunteers may have to be approved by the local authority if your playsetting is registered under the Children Act. Make contact with the National Council for Voluntary Organisations or your local branch if there is one (see also section 5.1.)

Meeting individual needs

All children have needs. Some children's needs are more difficult to meet within the playsetting. You may lack confidence in your ability to meet the needs of a child with disabilities or a particular medical condition. Acknowledge these feelings without guilt because it is only then that you will be able to ask for the support you need and gain confidence to overcome real or imagined obstacles.

Make contact with your local health visitors and any special schools, who will probably be in the best position to advise you of local resource centres and sources of suitable equipment

Some playsettings find that they do not get enquiries from children with disabilities or special needs. Making contact and publicising your playsetting in special schools and with social services and community health services may be one way to get applications from children with disabilities.

Make sure you get accurate information about a child's needs before making a decision about whether you can offer the child a place. As well as talking to the child and parents and carers, you may be able to get information and advice about particular disabilities or conditions from national or local support groups.

As playworker you are not only part of a playsetting but also part of wider network of organisations which support and promote children's wel-lbeing. There are many sources of support open to you in your work, but you may need to seek them out and actively promote and publicise what your playsetting has to offer.

Reference

Kapasi, Haki 1992: *Asian Children Play*. PLAY-TRAIN.

Further reading

Buck, Donne 1987: *Involving Volunteers in Children's Play*. The Volunteer Centre UK and Play Board.

Lowndes, B 1994: *Getting Your Message Across – publicity for community organisations*. Community Matters (tel: 0171 226 0189)

Lubelska, Anna (ed.) 1993: *Better Play*. National Voluntary Council for Children's Play. (See in particular the articles on promoting play, overcoming cultural barriers: Asian children play, play without frontiers and integrated play is better play.)

Petrie, Pat 1994: *Play and Care*. HMSO (See Chapter 3 on clients, customers and users and Chapter 6 on evaluation.)

The following are available from Kids' Clubs Network:

Here's How, a series of 20 practical information sheets and model documents to help your kids' club or holiday scheme get started.

Guidelines of good practice for out of school care schemes – Schools Out! 1993: Special issue.

Endword

Playwork and N/SVQs

In writing this book my main aim has been that it should be useful and interesting to you, the playworker. I have borne in mind that over the next few years many playworkers will be working towards an NVQ or SVQ in Playwork.

What are NVQs and SVQs in Playwork?

The playwork N/SVQs set out a national framework for what playworkers need to know, what they should be able to do and how they should be able to do it. They were developed by the Sport and Recreation Lead Body in consultation with many people involved in playwork. The underpinning values of playwork on which the qualifications are based are discussed throughout the book, and particularly in section 1.2.

NVQs consist of a number of 'Units of competence' covering different aspects of playwork. Each unit is assessed and credited separately so that credits can be built up over time to achieve the qualification. Each unit contains several 'Elements' of competence. These elements describe the functions which a competent playworker ought to be able to carry out.(Appendix 1 shows which sections of the book relate to particular units and elements of the playwork NVQs.)

Each unit also specifies the 'underpinning knowledge' which a playworker is expected to have and 'range statements' which describe the different aspects or situations in which the content of the unit applies.

NVQs are not training courses. You can get an NVQ without attending any course – but appropriate training will certainly help you to get underpinning knowledge and evaluate your practice.

What the NVQ levels mean

Currently there are playwork NVQs at levels 2, 3 and at level 4 for Play Development. This book addresses the units and underpinning knowledge at levels 2 and 3. The deciding factor as to whether you will aim at level 2 or 3 is likely to be your experience and the level of responsibility of your job. At level 2 you will be expected to take some some responsibility (as all playworkers must do) and to undertake a variety of complex and non-routine duties, including working within a team. At level 3 you are also expected to take a higher level of overall responsibility – for example as senior member of staff within a playsetting.

How do you get an NVQ?

To get an NVQ you need to register at an assessment centre. A trained and approved assessor will assess your work through observation in your workplace, asking you questions and by setting up situations where you can demonstrate your ability. Each element will be assessed, using 'Performance criteria' as specified in the Standards.

The NVQ assessor will be able to help you identify gaps in your knowledge and what evidence you need to show that you are competent in a particular area. You can collect evidence in a folder or portfolio. A portfolio contains records of the work you have undertaken – plans, notes, diary, photographs, letters, job descriptions, references, tapes – but you must clearly demonstrate your own role in the evidence you present.

Working through the activities in this book will help you collect such evidence. You can start a portfolio even if you are not currently planning to get an NVQ. Many playwork training courses have 'Building a portfolio' as part of the course. You can also purchase a Portfolio Building Pack from the North East National Centre for Playwork Education (see Appendix 2: Useful contacts).

In most cases I have not distinguished between what would be expected for level 2 and level 3 in the activities. What makes the difference is the level of responsibility at which the activities are carried out. In practice, clarification of roles and responsibilities requires negotiation and discussion, and some of the activities are designed to help you in this. I hope you enjoy them and find them useful.

When the assessor is satisfied that you have the skills, knowledge and understanding to carry out the work in each unit to the required standard you will be awarded an NVQ.

For further information about playwork NVQs and how to get one contact either the National Play Information Centre or one of the National Centres for Playwork Education.

N/SVQs and this book

If you are reading this book to help you gain an NVQ in playwork, here are two ways of looking at them which influence the way the book is structured.

NVQs as a jigsaw puzzle

The different standards and units which form the basis of these qualifications are to my mind like pieces of a jigsaw puzzle. You can start anywhere, but it doesn't form a proper picture until you have looked at how each piece fits into the whole. If you are using this book to help you work towards your NVQ in playwork you can think of chapter 1 of this book as the picture or the guide on the box of jigsaw pieces: you don't have to study it first, but it will help to make sense of how the pieces fit together if you do.

Playwork as an art

NVQs look technical to me. The skills and competences are broken down into small numbered components. This is a useful way of analysing what is actually involved and enabling you to reflect on and develop particular aspects of your work. But in looking at the detail it is important not to forget the whole – playwork is about working with children and doing several things at once. In taking an analytical approach to learning about playwork do not forget that playwork is also an art – filled with different textures, colours, moods, spontaneous and often unpredictable happenings, and feelings.

Whatever approach you take to your work and to learning about playwork, I wish you and the children you work with many moments of joy in your play because, without joy, play can quickly develop into something else.

Further reading

Shier, H. 1994: *Introduction to the Playwork NVQ*. National Play Information Centre (see Appendix 2). A straightforward guide to playwork NVQs with examples.

1992: *National Occupational Standards*. Crown Copyright. The complete NVQ Standards (for the whole of Sport and Recreation, including playwork) is available from the Sport and Recreation Lead Body.

Appendix 1: Playwork N/SVQs – quick reference guide

Level 2 (11 Units)

Unit		Element		Section
D28	Contribute to planning of a play opportunity	D28.1	Collect information to prepare a play opportunity	3.2
		D28.2	Suggest and agree the design of a play opportunity	3.1, 3.2, 3.3
		D28.3	Contribute to arrangements for a play opportunity	3.1, 3.2
D29	Facilitate a play opportunity to enhance the development of children	D29.1	Introduce children to a play environment	2.3
		D29.2	Enable children to develop through a play opportunity	2.2
		D29.3	Play with children	3.2, 3.3
		D29.4	Bring a play opportunity to an end	3.2, 3.3
		D29.5	Contribute to the evaluation of a play opportunity	3.3, 5.3
D30	Support children's social and emotional development	D30.1	Help children to relate to others	2.3
		D30.2	Help children to develop self-reliance and self-esteem	1.2, 2.3
		D30.3	Help children to recognise and deal with their feelings	2.3
		D30.4	Help children to adjust to the playsetting	2.3
		D30.5	Prepare children for moving on to new settings	2.3
E7	Contribute to the maintenance and improvement of a child-centred environment	E7.1	Contribute suggestions on the selection of resources for a child-centred environment	3.1, 3.2, 3.3
		E7.2	Help to organise a child-centred environment	3.1
		E7.3	Maintain the safety of a child-centred environment	4.2
H1	Contribute to the health and safety of self and others	H1.1	Take action to prevent accidents	4.2
		H1.2	Report and record accidents	4.1, 3.4
		H1.3	Follow emergency procedures	4.1
		H1.4	Respond to injuries and signs of illness	4.1

Level 2 *continued*

Unit		Element		Section
H4	Support the protection of children from abuse	H4.1	Identify signs of possible abuse	4.3
		H4.2	Respond to child's disclosure of abuse or neglect	4.3
		H4.3	Provide information to professional about child abuse	4.3
H6	Contribute to children's health and well-being	H6.1	Provide food and drinks for children	3.2, 4.1
		H6.2	Contribute to the maintenance of children's personal hygiene	2.2, 4.1
M3	Contribute to the promotion and improvement of service delivery	M3.1	Contribute to the display and distribution of promotional material	5.3
		M3.2	Deal with suggestions and complaints	5.2, 5.3
		M3.3	Report on aspects of service delivery which could be improved	3.1
		M3.4	Suggest changes to policy and practice	5.1, 5.3
P14	Establish and maintain relationships with children and parents	P14.1	Establish relationships with children	2.3
		P14.2	Maintain relationships with children	2.3
		P14.3	Communicate with children	2.3
		P14.4	Establish and maintain relationships with individual parents and carers	5.2
P16	Contribute to the management of children's behaviour	P16.1	Contribute to a framework for children's behaviour	2.4
		P16.2	Promote positive aspects of children's behaviour	2.4
		P16.3	Manage unwanted aspects of children's behaviour	2.4
P19	Support the work of a team	P19.1	Work as a member of a team	5.1
		P19.2	Contribute to team meetings	5.1
		P19.3	Contribute to the development of good practice of the team	5.1, 5.3
		P19.4	Help colleagues in their work	5.1
		P19.5	Respond to conflict in the team	5.1

Level 3 (15 Units)

Unit		Element		Section
D1	Prepare a programme of activities	D1.1	Collect information to plan and prepare a programme of activities	3.2
		D1.2	Identify the needs of participants	2.1, 2.2, 3.2
		D1.3	Negotiate a plan of activities/ opportunities to meet the participants needs	2.1, 2.2, 3.2
		D1.4	Make arrangements to enable the programme to take place	3.2, 3.4, 5.3
D2	Co-ordinate a programme of activities	D1.1	Co-ordinate and allocate programme resources	3.2, 3.4
		D1.2	Monitor and adjust the programme to meet new needs and circumstances	3.2
		D1.3	Conclude a programme	3.1, 3.2, 3.4
		D1.4	Evaluate the effectiveness of a programme of activities	3.2
D25	Prepare play opportunities to enhance children's development	D25.1	Collect information to prepare play opportunities	3.1, 3.2
		D25.2	Identify the play needs of the children taking part in play opportunities	2.1, 2.2, 3.1, 3.2
		D25.3	Design play opportunities to offer children developmental experiences	2.1, 2.2, 3.1, 3.2
		D25.4	Make arrangements for play opportunities	1.1, 1.2, 3.1, 3.2
D26	Facilitate play opportunities to enhance children's development	D26.1	Introduce children to the play environment	2.3, 5.2
		D26.2	Enable children to develop through play opportunities	2.1, 2.2, 2.3, 3.1, 3.2
		D26.3	Play with children	1.1, 1.2, 3.3
		D26.4	Bring play opportunities to an end	3.1, 3.2, 4.2
		D26.5	Evaluate the effectiveness of play opportunities	3.1, 3.2, 5.3
		D27.1	Help children to relate to others	
D27	Promote children's social and emotional development	D27.2	Help children to develop self-reliance and self-esteem	2.3
		D27.3	Help children to recognise and deal with their feelings	1.2, 2.3
				2.3
		D27.4	Help children to adjust to the playsetting	2.3
		D27.5	Prepare children for moving on to new settings.	2.3
		D27.6	Help children develop a positive self-image and identity	1.2, 2.3
E7	See level 2			
H1	See level 2			
H4	See level 2			

Level 3 *continued*

Unit		Element		Section
H5	Promote children's safety outside the play environment	H5.1	Identify risks to children's safety outside the play environment	4.1, 4.2, 4.3
		H5.2	Provide information about risks to children's safety outside the play environment	4.1, 4.2, 4.3
		H5.3	Provide information and advice to children on safety risks outside the play environment	4.1, 4.2, 4.3
H6	See level 2			
IN6	Administer provision	IN6.1	Receive and disburse monies	
		IN6.2	Implement admissions procedures	3.4 3.4, 2.3, 5.2
		IN6.3	Maintain records of information	
		IN6.4	Operate budgets	3.4
		IN6.5	Operate systems for the supply of materials and equipment	3.4
O5	Contribute to the planning, organisation and evaluation of work	O5.1	Contribute to planning work activities and methods to achieve objectives	5.3
		O5.2	Organise work and assist in the evaluation of work	5.3, 5.1
		O5.3	Provide feedback on work performance to teams and individuals	5.3, 5.1
P11	Work with colleagues in a team	P11.1	Contribute to the work of the team	5.1
		P11.2	Contribute to team meetings	
		P11.3	Contribute to the development of good practice of the team	5.1 5.1, 53.
		P11.4	Contribute to support for colleagues	5.1
		P11.5	Respond to conflict in the team	5.1
P14	See level 2			
P15	Provide for the management of children's behaviour	P15.1	Contribute to a framework for children's behaviour	2.4
		P15.2	Promote positive aspects of children's behaviour	2.4
		P15.3	Manage unwanted aspects of children's behaviour	2.4
		P15.4	Respond to persistent problem behaviour	2.4

Appendix 2: Useful contacts

Some organisations supporting play

HAPA Fulham Palace, Bishop's Avenue, London SW6 6EA. Tel: 0171 731 1435. Runs five adventure playgrounds for children with disabilities and special needs in London and a national information service which offers information and advice on all aspects of play and disability.

Kids' Clubs Network Bellerive House, 3 Muirfield Crescent, London E14 9SZ. Tel: 0171 512 2112. A nation-wide network of development workers, trainers and consultants. Promotes and supports out-of-school childcare, training for playcare workers and has a quality assurance scheme.

National Centre for Play Moray House College, Cramond Campus, Cramond Road North, Edinburgh EH4 6JD. Tel: 0131 312 6001 Ext. 292.

National Playbus Association AMF House, Whitby Road, Brislington, Bristol BS4 3QF. Tel: 0117 977 5375. Promotes use of mobile community resources.

National Play Information Centre 359–361 Euston Road, London NW1 3AL. Tel: 0171 383 5455. Information service for all matters relating to play, playwork and playwork training, including a comprehensive library/resource centre and booksales.

This is also the address for the National Voluntary Council for Children's Play and the International Association for the Child's Right to Play, and the Sports Council (Play and Recreation).

National Playing Fields Association 25 Ovington Square, London SW3 1LQ. Tel: 0171 584 6445. Aims to preserve and develop recreational and play facilities.

Playboard Northern Ireland Unit 2, Quayside Office Park, 14 Dargan Crescent, Belfast BT3 9JP. Tel: 01232 370865. Organisation supporting play in Northern Ireland.

Play for Life 31B Ipswich Road, Norwich NR2 2IN. Aims to stimulate fresh thinking about play for 5–12-year-olds and the production of life-affirming playthings.

Playlink 279 Whitechapel Road, London E1 1BY. Tel: 0171 377 0314. Grew out of the London Adventure Playground Association. Connects practical playwork experience to the broader policy issues affecting children's play.

Play Wales 10–11 Raleigh Walk, Cardiff CF1 5LN. Tel: 01222 498909.

Scottish Out of School Care Network 55 Renfrew Street, Glasgow G2 3BD. Tel: 0141 333 1435.

Training

DYNAMIX 14 Montpellier Terrace, Mount Pleasant, Swansea SA1 6JW. Tel: 01792 466231.

Early Years Trainers Anti-Racist Network (EYTARN) PO Box 1870, London N12 8JH. Tel: 0181 446 7056.

Playtrac Training Consultants Horizon NHS Trust Harperbury, Harper Lane, Radlett, Herts WD7 9HQ. Tel: 01923 854861. Specialises in training and resources for play with children with disabilities and special needs.

PLAY-TRAIN 31 Farm Road, Birmingham B11 1LS. Tel: 0121 766 8446. Consultancy promoting both quantity and quality of creative play opportunities and offering a range of playwork training courses tailored to meet needs of the client.

National Centres for Playwork Education Block D, Barnsbury Park Complex, Offord Road, London N1 1QG. Tel: 0171 457 5824/5592. Funded by the Sports Council, the four National Centres work closely with other organisations to develop training and qualifications appropriate to the playwork field. Contact the London address for contacts with the three other centres in the North-east, South-west and West Midlands.

Equal opportunities

See also other sections in this Appendix.

Commission for Racial Equality Elliot House, 10–12 Allington Street, London SW1E 5EH. Tel: 0171 828 7022.

Council for Disabled Children 8 Wakley Street, London EC1V 7QE. Tel: 0171 843 6061.

Equal Opportunities Commission Overseas House, Quay Street, Manchester M3 3HN. Tel: 0161 883 9244.

Health, safety and well-being

ACT Association for Children with life-threatening conditions and their families 65 St Michael's Hill, Bristol BS2 8DZ. Tel: 01272 221556.

Action for Sick Children Argyle House, 29–31 Euston Road, London NW1 2SD. Tel: 0171 833 2041.

Child Accident Prevention Trust 18–20 Farringdon Lane, London EC1R 3AU. Tel: 0171 608 3828.

CHILDLINE 0800 1111

Health and Safety Executive Rose Court, 2 Southwark Bridge, London SE1 9HS. Tel: 0171 717 6000.

Health Education Authority Hamilton House, Mabledon Place, London WC1H 9TX. Tel: 0171 383 3833.

KIDSCAPE 152 Buckingham Palace Road, London SW1W 9TR. Tel: 0171 730 3300.

NSPCC National Centre, 42 Curtain Road, London EC2A 3NA. Helpline: 0800 800500.

Royal Society for the Prevention of Accidents (ROSPA) Cannon House, Priory Queensway, Birmingham B4 6BS. Tel: 0121 200 2461.

Information, resources, materials and equipment

The organisations listed below are just a few of those offering non-discriminatory play materials, books and guidance. Many larger manufacturers and distributors of toys and equipment such as Galt and NES Arnold supply a good range.

Community Insight Pembroke Centre, Cheyney Manor, Swindon, Wilts SN2 2PQ. Tel: 01793 512612. For books for trainers and practitioners in community, education, childcare and play issues; Bookstall for conferences, etc.

Development Education Centre Gillett Centre, 998 Bristol Road, Birmingham B29 6LE. Tel: 0121 472 3255.

Planet c/o Harperbury Hospital, Harper Lane, Radlett, Herts WD7 9HQ. Tel: 01923 854861 ext. 4384. Play Resources for children with disabilities and special needs

Working Group Against Racism in Children's Resources (WGARCR) 460 Wandsworth Road, London SW8 3LX. Tel: 0171 627 4594.

Working Party on World Religion in Education c/o The National Society's RE Centre, 36 Causton Street, London SW1P 4AU. Tel: 0171 932 1190. Produces the SHAP Calendar of Religious Festivals.

Additional sources of information and advice

Children in Scotland (Clann An Alba) Princes House, 5 Shandwick Place, Edinburgh EH2 4RG. Tel: 0131 228 8484.

Children's Legal Centre 20 Compton Terrace, London N1 2UN. Tel: 0171 359 6251.

Daycare Trust (National Childcare Campaign) 4 Wild Court, London WC2B 4AU. Tel: 0171 405 5617.

Plant yng Nghymru (Children in Wales) 7 Cleeve House, Lambourne Crescent, Cardiff CF4 5GJ. Tel: 01222 761177.

National Children's Bureau 8 Wakley Street, London EC1V 7QE. Tel: 0171 843 6000.

Index